Management Accounting: A Strategic Focus

A MODULAR SERIES

Prepared for:
Professors Allen, Brownlee,
Haskins, and Lynch
University of Virginia, Darden
Graduate School of Business
First-Year Accounting

Shahid Ansari, Series Editor
California State University Northridge

Jan Bell
California State University Northridge

Thomas Klammer
University of North Texas

Houghton Mifflin Company   Boston   New York

Contents

Standard Costing as a Cost Management Tool 145

MODULE

The Kaleidoscopic
Nature of Costs

VERSION

1.2

AUTHORS

Jan Bell and Shahid Ansari
California State University Northridge

SERIES CONCEPT DEVELOPED BY:

Shahid Ansari • Jan Bell • Thomas Klammer • Carol Lawrence

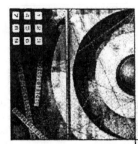

The Kaleidoscopic
Nature of Costs

THE MANY FACES OF COST

Alberto Mantillab, president of Andean Jewelry Inc., opened the weekly staff meeting of his top officers with the following news. "Folks, our distributors want further price reductions from us. I have explained to them that we're operating on razor-thin margins, but they tell us they have no choice. They tell me that they are competing for jewelry counter space in stores. Many of their competitors are importing from suppliers from the Far East. Without price reductions, they're not competitive. That means that we must find a way to reduce our costs further."

"Yes," broke in Maria Davidson, marketing manager of Andean Jewelry. "I've had the same complaints from almost all our customers. They tell me that while our unique Peruvian-styled gold and silver jewelry designs remain popular and customers frequently ask to see items, most are put off by the price and buy something else."

"Well," said Sham Patel, production manager, "we have invested a great deal in new capital equipment and I do not know how I can reduce these costs. Also, a large part of our costs is for gold and silver purchases. I have been trying to buy our materials and parts in large quantities to get purchase discounts and produce finished items in large batches to lower unit fixed costs."

"Maria, perhaps our costs are high because we make too many and too elaborate designs," interjected Alberto Mantillab. "Robert, I wonder if having huge amounts of inventory is a cost-effective solution." He then turned to Thomas Kim, the company's accountant. "Tom, do you know what we might save if we simplify designs? How much does it cost us to maintain these high inventory levels? Can we do something about reducing our marketing and administrative costs? Which reminds me, what is our margin compared to the distributors and the stores that sell our jewelry?"

"Mr. Mantillab," replied Tom, "I am not sure I can answer your questions from our existing accounting records. We have never systematically collected or analyzed our cost data, let alone the costs of outsiders like distributors and storeowners. Our cost statements are designed only for our banks and shareholders."

"The customer is speaking to us; we'd better respond," replied Mantillab. "We need to study our costs carefully and classify them in ways so we can determine where and why our costs are incurred and how to reduce them while still making quality jewelry."

The term *cost* refers to a sacrifice of resources. Whether we barter, pay cash, or finance our acquisitions, the amount expended for an item is its cost. For example, when you sign a lease and live in an apartment for a month, that month's rent is the cost of using the apartment. It does not matter whether you pay the rent in advance, at the end of the month, or in services rendered.

As the opening story illustrates, to manage costs, we must first measure and classify them. As you will see in this module, there are many different ways of classifying costs. Each classification provides useful information; each also has its limitations.

3

■ STRATEGIC IMPLICATIONS OF DIFFERENT COST VIEWS

In all organization, service, manufacturing, not-for-profit, and for-profit, managers are interested in using cost data for making strategic decisions and for managing costs. This requires measuring costs and classifying them by products, services, work processes, departments, and other cost objects of interest to managers. A good cost classification scheme provides a manager with insights about an organization's cost structure that enable him or her to achieve the strategic objectives of quality, cost, and time.

- ■ **Quality.** To ensure that products meet customer requirements, a cost system must measure and report the cost of providing the features and functions that customers want. Costs must be matched to customer willingness to pay. Only then can firms design products that maximize customer value.

- ■ **Cost.** To manage costs, managers must understand their cost structure. The cost classification system must help them answer questions such as: What causes costs to vary? Which costs are internal and under their control? What costs are outside with suppliers and others? What does it cost per unit to produce, sell, and administer the company? What is a customer's lifetime ownership cost for a product?

- ■ **Time.** The way a firm organizes its work processes to produce, market, distribute, sell, and service its product impacts the time it takes to meet customer orders. Rearranging work processes impacts time, and that in turn impacts cost. A cost classification system must make visible the impact of time on the cost of a product.

■ PURPOSE OF THIS MODULE

This module introduces and illustrates cost terminology and cost-classification schemes. The primary purpose is to acquaint you with the language of managerial accounting and to show that various cost classifications are essential to understanding and managing an organization's cost structure. After studying this module, you should understand:

- ■ The meaning of some basic cost terms.
- ■ The historical evolution of cost terms and classifications over time.
- ■ Cost classifications used for external financial reporting.
- ■ The difference between cost classification for external and internal managerial reporting.
- ■ The traditional management accounting cost classifications.
- ■ The emergence of new cost classifications in response to the changed business and manufacturing environment.
- ■ The technical, behavioral, and cultural impact of cost classifications.

■ THE KALEIDOSCOPIC NATURE OF COST

Remember as a child when you played with a kaleidoscope? Each turn of the lens presented a unique pattern. You may not have been aware at the time, but the kaleidoscope used the same pebbles to create each unique pattern. The turn of the lens caused the delightful variations. Each new view, however, obscured a previous pattern and hid from view the endless other

4

patterns. **Costs are very much like the pebbles in a kaleidoscope. Each time we arrange them in a different pattern (classification scheme), they give us a different insight. Each pattern, however, obscures others and can create the impression that it is the total picture.**

The accountant's classification system is the lens that arrays costs into different patterns. Unclassified, the cost pebbles simply tell what object was acquired, such as materials, supplies, wages, and rent. With each change in the accountant's classification system, costs array differently and give a new perspective that helps a firm's management to make strategic decisions and manage costs.

KEY POINT

> Since accountants can array the same costs in many ways, how a cost is to be used determines what cost classification is relevant. Different cost classifications reveal different information about a company's cost structure.

Accountants accumulate and classify costs with respect to different *cost objects*. A cost object is any item (i.e., activity, function, segment, product, or service) whose cost is to be determined. In practice, there are many different cost objects of interest to users and decision makers. This leads to many different ways of classifying costs.

To understand the most popular cost classifications used in practice, it is useful to look at their historical evolution. Different cost classifications we see today can be traced to three distinct time periods.[1]

- The first period coincided roughly with the beginning of the industrial revolution and goes through the first half of the 20th century. During this period, cost classifications were dominated by the needs of external financial reporting.
- The second era lasted roughly from the late 1950s to the late 1970s. This period saw the emergence of traditional management accounting cost classifications that were heavily influenced by mass manufacturing systems.
- Finally, the modern era, which started in the late 1970s, saw the advent of modern cost-classification systems influenced by the introduction of modern manufacturing methods and the changed global business environment.

THINK ALONG

> What are the cost classifications and terms you would expect to be important from an external financial reporting perspective? Why is it important to understand them?

■ EARLY COST CLASSIFICATIONS—THE EXTERNAL (FINANCIAL) PERSPECTIVE

Historically, cost classifications emerged as an offshoot of external financial reporting in the manufacturing sector. The primary purpose of cost data was to record and report the value of inventories on external financial statements. During these early years, cost data used for preparing external financial statements was also used for internal reporting to

---

[1] Our division of the emergence of cost classifications into these three time periods is only for convenience of exposition. It is not a strict historical recounting and represents when these cost classifications gained popular acceptance across a large number of organizations.

Exhibit 1
Andean Jewelry Ltd.
Income Statement
For the Year Ended December 31, 1999.

Net sales revenue	$7,913,900	100.0%
Cost of goods sold	4,537,806	57.3%
Gross margin	$3,376,094	42.7%
Operating expenses		
Marketing	858,709	10.9%
Administrative	1,313,618	16.6%
Total operating expenses	2,172,327	27.5%
Income before tax	$1,203,767	15.2%
Income taxes (40%)	481,507	6.1%
Net income	$722,260	9.1%

managers. Even today, as an external party, you probably will not have access to a firm's internal cost data. The language used in exter⸱ ⸱ ⸱a⸱ements is the basic language that you will have to understand if you want to analyz⸱ ⸱ost structure of a firm. To illustrate the basic cost classifications used by a manufactur⸱r o⸱ their external financial statements, we will use Andean Jewelry's income statement for this last year shown in Exhibit 1.

External financial accounting and reporting are governed by a set of rules known as generally accepted accounting principles (GAAP) in the United States. Most countries have similar rules that govern financial reporting. Accountants must follow these rules when reporting to external parties such as shareholders and creditors.

Cost classifications required to prepare external statements classify costs as assets or as expenses. An *asset* is a resource such as land, buildings, or machinery that has not been used up in producing goods or services for sale. It is sometimes referred to as an *unexpired cost*. An *expense* is a measure of resources used up in producing goods or services for resale. An expense is sometimes called an *expired cost*.

The income statement in Exhibit 1 is prepared in accordance with GAAP. It lists all the expenses (costs used up) in a period for generating revenues. The expenses or costs are classified by the major functions of a business—production and operations.

Cost of Goods Sold.

This category contains the cost of producing the products or services sold during the current period. For a typical manufacturer, this category contains a number of different sub-cost categories. The three most used are *direct materials, direct labor,* and *manufacturing overhead.*

Direct materials become part of the finished products. For Andean Jewelry, the direct materials cost would include the cost of gold, silver, precious stones, clasps, and chains used in jewelry.

Direct labor is the cost of laborers who directly work melting, forming, and finishing jewelry. In general, if workers "touch" a product to manufacture it or if they work directly providing a service, then their wages and benefits are directly traceable to the product or service.

Manufacturing overhead includes all other costs incurred in the production operation. Other names for manufacturing overhead are *factory overhead, indirect manufacturing costs,* and *factory burden.*

Exhibit 2 shows the typical manufacturing costs incurred by Andean Jewelry in 1999.

Exhibit 2
Manufacturing Costs Incurred
For the Year Ended December 31, 1999.

Cost Item	Amount
Direct materials used	$3,069,986
Direct labor	1,025,412
Total direct costs	4,095,398
Manufacturing overhead (indirect)	
Equipment depreciation	73,814
Rent and utilities	203,439
Repairs and maintenance	51,269
Supplies and tools	25,570
Supervision and maintenance wages	425,590
Factory employee benefits	83,525
Total indirect manufacturing costs	863,207
Total manufacturing costs	**$4,958,605**

Conversion cost is another term in manufacturing industries to describe costs used to convert materials into finished goods. It is the sum of direct labor and manufacturing overhead. In Exhibit 2, the amount of conversion cost is $1,888,619 (1,025,412 + 863,207). Finally, the sum of direct materials and direct labor ($4,095,398) is often called *prime costs*.

THINK ALONG

Why is the total manufacturing cost incurred in this period ($4,958,605) not the same as the cost of goods sold for this period ($4,537,806) shown in Exhibit 1?

The difference between the two numbers is due to inventories, that is, materials purchased but not used, units started but not finished, and goods produced but not sold. **The Appendix demonstrates how to calculate the cost of goods sold from the amounts spent on manufacturing costs in a period.**

Accountants often classify the three costs, materials, labor, and overhead, into *direct* and *indirect costs*.

Direct costs are costs that can be traced uniquely to a cost object. Since the cost of materials used in a product and "touch" labor (workers who work on the product) can be traced uniquely to products, the word *direct* is added before materials and labor costs.

Indirect costs are common to more than one cost object and either cannot be uniquely traced to a particular cost object, or the cost of tracing them to products exceeds the benefit of doing so. Traditionally, accountants consider all production costs other than materials and labor and all operating expenses as indirect costs.

Operating Costs.

This category includes the cost of other business functions such as marketing and administration.

Marketing costs include both the cost of obtaining orders from customers, *order-getting costs,* as well as costs to complete the sales transaction, *order-filling costs*. Order-getting costs include costs to advertise products, salesmen's commissions and salaries, and travel and entertainment expenses as well as other items. Order-filling costs include warranty repairs and office expenses associated with granting credit, invoice preparation,

7

Exhibit 3
Schedule of Marketing Costs
For the Year Ended 12/31/99.

Sales commission	$282,766
Sales salaries	191,295
Shipment and delivery	318,550
Telephone	16,725
Occupancy Costs	49,373
Total marketing expenses	**$858,709**

Exhibit 4
Schedule of Administrative Costs
For the Year Ended 12/31/99.

Design fees*	$130,703
Accounting and legal	67,986
Insurance and risk analysis	60,605
Office supplies	132,246
Administrative salaries and benefits	706,625
Office equipment and furniture depreciation	92,162
Taxes and licenses	50,214
Telephone	33,501
Miscellaneous	39,576
Total administrative expenses	**$1,313,618**

* Some students might classify design fees as a product cost. The classification in this module follows generally accepted accounting principles that require classification of research and development costs as a period and not a product cost.

shipping of merchandise, and payment collection. Exhibit 3 contains Andean Jewelry's cost report for marketing.

Administrative costs include the costs of other business support functions. This cost category typically includes executive and support salaries, research and development, accounting fees, information processing system costs, legal expenses, and so on. Exhibit 4 contains Andean Jewelry's administrative costs for last year.

The terms *product* and *period costs* are often used to distinguish between manufacturing and operating costs. This classification determines when costs are expensed on the income statement or classified as inventory on the balance sheet.

Product costs become expenses as products sell; they are included as inventory on the balance sheet if products remain unsold. Product costs include the manufacturing costs of units.

Period costs are the operating costs incurred to market products/services or administer the company. Period costs are expenses in the period the cost is incurred.

KEY POINT

The basic criterion for cost classification from an external financial statement perspective is whether a cost is an asset or an expense. Manufacturing costs of unsold units are assets even if we have **paid** for all these costs. They are also called *product* costs. Operating costs are expenses in the period incurred even if we have **not paid** for them. They are also called *period* costs.

Exhibit 5
GAAP Classification of Costs.

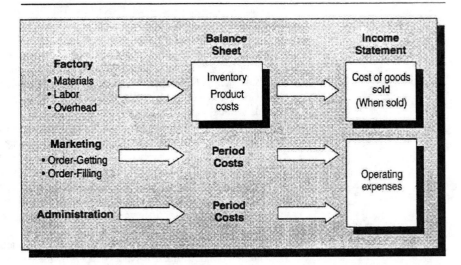

Exhibit 5 provides an overview of manufacturing and nonmanufacturing costs and their GAAP classification.

This distinction between product and period costs does not occur in service organizations, because services are not inventoried. Consider a haircutting establishment such as Regis or Super Cuts. The cost of providing a shampoo and haircut includes materials, supplies, equipment, labor, and other support costs; all these are expensed in the period in which they are incurred.

THINK ALONG

> Would you expect different cost classifications and terms for internal (management) reporting? If so, why? How might they be different?

■ TRADITIONAL MANAGEMENT ACCOUNTING COST CLASSIFICATIONS

A manager cannot run his or her business with the cost classifications developed for external financial reporting. As the opening story pointed out, a manager needs to know, among other things, whether a product or service is being produced at a competitive cost, what the cost impact is of increasing production, which customers or channels are profitable, and what the cost is of alternatives not adopted. None of these questions can be addressed by the cost classifications described so far. They require different cost classifications.

This is the role of management accounting cost classifications. Management accounting views costs from a much broader lens than external financial reporting does. In the early years, the cost classifications developed by management accountants were heavily influenced by the economic theory underlying mass production systems. This thinking encouraged managers to understand the difference between an *actual* outlay and *opportunity* costs, the *behavior* of costs, the *traceability* of costs, and the *responsibility* for costs.

9

Actual and Opportunity Costs.

An *outlay cost* is an out-of-pocket sacrifice. The financial accounting system captures outlay costs. The timing of the cost outlay can vary. The costs may have occurred in the past, or they could occur in the present or in the future.

For example, if a health care provider uses existing medical equipment to examine a patient, a portion of the equipment cost is a cost of providing patient care. It represents an outlay cost incurred in the past. The cost of wages of the health care provider is also a cost of providing patient care. It represents a present outlay cost. If the health care provider discards medical supplies and wastes in a bio-hazardous materials disposal unit, the facility will incur a cost in the future to have these wastes disposed of properly. This future outlay cost is also a cost of providing patient care. Management accountants carefully measure the cost of a health care episode considering all these outlay costs.

An *opportunity cost* is a different cost of concern to management accountants. The financial accounting system does not capture these costs. Opportunity costs recognize that by taking one course of action or alternative, you give up others. An opportunity cost measures the sacrifice you incur by forgoing your next best alternative course of action.

For example, assume that you buy a $5 power-ball lottery ticket for a chance at a $120 million jackpot. Prior to the lottery, a person in a state not selling lottery tickets offers you $500 for your ticket. If you keep your ticket, the cost of playing the lottery is $500, not the $5 outlay cost. The amount that you forgo by not selling the ticket is its opportunity cost.

Management accountants often consider opportunity costs in decision making. Consider an offer from a company to rent a portion of your warehouse space for $5 per square foot. You built this space for $2 per square foot several years ago. If you decide to use this space internally, then the cost of using the space is $5, not $2. The relevant cost measurement is the opportunity cost, not the past outlay cost.

Cost Behavior.

Management accountants are very interested in knowing how costs behave when production volume changes. They want to know whether a cost is *fixed, variable,* or *mixed.*

A *fixed cost* is constant in total regardless of the number of units produced within a relevant range of operations or within a certain time period. Think about a "forming" machine. Assume that it cost $50,000 and has an expected life of five years. Using a systematic method of charging some of the cost to each year of its use (*depreciation*), an accountant might calculate the cost of its use to be $10,000 per year. This $10,000 is the same regardless of the number of units Andean Jewelry produces. Similarly, the rent on the factory building is fixed by the lease term and will not change no matter how many units are produced in that year.

A *variable cost* is a cost whose total changes directly and *proportionally* with volume produced. Consider the raw materials used to manufacture jewelry. Assume that a necklace requires $235 per piece for gold, clasp, and stone. The total material cost is $235 if we make one unit and $23,500 if we produce 100 units.

A *mixed cost* has elements of both fixed and variable costs. A mixed cost typically has a fixed base and then increases above that base with volume changes. Consider

Andean Jewelry's utility bill. Even if Andean Jewelry doesn't operate, some utility costs are incurred. However, as they produce more products, they use more machinery, heat, air conditioning, and lights. Thus, above a fixed base cost, utilities will vary with production volume. Many retail store leases contain a clause that includes a base rent and an additional rent above a certain sales volume.

THINK ALONG

> Why are management accountants interested in knowing which costs are fixed and which ones are variable?

Management accountants are interested in fixed and variable costs because of what economists call *economies of scale*. This concept captures the fact that as the number of units produced increases, the cost per unit declines since only variable costs increase and fixed costs remain the same. For example, in the case of the "forming" machine, the cost per unit is $10 ($10,000/1,000) if we produce 1,000 pieces of jewelry and $5 per unit if we produce 2,000 pieces of jewelry.

The idea of scale economies is tied closely to the another economic concept—*marginal cost*. Marginal cost is the additional cost incurred when a company produces one additional unit. Typically, variable and marginal costs are the same. However, if a company is at its maximum production capacity, then marginal cost and variable cost are not equal. The additional cost to produce one more unit at maximum capacity includes both variable cost and an increase in fixed costs. Management accountants label as *incremental* the increase in costs (or revenues) that includes all elements that change.

Exhibit 6 shows how management accountants might classify the manufacturing costs in Exhibit 2 into the three categories of fixed, variable, and mixed costs. The exhibit further classifies mixed costs into fixed and variable elements.

Exhibit 6
Behavior of Manufacturing Costs.

Cost	Amount Incurred	Nature	Variable Cost	Fixed Cost
Materials used	$3,069,986	Variable	$3,069,986	0
Labor	1,025,412	Variable	1,025,412	0
Depreciation	73,814	Fixed	0	$ 73,814
Rent	150,000	Fixed	0	150,000
Utilities	53,439	Mixed	43,000	10,439
Repairs & maintenance	51,269	Variable	51,269	0
Supplies & tools	25,570	Variable	25,570	0
Supervision & maintenance wages	425,590	Mixed	104,350	321,240
Factory employee benefits	83,525	Variable	83,525	0
Total	$4,958,605		$4,403,112	$555,493

> What would you predict total costs to be if volume (number of units produced) increased by 20 percent next year?

NOTE PAD

11

Many people would answer this by increasing variable cost by 20 percent, or $4,403,112 \times 1.20 = \$5,283,734$, and adding that amount to fixed cost of \$555,493, to yield a cost estimate of \$5,839,277. This is the conventional way of using these costs. We feel it is too simplistic. A proper analysis is to consider the *decision horizon, cost divisibility,* and *management policies.*

Decision horizon.

When the planning period or decision horizon is short, all costs are fixed. When the planning period or decision horizon is long, all costs are variable. For example, consider a decision that affects production during the next hour. Labor costs are fixed. They will not vary with whatever production level workers achieve. All services are contracted for in the next hour. If, on the other hand, the managers at Andean Jewelry are looking at decisions that affect production five years from now, then all costs are variable. Managers can change the entire cost structure, given a long time. In Exhibit 6, we use a one-year time period since managers normally plan for a twelve-month period. A one-year time horizon is normal when classifying costs as fixed, variable, or mixed.

Cost divisibility.

The term *divisible* means that a cost can be acquired in relatively small increments. Supervision is an example of divisible fixed costs. The \$321,240 in the fixed column is the salary of several supervisors. To handle the increased volume, additional workers will be hired and we will need additional supervision time. Assume we need two additional supervisors to handle the workers hired to produce the 20 percent additional volume. However, we can hire the supervisors one at a time. That is, if the volume increases by 10 percent, we can hire only one supervisor. Highly divisible fixed costs behave more like variable costs than fixed costs.

Indivisible means that the cost item can be acquired only in large chunks. Consider the case of the forming machine. The forming machine is indivisible. Assume it can produce 100,000 units and we are using it fully. Then a 20 percent increase in volume can be met only by acquiring another forming machine (with a capacity of 100,000 units) even though we need only 20,000 units. If we assume that capacity is available, a 20 percent increase in volume may mean no increase in cost.

Management policy.

Management decisions can make a cost that is fixed for one business variable for another. For example, when a law firm has documents copied by an external provider (like Kinkos), its copying costs are variable. If the law firm acquires its own copying equipment and hires personnel to run a copy shop internally, a portion of the cost becomes fixed. Similarly, many businesses do not like to lay off workers. For these businesses, direct labor would not be considered a variable cost.

KEY POINT

> Costs are not inherently fixed or variable. Their behavior depends on the decision period, cost divisibility, and management decisions.

A Responsibility View of Costs.

Management accountants are very interested in reducing the costs of operations. Traditionally, they have done this with responsibility accounting using controllable costs, budgets, and standards.

Responsibility accounting is a vertical look at costs along formal organizational lines. Most organizations use the formal lines of authority to report actual spending. A *responsibility center* is a unit in an organization with a manager who is responsible (accountable) for outcomes. This means that there are several responsibility centers within each functional area. For instance, within production, accountants prepare separate reports showing the melting and forming department managers how much each spent on materials, labor, and overhead items. Note that the GAAP cost classifications in Exhibit 1 reflect basic functional responsibility for cost. The plant manager is responsible for cost of goods manufactured, the marketing director is responsible for marketing costs, and the president is responsible for administrative costs.

Controllable and *noncontrollable costs* are closely related to the idea of responsibility. A controllable cost is defined as a cost that can be influenced by the actions of a manager. For example, if the purchasing manager requests a contract review by a corporate attorney, accountants classify the legal charge as a controllable cost, since management had the right to request or not to request a review. It does not matter that the purchasing manager cannot control the number of hours of review spent by the attorney, or the wages paid to the attorney. Under the concept of responsibility accounting, it is argued that managers must not be held accountable for costs that are not under their control.[2]

Standard costs and *budgets* are another traditional means by which management accountants manage costs. A standard cost is a predetermined cost for a product or service based on estimates using assumed levels of efficiency. Consider the situation at Andean Jewelry. Assume that the workers in the assembly department normally assemble two necklaces per hour, and that the hourly wage and benefit rate is $12 per hour. If 160,000 necklaces were produced, the direct labor cost should be $960,000 at this standard cost per unit (($12 per hour ÷ 2 pieces per hour) × 160,000 necklaces). The $960,000 is the standard labor (or the *budget earned*) for the assembly department.

Assembly's actual direct labor was $1,025,412 (see Exhibit 2) for the 160,000 pieces of jewelry. That means that workers spent $65,412 more than their budget. The $65,412 ⁞ called an unfavorable cost *variance,* and the manager of the assembly departmer accountable for this variance. Top management evaluates a lower-level employee p how well he or she controls costs in his or her responsibility center. If the produ of jewelry exceeds the expected or budgeted cost, an unfavorable evaluation

THINK ALONG

Is knowledge of who is accountable for a cost and establishment of a sta budget sufficient to manage costs?

■ CONTEMPORARY MANAGEMENT ACCOU COST CLASSIFICATIONS

The cost classifications from the mass production era were ba economies of scale and responsibility accounting. These co long as firms produced identical (or nearly identical) prod dedicated, indivisible production equipment and specia The usefulness of these classifications is greatly diminish environments in which firms use divisible capital equipme

---

[2] In actual practice, if a cost is on a responsibility center's report, the manager i controls the cost.

products, and have a flexible workforce organized into teams. Increasing volume (scale economies) is no longer the only or even the most important way to reduce unit costs. Furthermore, responsibility for cost lies with teams and not functional managers.

The growth in service organizations, as well as new manufacturing methods, and the increasing global competitive business environment require managers to understand costs. They need to know what causes costs and how to focus spending so value to customers is maximized. A number of different cost concepts have emerged during the last two decades. These new cost classifications focus on cost drivers, recognize the horizontal work-flow linkages within and across organizations, take a long-term view of costs, and put customer value at the center of cost analysis. Six cost classifications of particular importance for modern cost management are *cost-driver analysis, value-chain costing, activity-based costing, life-cycle costing, feature costing,* and *function costing.*

Cost-Driver Analysis.

A *cost driver* is any factor that causes a systematic variation in costs. As demonstrated earlier, production volume is an example of a cost driver. There are many other cost drivers. They include the number of production batches, number of orders, number of shipments, experience with a product or process, the type of technology being used, and many others.

The purpose of cost-driver analysis is to classify and analyze costs by common drivers. This helps managers understand which factors are critical for their cost performance and should be the primary focus of their cost-management efforts.

Consider the case of state universities. They are typically funded by a formula based on *"full-time equivalent students" (FTES)* enrolled. An FTES is measured by adding together student credit hours (15 student credit hours equals one FTES). For example, assume that a university has two students, one student taking a 9-unit course load and the other taking a 6-unit course load. The university will receive funding for one FTES [(9 units + 6 units)/15]. Its costs, however, do not increase in proportion to increases in FTES.

One cost driver in a university is the *variety of course offerings.* This will drive the cost of hiring teachers. For example, if the student with the 9-unit load takes the same two courses as the student with the 6-unit load, then we need to staff only three 3-unit course sections. If they take different courses, we need to staff five 3-unit courses. The *number of students* drives the costs of registration and parking. Thus, we have higher costs if we have two part-time students as opposed to one full-time student with a 15-unit load. *Capital intensity of a discipline* is another cost driver. If one of our two students is a science major and the other is a humanities major, then the science student is more costly since his or her instruction requires more capital equipment.

Consider circuit board manufacturing. Some important manufacturing cost drivers are number of chip insertions, type of chips inserted, and number of test hours. If designers can design circuit boards that require fewer insertions, use simpler chips, and take less time to test, the cost of the boards can be reduced.

Value-Chain Costing.

Value-chain costing is the process of decomposing the cost of a product or service into the various steps involved in providing that product from the most elementary raw material to its disposal. For example, the value chain for writing paper starts with growing *trees* in the forest. The trees are *cut* and *transported* to a mill where they are *converted* into pulp. Further *processing* turns pulp into paper. Finished paper is *distributed* wholesale, and then

Exhibit 7
A Simplified Value Chain for White Paper.

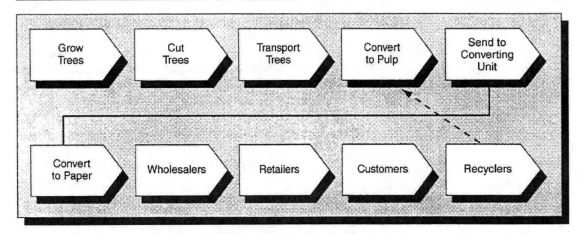

retail, and to final customers. Finally, the paper is *recycled* after it is used. Exhibit 7 depicts the value chain for writing paper.

Sometimes the same organization performs several value-chain steps, and sometimes these steps are spread across multiple organizations. For example, Weyerhaeuser Corporation performs all of the steps in Exhibit 7 from growing trees to selling to wholesalers. Other paper companies rely on a network of suppliers, dealers, and retailers to perform these same steps. These legally separate organizations are interdependent with respect to satisfying the ultimate customers' product and service needs. These legally separate organizations comprise an *extended enterprise.*

Regardless of how many firms are involved in the value chain, the final price customers pay is a function of the costs and profit margins added at each step of the value chain. A value-chain approach to cost management analyzes costs across the linked extended enterprise. From the viewpoint of an individual firm, such as a paper converter, *value-chain cost analysis* shows what part of a customer's price is the converter's internal cost and profit margin and what part is the cost and margin of other firms in the extended enterprise.

Assume that customers pay $3.00 for 1,000 sheets of white paper at a retail store. Assume further that the converter finds out that their own cost is $0.286 and their profit margin is $0.0144. The total, $0.30, accounts for only 10 percent of the total paper price and includes a 5 percent profit margin on sales. Assume that value-chain analysis further reveals that the profit margin of the paper mill is 20 percent, and that transportation of pulp accounts for 50 percent of the converter's production cost.

THINK ALONG

If customers think that the price of white paper is too high, how can the converter use value-chain information to manage costs?

Even the simple example of value-chain analysis above helps a converter get two major insights. First, it shows that since most of the cost for white paper is outside the conversion process, the converter alone can do little to reduce costs. The converter must work with other members of the extended enterprise. Since pulp producers have a higher profit margin, the converter may try to persuade pulp producers to reduce their margins, or the converter may buy a pulp operation to become an integrated producer. Second, since transportation of pulp accounts for the bulk of their cost, they may want to relocate next to the paper mill.

In general, value-chain analysis helps to determine

- What part of the value chain accounts for most of the costs and therefore is the best place for cost-management efforts.
- How actions by upstream value-chain members (such as tree growers and pulp and trucking companies) impact downstream costs (such as converting, storing, and packing).
- Whether some part of the value chain has more profitability so vertical integration may be an appropriate cost-management strategy.

Performing value-chain analysis is not an easy task. Not all suppliers share information, and performing value-chain analysis takes skill. A detailed discussion of how to perform this analysis is beyond the scope of this module.[3]

Activity-Based Management and Costing.

Value-chain analysis shows the larger picture of how organizations and major functional units within organizations (such as production, distribution, and support) are linked to provide customers with products and services. *Activity-based management* and *costing* show the linked set of work tasks within and across an organization that produce products and services.

An *activity* is a series of work *tasks* that have a defined input and output. For example, "serving food" in a restaurant is an activity. It starts with a customer order (input) and includes tasks such as writing down the order, giving it to the cook, and picking up the plates when ready. It ends with placing the food on the table (output). Activities use *resources* such as people, space, materials, supplies, utilities, computers, and so on. The resources consumed by an activity are the cost of that activity.

A set of linked activities is a process. In the restaurant example, the four activities of "reserving tables," "serving food," "cleaning table," and "billing customers" constitute the customer-service process.

Activity-based management (ABM) is the systematic documentation of the major activities in an organization. The documentation is designed to uncover what causes each activity to begin (its *driver*), the cost of the activity, how much time it takes, and how well it is performed (quality). ABM allows organizations to redesign work and improve the cost, quality, and time for performing activities.

One way in which ABM helps cost management is by eliminating unnecessary tasks in activities. For example, filing paperwork that no one uses is unnecessary and can be eliminated. Another way to reduce cost is to eliminate activities that are not of value to customers (*nonvalue-added activities*). Inspection is the classic example of an activity that customers don't value. They want quality products, not inspected products.

THINK ALONG

> How might Andean Jewelry use ABM to reduce costs?

Assume that Andean Jewelry conducts an analysis of its manufacturing activities.[4] The results of the analysis are presented in Exhibit 8. To understand these results, review the

---

[3] For a comprehensive discussion of the value-chain concept as a way to manage costs, see John Shank, *Strategic Cost Management*, Wiley, 1993.

[4] This module simply introduces the concept of ABM and its managerial usefulness. For a detailed discussion of this topic, including how to derive the cost of activities, see the *Activity-Based Management* module in this series.

Exhibit 8
Activity Classification of Manufacturing Costs.

Activity	Cost	Cost Driver	Cost per Unit of Driver
Melting	$218,100	Melting hours (Total 21,810)	$10 per melting hour
Forming	588,834	Number of forming hours (Total 32,713)	$18.00 per forming hour
Inspection	157,024	Number of inspection hours (Total 9,814 hours)	$16 per inspection hour
Rework of defective units	924,661	Number of defective units (Total 10,468 units)	$88.33 per unit
Total Conversion Costs	**$1,888,619**		

THINK ALONG

What insights do you gain from Exhibit 8?

manufacturing costs in Exhibit 2. Total manufacturing costs are $4,958,605. Classified by object of expenditure, they consist of $3,069,986 for direct materials, $1,025,412 for direct labor, and $863,207 for manufacturing overhead. Exhibit 9 reclassifies the direct labor and manufacturing overhead costs (the *conversion costs*) of $1,888,619 according to four manufacturing activities.[5]

It is clear that reworking defective units is a very costly activity. Andean Jewelry can cut their conversion costs by more than half if they could eliminate rework and inspection. Both of these are nonvalue-added activities. Customers want quality products, not inspected and reworked products. If the company can build quality jewelry without inspecting and reworking, they can increase customer satisfaction (quality) and lower costs.

Activity-based costing extends the information obtained from ABM analysis to compute the cost of cost objects such as products, customers, distribution channels, environmental compliance, and so on. Assume that Andean Jewelry produces two different types of necklaces—silver and gold. A silver unit requires 8 minutes to melt, 20 minutes to form, and 6 minutes to inspect. Approximately 8 percent of the units have to be reworked. Assume further that it takes twice as much time to melt and form a gold necklace but the same time to inspect and rework them.

NOTE PAD

What is the conversion cost for a silver necklace and a gold necklace?

The cost for the two units is shown in Exhibit 9.

Exhibit 9
Activity-Based Product Costing.

Activity	Conversion Cost of Silver Necklace	Conversion Cost of Gold Necklace
Melt	$10 × 8/60 hours = $1.33	$10 × 16/60 hours = $2.66
Form	$18 × 20/60 hours = $6.00	$18 × 40/60 hours = $12.00
Inspect	$16 × 6/60 hours = $1.60	$16 × 6/60 hours = $1.60
Rework of defective units	$88.33 × 8% = $7.07	$88.33 × 8% = $7.07
Conversion costs per unit	$16.00	$23.33

[5] To keep the example simple, this analysis focuses only on manufacturing activities performed by Andean Jewelry. It does not include marketing and administrative activities within Andean Jewelry, nor does it extend to Andean Jewelry's extended enterprise.

How might you use the data in Exhibit 9?

This data might be used to assess product profitability or to redesign necklaces to use less of each activity and cost less. Further, the information might be useful to benchmark the unit cost of the activities against other organizations.

Life-Cycle Costing.

Modern organizations recognize that costs have to be managed over the life of a product or a process. This has given rise to the importance of *life-cycle costing*. Life-cycle costing can be from the perspective of a customer or a producer.

A *customer's life-cycle cost* is the total amount of outlay over the entire life cycle of a product from its inception to its abandonment. It includes both *one-time* and *recurring* costs and is called the *cost of ownership*. Consider a car from a customer's perspective. Life-cycle costs include the one-time purchase price; the recurring outlays for gas and oil, repairs, maintenance, taxes, registration, and insurance; and the cost of abandonment or resale value. Car companies often advertise lower cost of ownership to win customers.

Exhibit 10 shows the typical cost of ownership for a car in the state of California under a number of assumptions. The car is driven 15,000 miles per year and is serviced twice at 7,500-mile intervals at a cost of $75 per service. The average gas price is $1.45 per gallon over the five-year life and the car averages 20 miles per gallon. Repairs will be nothing in year one, $250 in year two, and will increase to $350 a year thereafter. Insurance runs approximately $900 per year and taxes and licenses are $650 per year. At the end of the five-year life, the owner will receive $2,500 from selling the car.

What is the cost of ownership of the car?

A *producer's life-cycle cost* is the cost for all activities that occur over the entire life cycle of a product from its inception to its abandonment. It considers both *one-time* and *recurring* costs. One-time costs are costs such as those associated with product and process design or with designing a marketing plan. Recurring costs include manufacturing costs and the costs of selling and supporting the product. A product will yield a return only if lifetime sales revenue exceeds life-cycle costs.

Exhibit 10
Cost of Ownership of a Typical Four-Door Sedan in California.

Purchase price	$14,200
Gas (1.45 × 15,000/20 × 5)	5,438
Maintenance (2 × 75 × 5)	750
Repairs ((350 × 3) + 250)	1,300
Insurance (900 × 5)	4,500
Taxes & licenses (650 × 5)	3,250
Salvage value on sale	(2,500)
Total cost of ownership	$26,938
Cost of ownership/mile	$0.3592

For example, an oil company incurs a one-time cost of finding oil and drilling a well, the ongoing operational cost of pumping the oil out of the ground, and finally a one-time cost of returning the site to an environmentally suitable condition. In its early years, the oil well is more productive. The ratio of oil pumped to other substances, such as water, is high. As the well ages, more water and other substances are pumped and less oil is recovered. Drilling this oil well is economically good only if the lifetime yield of oil at the market price is more than the lifetime cost of drilling and pumping it.

Exhibit 11 shows the assumed life-cycle cost of an oil well. Assume that an oil company spends $54,500,000 to explore for oil and develop a field. In this development stage, no oil is pumped. In its first year, the field produces 20,000,000 barrels/year at a cost of $5.84 per barrel. In the last productive year, only 5,000,000 barrels are pumped, at a cost of $19.90 per barrel. Note that over time, it costs more to produce oil. Finally, there is a $10,000,000 environmental clean-up cost to abandon the field.

If oil sells for an average of $13 per barrel over the field's life, sales revenue is $520,000,000 (40,000,000 barrels times $13), life-cycle cost is $416,500,000, and life-cycle revenue is $103,500,000, or a 25 percent return on sales. This information is more valuable than any one year's results in evaluating the field's profitability.

Exhibit 11
Life Cycle Costs of Oil Wells (000s omitted)

Activity	1998	1999	2000	2001	2002	Total
Find & develop field	$50,000					$50,000
Production		$100,000	$115,000	$90,000		305,000
Transportation		15,750	20,250	9,000		45,000
Business support	4,500	1,000	500	500		6,500
Abandonment					$10,000	10,000
Total cost	$54,500	$116,750	$135,750	$99,500	$10,000	$416,500
Barrels produced		20,000	15,000	5,000		40,000

Exhibit 12 shows how the productivity and cost of operations behave over the life of an oil well.

Exhibit 12
Life-cycle Operating Costs and Productivity of Oil Wells.

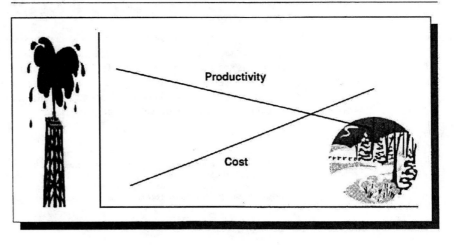

Does a customer's cost of ownership or a producer's life-cycle costs provide enough information to develop products and services desired by customers? Does it assure that an organization will spend its resources in a way that satisfies customers?

THINK ALONG

Feature and Function Costing.

Feature and function costing exists to provide customer focus to an organization. It helps an organization assess whether it is spending on features desired by customers. A *feature* is a physical or esthetic characteristic of a product that satisfies a customer's want or need; it is a customer's view of a product. A *function* is an internal property of a product or process; it is the product designer's view of the same product. Consider a product such as a lawn mower. Features that customers may want in a lawn mower are "handles easily," "cuts grass evenly," "large bag capacity," and so on. Functions that product designers build into a lawn mower are "power," "torque," and "rotation."[6]

Function costing informs product or process designers how much they are spending to deliver a particular functionality. Their job is to provide the desired functionality from a product or process at lowest possible cost. Exhibit 13 shows the cost of the functions in a lawn mower. (For simplicity, we will assume these are all of the functions in the lawn mower). To calculate these costs, the lawn mower manufacturer must add together the cost of all materials, components, and activities needed to perform a function. For example, the function "power" comes from the motor. The motor is assembled, tested, balanced, and installed before it can supply power. The cost of all these activities is the cost of supplying power.

Exhibit 13 shows the cost of each function. The function costs include only *attributable* costs—that is, cost items that can be avoided if the function were to be excluded. Exhibit 13 shows the lawn mower manufacturer that providing power is the most costly function in the product. To reduce the cost of lawn mowers, the firm must find lower-cost ways of providing power.

Feature costing relates spending to features important to a customer. Recall that one feature that is important to customers is "cuts grass evenly." Now assume that the engineers tell us that to cut grass evenly, we need power and blade rotation speed. This means that the cost of cutting grass evenly is $100 ($80 + 20), or 74 percent of the total cost.[7]

To create value, the lawn mower manufacturer must align spending with features that are important to customers. Assume that marketing research shows that half of the money customers spend on a lawn mower is for the feature cutting grass evenly. (This information may come from a customer survey that asks for the relative importance of each feature.) If customers give only 50 percent importance to this feature, then at 74 percent, we are spending too much money. Value creation is negative.

---

[6] It is customary to express functions as verb-noun combinations. This helps to distinguish a physical part such as a motor from the function of that motor, which is to supply power or a task such as data entry from its function "update records."

[7] It is not easy to match functions to features, and often one function addresses several features. We have kept this example simple only to illustrate the concept. For a more complete discussion, see the *Target Costing* module in this series.

Exhibit 13
Cost of the Lawn Mower's Functions

Cost items	Functions			
	Power	Torque	Rotation	Total
Materials and parts	$50	$15	$5	$70
Assembly	13	13	8	34
Balance	5	2	5	12
Test	12	5	2	19
Totals	$80	$35	$20	$135

■ EVALUATION OF A COST-CLASSIFICATION SCHEME

How do we evaluate and decide what cost-classification scheme best suits our needs? As you have seen, there are many ways to classify costs. A good classification scheme should have good technical, behavioral, and cultural properties. A scheme that works very well on one attribute, but performs poorly on the others, should be avoided.

Technical Attributes.

Technically, a cost-classification scheme must provide information that has *decision relevance* and helps us understand how choices and actions in our *work processes drive or cause* costs to be incurred.

Decision relevance.

Until the 1970s, it was common for accountants to respond to internal managerial cost-information needs with cost concepts meant for external financial reporting. This practice resulted in seriously flawed management decisions. For example, product cost data for inventory measurement was used to make pricing decisions, resulting in an inward rather than market-based pricing system. Standard costing systems designed to measure inventory costs were used to manage costs. This created a mentality of managing costs after it was too late. During times of economic downturn, managers built inventory even if it could not be sold.[8]

The fixed–variable cost classification also has resulted in flawed decisions. Many managers tend to use variable costs as an excuse for pricing products below full cost. Further, fixed costs are treated as "sunk" and regarded as irrelevant for decision making and cost management. The result is decisions that have hurt the long-term profitability of many corporations. The fixed–variable cost classification also puts excessive focus on production volume as a cost driver. Today, most organizations recognize that costs vary with cost drivers other than volume.

---

[8] It is beyond the scope of this module to explain fully the link between these flawed decisions and accounting data. However, there are several discussions of this in the literature. See Robert Kaplan and Tom Johnson, *Relevance Lost: The Rise and Fall of Management Accounting,* Harvard Business Press, 1987, for a good discussion of some of the reasons and consequences of providing flawed management accounting data to decision makers.

21

Contemporary management accounting classifies costs by cost drivers, activities, product features, process functions, value-chain steps, life cycle, and many other ways important to management. These classifications are complex and new and require in-depth knowledge of business. They allow managers to turn the cost kaleidoscope whichever way enlightens their strategic decision making.

Work process understanding.

A good classification method helps managers understand what *drives* or *causes* costs to change. Classifications link work-related decisions and actions to costs incurred within the organization. Understanding the link between what we do while we work and the kinds and amounts of costs incurred enables cost management. In a bank, knowing the cost of personal-telling versus machine-telling activities assists cost management. Bank personnel can offer incentives that redirect customers to use machine telling. Cost classifications by activity, value chain, life cycle, and functions relate cost to work processes in organizations. In addition, cost classifications by cost drivers help managers understand the key causes for cost variation in their systems.

Behavioral Attributes.

Cost classification can affect behavior of people in organizations. This is because each cost classification scheme makes *visible* a different aspect of the cost structure and *focuses attention* on a different management problem. If chosen carelessly, cost classifications can lead to dysfunctional behaviors.

Consider value-chain costing. It focuses the attention of managers on the external relationships that cause costs. This often leads to the building of strong ties with suppliers or dealers to improve cost performance. Many companies have managed their value chains to drive costs out of the entire value chain. Wal-Mart is tightly linked to its value-chain members. It offers suppliers a price for merchandise based on Wal-Mart's knowledge of quantities and prices that customers desire. Wal-Mart carefully tracks sales volume and restocks merchandise quickly to avoid stock-out conditions.

Life-cycle cost classifications encourage managers to take a long-term perspective of costs and to consider more cost elements in making decisions. Managers begin to understand that to earn a profit, all costs, from birth to death, have to be paid for out of cash flows generated by product sales. This may discourage short-term manipulation of data by those championing a new product or service.

Feature costing focuses attention on the voice of the customer in product design. If customers don't desire certain features or value them as much, then feature costing signals them as cost-reduction areas. Similarly, functional costing helps product designers to open their thinking beyond the physical product or process step to the function delivered. The message is that we need to deliver functions cost effectively.

Cost classifications can also lead to dysfunctional behaviors. The best example is the fixed–variable cost classification system so popular in most traditional management accounting texts. The term *fixed* conveys a message that the cost cannot be managed since it does not change. This often prevents managers from looking for creative ways to change fixed costs. This overemphasis on fixed and variable cost classification often obscures the more complex relationships between costs and their drivers and gives managers an overly simplistic view of their cost structure.

22

Cultural Attributes.

A cost-classification scheme is a way of organizing cost data. The organization reflects our mental view of costs and captures the cultural lens through which we view it. You will recall that early cost classifications were heavily influenced by external reporting needs. The terms *inventory costs* and *direct labor* were part of our language. However, they came to be more than language used. These terms shaped the way we viewed these items. For example, we regarded inventory as an asset until we learned from just-in-time manufacturing firms that inventory can be a liability from an operational perspective. Similarly, our unthinking acceptance of direct labor as a variable cost has bred an attitude of people as expendable. Many organizations spend more time and effort analyzing machinery purchases (because they are capital equipment) than they do in hiring and training the right people (because labor is a short-term variable cost). Similarly, classifying a cost as overhead may reduce an employee's perception of the value of the work performed.

Cost classifications also reflect an organization's belief about how to manage work. Responsibility accounting embeds a value of individual responsibility and accountability. Under this mindset, when things go wrong, blame is assigned to people rather than the way we organize work. As opposed to this, activity-based and value-chain costing expand the mindset to look beyond people to the processes and extend the reach to organizations beyond our own boundary. Rather than individual responsibility, they are more likely to create a mindset that encourages teamwork.

■ LESSONS LEARNED

- ■ Cost classifications are different ways of arraying the same costs.
- ■ Financial accounting classifications have historically dominated the discourse around appropriate cost classifications.
- ■ Cost classifications needed for external financial accounting are not very useful and often misleading for managerial decision and cost-management needs.
- ■ Traditional managerial accounting cost classifications emerged during the era of mass manufacturing. They emphasize volume as a cost driver and cost control through individual responsibility.
- ■ Contemporary management accounting cost classifications better capture the richness of contemporary business environments. They emphasize strategic decision needs and cost management through process management both within and across the value chain.
- ■ A poor cost-classification scheme can lead to dysfunctional behaviors.
- ■ A cost-classification system is also a mental model of cost reality. A good mental model creates the right values for cost management.

23

APPENDIX

■ REPORTING PRODUCT COSTS IN EXTERNAL INCOME STATEMENTS

Management accountants traditionally prepare cost-of-goods-manufactured schedules to back up the income statement calculation of cost of goods sold and to compare unit costs of goods manufactured from one period to the next for cost control. In any period, the difference between manufacturing costs incurred and the cost of goods sold is because of inventories—that is, costs spent on units that are not yet ready for sale or have not been delivered to customers.

The three inventories that exist in manufacturing firms are *raw materials, work-in-process* and *finished goods*. Before production begins, raw materials inventory exists. It includes items that will become the final product as well as supplies used in production. For example, Andean Jewelry has approximately six weeks of inventory of gold, silver, and stones at all times. These, along with production supplies, constitute Andean Jewelry's raw materials inventory.

Work-in-process inventory exists if there are partially manufactured items when financial statements are prepared. Work-in-process inventory causes the use of materials, labor, and overhead. The costs associated with the partially completed products are included on the balance sheet in work-in-process inventory. For example, if Andean Jewelry normally has unfinished items on each work bench at the end of each day, then a work-in-process inventory exists.

Finally, when the manufacturing process is complete, items become finished goods. Finished goods inventory includes all jewelry that is awaiting shipment to distributors.

Exhibit 14 shows a typical cost-of-goods-manufactured and cost-of-goods-sold schedule for Andean Jewelry that backs up the income statement shown in Exhibit 1.

Note that total manufacturing costs this period were $4,958,605. Cost of goods manufactured totaled $4,949,173, and cost of goods sold (see Exhibit 1) was $4,537,806. These different terms, while similar in their sound, measure three different variables.

THINK ALONG

When will the manufacturing costs incurred, cost of goods manufactured, and cost of goods sold be the same?

For a modern manufacturing organization that uses just-in-time manufacturing, the inventories of raw materials, work-in-process, and finished good, are negligible. Therefore, the three amounts will be virtually identical. You can verify this by assuming that all of the beginning and ending inventories of raw materials, work-in-process, and finished goods are zero in Exhibit 14.

THINK ALONG

Remember in the opening story that the president of Andean Jewelry was concerned about the cost impact of inventories. Was he right?

Exhibit 14
Schedule of Cost of Goods Manufactured and Sold

Direct materials:	
Beginning inventory, January 1	$ 179,191
Add: Purchases	3,261,273
Direct materials available	3,440,463
Less: Ending inventory, December 31	(370,477)
Direct materials used	$ 3,069,986
Direct labor	$ 1,025,412
Manufacturing overhead:	
Equipment depreciation	73,814
Rent & utilities	203,439
Repairs & maintenance	51,269
Supplies & tools	25,570
Supervision and maintenance wages	425,590
Factory employee benefits	83,525
Total manufacturing overhead	$ 863,207
Total manufacturing costs	**$4,958,605**
Plus: Beginning work-in-process inventory, January 1	188,641
Less: Work-in-process inventory, December 31	(198,073)
Cost of goods manufactured	**$ 4,949,173**
Plus: Finished goods inventory, January 1	1,127,211
Less: Finished goods inventory, December 31	(1,538,577)
Cost of goods sold	**$ 4,537,806**

The president of Andean Jewelry was rightly concerned about the buildup in inventories. Inventories cost money and tie up capital. They also require space to store and security against theft. The higher inventory levels reduce per unit cost temporarily by absorbing more fixed manufacturing overhead. However, if unsold, this cost decrease is actually a long-term cost increase for an organization.

25

■ PROBLEMS AND CASES—INTRODUCTORY LEVEL

1. Self-test Questions.

a. What does the term *cost* mean?

b. Does when or how we pay for an item influence its classification as a cost?

c. What does the kaleidoscopic nature of cost mean?

d. How are costs arrayed in different ways?

e. What determines how to array costs?

f. What is a cost object?

g. Different cost classifications we see today can be traced to three distinct time periods. Identify those and indicate what factors influenced managerial cost classifications during each period.

h. What is an expense?

i. What is cost of goods sold and what items of cost does it contain?

j. What is conversion cost?

k. What do the terms *direct* and *indirect cost* mean?

l. What kinds of marketing costs exist?

m. What are administrative costs?

n. What is the difference between a product and a period cost?

o. What is the difference between an outlay and an opportunity cost?

p. What are fixed, variable, and mixed costs?

q. What is a cost driver?

r. What is value-chain costing?

s. What is the purpose of activity-based management and costing?

t. From a customer's perspective, what is life-cycle costing?

u. From a producer's point of view, what is life-cycle costing?

v. What do the terms *feature* and *function* mean?

Problems and Cases.

2. Below are costs that a company might incur. Complete the table by filling in whether the item is a product, marketing, or administrative cost.

Cost Item	Type of Cost
Credit check prior to sale	
Rent for finished goods warehouse	
President's salary and benefits	
Lumber used to manufacture bookcases	
Supervisory salaries in the factory	
Depreciation on computers used in administrative offices	
Depreciation of sample displays	
Research costs for new products	
Commissions to salespersons	
Utilities cost for factory	
Shipping cost to customers	
Shipping cost for incoming lumber	
Software cost of a production-scheduling program	

3. Classify the following costs as fixed, variable, or mixed:

Cost	Classification
Office salaries and benefits	
Wages of factory workers	
Salaries paid to doctors in a hospital	
Depreciation on computer systems	
Utilities	
Property taxes	
X-ray film in a hospital	
Advertising of products	
Shipping costs	
Depreciation on airplane engines	

4. Below are two columns of information. The first column contains costs for activities. The second contains a list of cost drivers. For each activity cost listed in the first column, choose a driver from the second column that most likely causes the cost of that activity. You may use drivers more than once; not all drivers have to be used.

Cost Item	Cost Drivers
Credit and collection cost	Sales dollars
Selecting and packaging merchandise for shipment	Units of products sold
Maintaining personnel files for payroll and benefits	Number of unique products
Cost of assembly operations performed in a production environment with diverse products	Number of batches of products produced
Costs of maintaining a 24-hour support line for a computer software package	Number of assembly operations performed
Inspection of highly diverse products	Number of assembly operations per product
Setting up equipment for different products to be produced	Payroll dollars
Costs of maintaining patents (applying, defending, etc.)	Number of employees
Advertising	Number of unique parts/items ordered
Purchasing merchandise for use in production	Number of items purchased

5. A hotel used its past experience to determine that monthly housekeeping costs are determined by the formula $18,500 + $2.50X where X represents the number of rooms rented in the month. During July, 7,200 rooms were rented.

  a. What are the activity and activity driver in this problem?

  b. What was the expected monthly housekeeping cost in July?

  c. What was the housekeeping cost per room?

  d. What was the fixed housekeeping cost per room?

  e. What was the variable housekeeping cost per room?

  f. Brainstorm. What other possible drivers might exist for housekeeping costs?

6. The following costs are for a law firm providing services to several clients. Classify these costs as to cost behavior—fixed or variable—and as to whether they are direct or indirect with respect to a client's case.

27

Cost	Fixed	Variable	Direct	Indirect
Lawyer's salary				
Lexis-Nexis research charges				
Experts and consultants				
Deposition transcription fees				
Service and filing fees				
Secretarial support salary				
Supplies				
Occupancy cost				
Photocopying				

7. Classify the following cost items as either product or period costs.

Cost Item	Product	Period
Research costs to discover new products		
Seats used on bicycles		
Shipping costs for finished items		
Package (bottle) for spring water		
Warranty repairs		
Factory supervision		
Depreciation on production scheduling software		
Depreciation on an executive conference center		
Costs of setting up machinery to produce different products		

8. Appendix A. Gaines manufactures women's hosiery. At the beginning of January, the following inventories existed:

Finished goods inventory	$ 5,200
Raw materials inventory	10,400
Work-in-process inventory	7,200

During January, direct labor cost was $22,700, manufacturing overhead was $78,000, and raw material purchases amounted to $86,400. The inventories at the end of January were

Finished goods inventory	$ 8,200
Raw materials inventory	12,600
Work-in-process inventory	5,400

a. What were the total manufacturing costs incurred in January?

b. Prepare a cost-of-goods-manufactured statement for January.

c. Prepare a cost-of-goods-sold statement for January.

d. If 370,000 pairs of hose were manufactured in January, what is the per unit cost of goods manufactured?

9. A company that manufacturers candies is adding a new truffles line. They are considering different ways of dipping their truffles in chocolate. Hand dipping and machine dipping are the methods available. If hand dipping is chosen, employees could be paid hourly wages (or given incentive pay based on production) and let go if sales decline. Hourly wages with an incentive would be about $9 per hour. Alternatively, employees could be paid a $1,600 monthly salary and guaranteed full-time employment. An employee typically can dip 100 pounds of chocolate per day. If machine dipping is chosen, the smallest machine costs $750,000 and is capable of dipping 1,000 pounds of chocolate daily for 10 years. This company expects to work 287 days a year and sell 100,000 pounds of chocolate.

   a. What is the labor cost per pound if hourly employees hand dip chocolates? How many labor hours would be required?
   b. How many salaried employees would be needed to hand dip chocolates?
   c. What is the labor cost per pound if salaried employees perform the job?
   d. What is the cost per pound if the chocolates are machine dipped?
   e. Discuss the cost behavior of dipping chocolates under each of the three alternatives. (Consider the cost per pound if production goes to 115,000 pounds, for example.)

10. Responsibility accounting is a vertical look at costs along formal organizational lines. It captures costs by the responsibility center (RC) that expended it and classifies the items as controllable or noncontrollable by that unit's manager. Using that classification scheme, classify the following items.

Cost	Assembly (RC)	Painting (RC)	Purchasing (RC)	Controllable	Noncontrollable
Small tools used in assembly					
Occupancy charge for painting stalls					
Paints, oils, and solvents					
Supplies for purchases					
Purchasing manager's salary					
Salary of painters					
Telephone use by purchasing					
Salary for manager of assembly					
Training new assembly workers					

11. Assume that your company has two different circuit boards that it regularly produces. These vary greatly in their complexity. Accordingly, accountants installed an activity-based costing system. Assume that the following cost drivers and costs emerged from that system:

Activity Cost Pools	Activity Driver	Cost per Driver
Assembly	Number of pin insertions	.18
Testing	Number of burn-in hours	.22
Soldering	Number of dips	.11

Determine the conversion cost of the two different circuit boards, if each board has the following characteristics:

Activity Driver	Simple Board	Complex Board
Number of pin insertions	20	50
Number of burn-in hours	2	10
Number of dips	3	5

12. An activity-based management study uncovered the following about manufacturing operations:

Activity	Percent of Total Manufacturing Cost
Procuring materials	8%
Materials movement	17%
Quality control (inspection, rework, etc.)	37%
Assembly	22%
Final finishing	16%

Think about each activity from a customer's perspective. Which are of value to the customer? Which does the customer not care about? What would you recommend based on your preliminary assessment?

13. The following is a list of departments (a functional view of an organization) combined with activities (a horizontal or work-flow view of an organization). Go through the list and separate the items into departments and activities. Then, place each activity under the department that you believe might be the place where many tasks in the activity occur.

Quality assurance

Credit checks

Picking and packing items for shipment

Human resources

Routing shipments

Defect rework

Credit and collection

Personnel file maintenance

Inspection

Transportation

Preparing customer deposits

Employee selection

14. List the life-cycle costs (from a customer's perspective) of owning a refrigerator. List the life-cycle costs the manufacturer of the refrigerator might incur.

15. From a marketing view, products' lives are divided into stages: introduction, when sales are low; growth, when sales growth is rapid; maturity, when sales have peaked; and decline, when sales are declining. Below is a table of costs that a producer might incur over the life of a product. Think about each cost listed in the table, and indicate whether you think the cost would be high, moderate, or low in each stage of a product's life. Be prepared to discuss your classification in class. Advertising cost is filled in as an example for you.

| Cost | Stage of Life | | | |
	Introduction	Growth	Maturity	Decline
Advertising	Moderate	High	Moderate	Low
Product R & D				
Process R & D				
Product costs				
Warranty costs				
Plant & equipment expenditures				
Business support costs				
Delivery costs				

16. A feature is a physical or esthetic characteristic of a product that satisfies a customer's want or need. A function is the product designer's view of the same product. The following is a list of features or functions of a car. Classify these items by whether they represent a feature or a function.

Description of Item	Feature	Function
Fun to drive		
Torque		
Seating capacity		
Sporty		
Acceleration rate		
Tensile strength		
Safe		
Handles curves well		

17. For what features do you shop when buying a pencil? What components or parts does the designer use to satisfy the customer? An example of a customer requirement may be comfortable grip. One way product design engineers provide grip is by using rubberized paint.

31

18. An automotive executive for a luxury car line proposed pricing the cars inclusive of normal purchase price and all service costs for 3 years (the average life the company's customer owns the car). Gasoline, tolls, parking, and insurance were the only items excluded in the package price. The executive was convinced that their luxury car was less expensive to own than its competitors, and this package price would demonstrate that point. What concept do you think motivated this novel pricing proposal?

■ PROBLEMS AND CASES—ADVANCED LEVEL

19. Appendix A. Various accounts for the Blooming Rose Company for 1999 follow:

Work-in-process inventory, January 1	34,000
Finished goods inventory, January 1	22,000
Raw materials inventory, January 1	10,000
Sales	515,000
Depreciation, factory	25,000
Depreciation, administration & marketing	12,000
Utilities, factory	25,000
Utilities, administration & marketing	3,000
Maintenance, factory	42,000
Advertising	37,000
Credit & collection	12,000
Delivery	5,250
Sales commissions	25,750
Direct labor	72,000
Indirect labor	15,000
Factory supplies	15,000
Raw material purchases	127,000
Factory insurance	2,000
Finished goods inventory, December 31	42,000
Work-in-process inventory, December 31	40,000
Raw materials inventory, December 31	5,000

a. Calculate the manufacturing costs of the period.

b. Prepare a schedule of cost of goods manufactured for 1999.

c. Prepare an income statement for 1999.

d. Assume that the company produced 14,700 ceramic flower pieces in 1999. What was the product cost per unit? What was the direct materials cost per piece? What was the factory depreciation per piece?

e. Assume that the company expects to produce 17,000 units in 2000. What are the unit and total cost for direct materials and for factory depreciation that you expect? Explain your answer.

20. Appendix A. Marmalade Kitchens had the following account balances at the end of the year:

Purchases of raw materials	$507,500
Selling and administrative salaries and benefits	192,500
Factory maintenance	45,000
Direct labor	?
Occupancy cost, factory	90,000
Advertising	120,000
Factory utilities	67,500
Indirect labor	90,000
Sales commissions	80,000
Factory rent	216,000
Administrative office rent	120,000

Inventory balances and other selected cost categories were as follows:

Item	January 1	December 31	For the Year
Raw materials inventory	60,000	20,000	
Work-in-process inventory	72,000	88,000	
Finished goods inventory	40,000	50,000	
Total manufacturing costs			1,310,250
Goods available for sale			1,334,250
Cost of goods sold			1,284,250

a. Prepare a cost-of-goods manufactured schedule. Hint: You'll have to work all the way through cost of goods sold to fill in all blank items you need.

b. Go through each cost item in total manufacturing cost and classify as fixed or variable. Explain what assumptions you had to make to classify costs into these categories. Refer to the discussion of business practices, time period, and divisibility of cost in the module.

c. Assume that these costs were incurred to produce 165,000 cases of marmalade. Calculate the per unit product cost of a case of marmalade.

d. If production next year falls to 150,000 cases, what would the per unit case cost be?

21. Marketing tests determine customers' importance ranking of the features of a pencil sharpener produced by your company. Accountants and engineers calculated the percent of total cost spent on each feature. That data is provided below. What does it tell you about your pencil sharpener?

Feature	Percent of Customer Importance	Percent of Product Cost
Attractive desk-top styling	20%	30%
Easy-to-clean filings	25%	5%
Sharpens cleanly & quickly	20%	30%
Automatic stop without breaking lead	30%	10%
Secures to desk without moving during use	5%	25%

22. Assume that you work for a local newspaper as an administrative assistant. The editor is concerned about costs. The accountant has suggested raising the price of the daily paper from \$.35 to \$.50 because of costs. The editor is concerned about declining subscriptions and cost complaints from local residents if prices increase. The accountant prepared a cost analysis based on an idea from value-chain analysis. He explained that he classified each cost incurred by whether it was controllable internally or externally with other value-chain members. The editor requested you study the report and write a memo to him making recommendations on how to proceed. (In your solution, focus on your knowledge of cost and where it is incurred. Don't address increasing subscriptions, classifying costs as fixed and variable, or earning revenue from advertisements.)

The Daily Chronicle Annual Costs Classified by Value Chain

Cost Item	Amount	Internal	External	Comments
Paper, ink	$375,000		$375,000	One supplier used
Administrative salaries & benefits	$40,000	40,000		
Journalist & editorial salaries and benefits	150,000	100,000	50,000	We use the services of 5 free-lance people whom we pay by the story or picture.
Typesetting & printing	250,000		250,000	One supplier used
Subscriptions & wire services	25,000		25,000	Represents over 100 different suppliers
Utilities, rent, & operating costs	50,000	35,000	15,000	Rent is under control of building owner; we control use of utilities, telephones, and other operating costs.
Delivery	200,000	125,000	75,000	We have our own delivery persons for local daily delivery; other papers are mailed.
Total	1,090,000	300,000	790,000	
	100%	27.5%	72.5%	
Number of daily subscriptions	7,500			

23. The Watermaster Company produces a kayak that is in great demand. The company sells its kayaks through sporting goods stores. It has orders that completely use its 17,000-unit capacity. Customers pay Watermaster \$125 per kayak. Annual cost data at full capacity follows:

Cost Item	Amount
Materials used (plastics, seats, etc.)	$382,500
Sales commissions	150,000
Touch labor	186,750
Advertising	93,750
Utilities, factory	24,000
Utilities, office	6,000
Depreciation on factory equipment	275,750
Depreciation on office equipment	12,000
Salaries, office	125,000
Salaries, factory supervision	75,000
General office supplies	15,000
Packing and shipping to customers	150,000
Insurance, factory	32,000
Insurance, other	5,000
Warranty repairs	30,000
Total	**$1,562,750**

a. Prepare an answer sheet with the following column headings. Enter each cost item on your answer sheet, placing the dollar amount under each appropriate heading. An example is provided for the first cost item.

Cost item	Cost Behavior		Selling or Administrative	Product Cost	
	Variable	Fixed		Direct	Indirect
Materials used	$382,500			$382,500	

b. From the perspective of management, what does each kayak cost? From the perspective of an accountant, what is the product cost of a kayak?

c. Assume that production drops by 2,000 units. Using the cost behavior classifications above, predict the new total cost. Will the unit cost increase or decrease? Explain the economic theory behind the change.

d. Refer to the original data. Your neighbor, an accountant, would like to buy a kayak from you at cost. What amount might he expect to pay? What cost term could you use to charge your neighbor the same amount that you charge regular customers?

24. Tom Brunridge, a dentist in your area, wanted help in determining the cost of routine dental cleanings in his office. He is uncertain how to proceed, but provided you with some details. Two years ago, he paid about $50,000 for outfitting **each** cleaning room with chairs and equipment. He pays 2 dental hygienists an annual salary (with benefits) of $38,000 each. Approximately 50 percent of his total office staff expense, $60,000 a year, relates to scheduling these appointments, filling out dental insurance paperwork, and updating files. About 20 percent of his annual lease payment ($15,000) relates to the space used for dental cleanings. In a typical year, approximately 5,000 dental cleanings occur.

a. What is the cost of a dental cleaning, assuming that each cleaning room will require re-outfitting after five years of service?

b. Classify the costs incurred into fixed, variable, and mixed cost categories.

Cost Item	Amount per Year	Classification
Outfitting rooms		
Hygienists' salaries & benefits		
Office support		
Leased space		
Total		

c. What other costs might be associated with dental cleanings that are not in the above list?

d. Consider the type of costs Dr. Brunridge has in his list. Compare the nature of the fixed-cost items in terms of their divisibility.

Cost Item	Amount per Year	Divisibility
Outfitting rooms		
Hygienists' salaries & benefits		
Office support		
Leased space		
Total		

e. Assume that a patient is looking for two different features in obtaining dental cleanings: (1) ease of making appointments and doing insurance paperwork, and (2) sanitary, competent dental hygiene service. Discuss which cost items provide each of these features.

25. Robinson Orthodontics currently performs its own full mouth and cranial x-rays prior to orthodontic service. Most other orthodontists use an outside supplier for this service. Since Robinson had idle space and worker time, it seemed logical to perform x-ray services internally. Dental assistants take the orthodontic x-rays during their regularly scheduled day. An orthodontist approached Robinson with an offer. He would like to rent the space and share the front office administrative staff. The orthodontist offered $48,000 a year in rent (covering space, utilities, telephone, and office staff). The new orthodontist would outfit his own office space. Robinson hired you to analyze the offer and help management decide what action to take. The following is a table of data you put together to help with your analysis.

Item	Description
Current annual rental cost	$18 per square foot per year
Number of square feet to use as rental or as x-ray	240 square feet
Charge for orthodontic x-ray series from outside supplier	$125 per patient
Average number of orthodontic x-ray series in a year	135
Cost of x-ray film, development chemicals per series	$25
Number of minutes of assistant's time per series	30
Assistant's salary and benefits	$32,000 annually (assume a 2,000-hour work year)
Depreciation on dedicated x-ray equipment per year	$2,000 annually (this equipment would last about 3 more years and has no resale value)

a. Calculate the full cost of performing a full set of orthodontic x-rays internally.

b. Compare the incremental cost of performing a full set of orthodontic x-rays internally to using an outside supplier. Be careful in your analysis. Remember, if a cost item would be the same regardless of the action you take, it is not included in the analysis. Also, remember to include opportunity costs.

c. What assumptions did you have to make to do this analysis?

26. Texaco evaluates the performance of its managers by comparing budgeted profit to actual profit. Consider the results from the Mobile Refinery:

	Mobile Refinery	
	Budget	Actual
Sales	$10,500,000	$10,250,000
Cost of goods sold	6,300,000	6,252,000
Marketing	210,000	210,000
Depreciation on refinery & equipment	1,100,000	1,050,000
Manager's salary	250,000	250,000
Other operating costs	950,000	1,000,000
Share of corporate overhead cost	750,000	786,000

a. Prepare an income statement for the refinery with two columns, one for budget and one for actual results.

b. Calculate the budgeted versus actual return on sales.

c. Is this income statement the one that you would use to evaluate the performance of the manager? Why or why not?

d. If the income statement in (a) is not the income statement that you believe is appropriate to evaluate the manager's performance, recast it into a form that you would use to evaluate the manager's performance. Briefly explain why you included or excluded each item in the table above.

27. General Motors is currently investigating building more flexible manufacturing plants for its small cars. These new plants would use less production line labor and more machinery. Accordingly, their cost structure will change; some items that were previously variable will become fixed. Below is a table showing the old cost factors compared to the new cost factors.

Factors	Old	New
Robots	Not employed.	Substitute for labor in many repetitive tasks.
Direct labor	Most production jobs performed by hourly workers who work in pace with a production line.	Mostly replaced by robots; remaining labor must be flexible learning to operate multiple machines and change their setup. Paid salary.
Equipment	Dedicated to performing the same task repeatedly; high cost to change setups for model changes.	More flexible. Can switch back and forth between models with minimum setup.
Setup	Performed by engineers; extensive and involves testing on materials for proper settings.	Performed by line workers by changing software and settings.
Direct materials	No change.	No change.
Supervision	Supervisors for every 12 laborers.	Few supervisors. Workers are empowered to make decisions.
Building space	Requires more square feet per car.	Requires less square feet per car.
Utilities	Used for machinery.	Used for robots and machinery.

a. Think about each cost factor listed above. Classify it as fixed, variable, or mixed in the old and in the new production environment.
b. Which cost structure is more susceptible to demonstrating economies of scale, the old or the new production environment? Why?
c. Which cost structure is more suitable for satisfying customer's demand for a wide variety of car models, colors, and option packages?

28. Adventures, Inc., manufactures mountain bikes. Currently, after tube kits are assembled, an inspector checks each assembled frame. The company employs two inspectors; each earns $36,000 a year plus 25 percent benefits. Inspectors use equipment that is depreciated $20,000 per year. Inspection supplies total $4,500 annually. Inspectors use space in the common production facility. Approximately 10 percent of the space is dedicated to inspection. The occupancy cost (rent, heat, light, parking, etc.) for the common production facility is $94,800 annually. (Space cannot be sublet.) Material movers move bikes to and from the inspection area. Approximately 25 percent of material movers' time is devoted to this task. Material movers' cost is $72,000 a year plus 25 percent benefits.

a. Adventures, Inc., is interested in the cost of the activity, inspecting assembled frames. Calculate that amount for them.

b. Consider the cost elements calculated in (a). Divide these into the following four groups: (1) direct costs that will vary with the level of the activity, (2) direct costs that are fixed (indicate whether they are divisible or indivisible), (3) common costs assigned to the activity that are divisible, (4) common costs assigned to the activity that are indivisible.

c. Assume that Adventures is considering reorganizing work by having assemblers inspect their own work. What will be the likely cost impact of this decision in 3 months and in 2 years?

Essay or Research Projects.

1. Many organizations place heavy emphasis on how costs behave with changes in production or sales volume. They classify all costs as fixed or variable and use this when modeling costs and profits. Discuss how and when this analysis can lead to bad decisions. (Problem contributed by Dan Swenson, University of Idaho.)

2. Each student should select a term or concept in the module (e.g., economies of scale or cost driver). Use the search engines on the Web to find out more about the term or concept. Students should give no more than a 5-minute oral presentation on their topic, using no more than 3 overhead slides. The presentation should include an annotated list of useful URL. (Project contributed by George Fiebelkorn, Marymount University.)

Case 1: Plant World Inc.©

Plant World sells a complete line of garden products.

Exhibit 15
Product Line Income Statement.

Revenue (1,000,000 cards @ $1.75/card)	**$1,750,000**
Variable costs	
Sales commissions (10% of revenue)	175,000
Shipping costs	325,000
Printing costs (0.682 unit × 1,000,000)	682,000
Total variable costs	1,182,000
Contribution margin	568,000
Fixed costs	
Order-filling costs (13 employees @ average of $23,040 per employee)	299,520
Product development cost ($88,000 amortized over three years)*	29,333
Marketing/advertising costs	35,000
General business support costs	312,000
Total fixed costs	675,853
Net profit	**($107,853)**
Return on sales	**−6.16%**

* The entire $88,000 is expensed in the first year on the company's external income statement.

© Copyright Dr. Shahid L. Ansari, 1997.

39

Management is concerned about the losses from the laminated card line. All product lines in the company are expected to earn at least 10 percent return on sales. The managers have been discussing ways to improve the profitability of the card line.

One alternative being proposed by the marketing manager would double the sales from its current level of 1,000,000 cards sold. To do this, however, the marketing manager wants to spend an additional $35,000 on advertising and sales promotion, reduce the price to $0.99 per card, and sell through nurseries instead of direct mail. She further indicated that marketing through nurseries means that the average number of cards per order will increase from the current 10 to 100 cards per order. The increase in order size means that Plant World could print the cards in batches of 100,000 instead of the current 20,000.

The owner of the supplier printing press company is currently charging Plant World $0.682 per card. The supplier has indicated that he typically requires a 25 percent profit on sales, and so he marks up all jobs by 33.3 percent above his cost. His variable cost of paper, laminate, and ink is $0.387 and the setup cost for each batch is $2,500. With the larger batch size of 100,000 cards, the supplier calculates that he can lower his price by 15 percent to $0.580 per card ($0.682 × 85%).

A revised analysis based on the new selling price of $0.99 per card, the reduced printing cost of $0.580 per card, and the increased fixed marketing costs of $35,000 is shown in Exhibit 16. The projected income statement increases all other variable costs in proportion to the increase in the volume of sales (that is, double). Fixed costs, with the exception of the incremental marketing costs, are unchanged.

A further analysis of fixed costs shows that the salary costs of $299,520 for order-filling employees is based on an average salary of $18,000 per year plus another 28 percent of this amount for fringe benefits. It takes an employee an average of 15 minutes to fill an order. Each employee works for 50 weeks per year and 40 hours per week.

The "general business support costs" of $312,000 include the costs of providing all employees (including order-filling employees) with space, furniture, utilities, supplies, and computer support. These costs average approximately 60 percent of the salary cost of an employee. These support costs are expensed as general and administrative costs on the external financial statements.

Based on Exhibit 16, the laminate cards are not a profitable item and management feels that this product line should be discontinued.

Exhibit 16
Projected Income Statement

Revenue (2,000,000 cards @ $0.99/card)	$1,980,000
Variable costs	
Sales commissions (10% of revenue)	198,000
Shipping costs (double due to doubling in volume)	650,000
Printing Costs (0.682 unit x 85% x 2,000,000 units)	1,159,400
Total variable costs	2,007,400
Contribution margin	(27,400)
Fixed costs	
Order-filling costs (13 employees @ average of $23,040 per employee)	299,520
Product development cost ($88,000 amortized over three years)	29,333
Marketing/advertising costs	70,000
General business support costs	312,000
Total fixed costs	710,853
Net profit	($738,253)
Return on sales	-37.29%

Required:

1. In your opinion, are the cost classifications used in Exhibit 16 appropriate?
2. Do you agree with the analysis in Exhibit 16 and the conclusion reached by management?
3. If not, what alternative course of action would you recommend?
4. What is the profit margin for this product line that you will use to evaluate whether the decision to enter this product line was sound?
5. What is the profit margin for this product line that you will use to decide whether to discontinue this product line?

Case 2: Kaleidoscope Inc.©

Kaleidoscope Inc. manufactures three models of decorative brass kaleidoscopes (economy, standard, and deluxe). Its income statement for the year 2003 is shown in Exhibit 17. In 2003, the company sold 163,569 units of all three models combined. The kaleidoscopes are sold through specialty boutiques in major shopping malls. The shops, which are independently owned, typically add a 100 percent markup to their purchase price from Kaleidoscope Inc. The shops send defective kaleidoscopes back to the company for repair. After the warranty period, the costs of repair are charged to the customer. Warranty repairs costs typically average $1 per kaleidoscope. Customers spend approximately $10 per kaleidoscope for repairs, refurbishment after the warranty expires, and $30 each four years to have the brass polish restored. The life of the product is typically 12 years. The *weighted-average retail price* of all kaleidoscope models is $80.

The company assembles kaleidoscopes from purchased parts. The plant is modern and the company operates a just-in-time manufacturing system. It purchases parts from two tier 1 suppliers and one recycler who takes apart old kaleidoscopes and salvages them for usable parts. Both these suppliers have had long relationships with Kaleidoscope and have long-term commitments for supply of parts. Each supplier, in turn, purchases 60 percent of their raw materials from their tier 2 suppliers. The company uses an outside design house for product design and a shipping and distribution company to ship its products to shops.

Internally, the company is divided into 3 departments: assembly, sales, and administration. The assembly department requires skilled labor. The company has spent a considerable amount for training its workers. Further, because the company operates in a small town, it does not believe in laying off workers. The assembly department occupies 40 percent of the common rented building for space. Sales occupies 20 percent, and administration occupies the remaining. Administration does not include accounting and legal. These services are purchased from independent practitioners as needed.

The company is trying to understand its cost structure and feels that their current income statement format (see Exhibit 17), developed for external reporting purposes, does not provide the insights about their cost structure that they need to manage the business. Kaleidoscope is intrigued by the many different ways of arraying costs and wants to understand the insights each cost view provides.

© Copyright Shahid L. Ansari. 1998.

41

Required:

1. Prepare a flowchart of the company's value chain starting with suppliers and ending with the customer. Put as much factual detail in the flow chart as you can.

2. Prepare a statement that lists the costs by whether they are part of the company's internal value chain or external value chain.

3. Assume that the company is trying to set margins and prices. What is the product cost per unit? (For this question, you can assume they only sell one product so you can sum the units for the three models.)

4. For the previous question, what is the product cost that the company will report on its external balance sheet?

5. What does this product cost a customer from the time he or she purchases it to the time that he or she disposes of it (that is, the life cycle or cost of ownership)?

6. Assume that this next year, production and sales are expected to increase by 20 percent. List all costs that will change. Also state whether the change will be less than, greater than, or equal to 20 percent and the basis for your answer. If production and sales decreased by 20 percent would all costs that you identified as increasing by 20 percent also decrease by 20 percent? Why or why not?

7. Review your answers to questions 2–6 above. What conclusions can you draw about the cost structure of the company from this analysis of its costs? What insights have you gained about cost management?

Exhibit 17
Kaleidoscope Inc.
Income Statement
For the year ended December 31, 2003

Net sales revenue:	$6,542,760
Cost of Sales	
Purchased Parts	2,563,331
Recycled Parts	456,873
Direct Labor	560,800
Design Charges	87,135
Depreciation	23,564
Equipment Rental	25,645
Insurance—Medical, etc.	124,789
Payroll Taxes	75,680
Rent on Plant	135,000
Repairs & Maintenance	36,621
Warranty Repairs	168,554
Supplies & Tools	18,264
Supervisory Salaries	354,658
Utilities	34,689
Total cost of sales	4,665,603
Gross Margin	1,877,157
Operating Expenses:	
Sales Commission & Salaries	121,844
Salesmen Salaries	60,863
Shipments & Delivery	43,813
Depreciation—Office Equipment	18,900
Accounting & Legal Fees	45,324
Insurance	35,650
Miscellaneous Expenses	27,294
Office Supplies	9,446
Administrative Salaries	542,980
Payroll Taxes, etc.	18,600
Pension Plan	98,745
Operating Taxes & License	32,396
Telephone	33,484
Total operating expenses	1,089,339
Operating Income	$787,818

MODULE

Cost Measurement Systems: Traditional and Contemporary Approaches

VERSION

1.2

AUTHORS

Shahid Ansari, California State University Northridge

Carol Lawrence, University of Richmond

SERIES CONCEPT DEVELOPED BY:

Shahid Ansari • Jan Bell • Thomas Klammer • Carol Lawrence

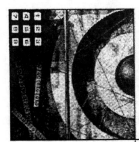

Cost Measurement Systems: Traditional and Contemporary Approaches

TWO PERSPECTIVES ON COSTING

"It's really not fair to compare the cost of the job we're working on now for a wastewater treatment plant in Sweden with the job we just finished for a sugar mill in Zimbabwe. The Sweden job requires heavy-duty surface finishes to withstand the exposure to severe winter weather. We've had real problems with the new weatherproof paint we're trying." The production manager of **Alfa Laval** offered this explanation at the monthly staff meeting as managers reviewed the latest cost reports. The company's plant in Richmond, Virginia, makes equipment for industrial processes that require heating and cooling of liquids during processing.

Meanwhile, across town at the **A.H. Robins** plant that produces over-the-counter and prescription cold and flu medicines sold under the brand names Robitussin and Dimetapp, managers were also reviewing cost reports. Costs in the mixing department were slowly inching upwards. The plant manager protested, "But the cost increase is only *2 cents!*" The controller responded, "With the huge quantities we produce, 2 cents per bottle adds up in a hurry. That 2 cents a bottle will increase our total cost by $360,000 this quarter, and if this keeps up, total cost for the year will be $1,440,000 more than last year!"

Everyone agreed with the plant manager when he commented, "You know, it seems we get lots of information from our accounting system, but it doesn't really tell us what we need to know. I want to know how to manage our costs proactively, not just find out after the fact they were too high!" The controller spoke up, "I know our accounting system has to change. Perhaps we can incorporate some of the more contemporary approaches to cost measurement."

A cost measurement system records, tracks, and reports information about the resources consumed by an organization in providing its customers with the goods or services they want. The primary reasons for measuring costs are to make informed strategic choices and to manage costs. A cost measurement system is part of a **strategic management accounting system**. Other functions performed by a comprehensive strategic management accounting system include the following elements:

- *Competitor cost estimation* that estimates the cost at which competitors are providing similar goods and services.
- *Value chain costing* that helps management understand what each member of the value chain[1] contributes to the total cost of providing a product or service to a customer.
- *Strategic cost analysis* to help management estimate the impact of pursuing different customers or markets or of investing in different production technology.

---

[1] The value chain is the linked series of activities required to provide a service or product to a customer. A comprehensive view of the value chain would begin with the extraction of raw materials and include all steps through production, delivery, use by the customer, and recycling or final disposal.

■ STRATEGIC IMPORTANCE OF COST MEASUREMENT SYSTEMS

Information provided by a cost measurement system helps managers achieve their major strategic objectives of providing customers with high-quality products or services, at a reasonable cost, and in a timely fashion.

- **Quality.** Providing customers the features and reliability they want at affordable prices can be a major challenge. A cost measurement system provides data that allows managers to understand the cost of providing customers with current levels of quality. In addition, a well-designed cost measurement system should provide information to estimate the cost of adding new features desired by customers.

- **Cost.** The purpose of measuring costs is to manage costs. A cost measurement system helps management to understand how each of the various cross-functional processes used to produce, deliver, and support products or services contributes to costs and what factors cause costs to change. This information helps managers to focus their cost management efforts on areas that produce the greatest benefit.

- **Time.** Both of the firms in the opening story face key strategic issues on the time dimension of the strategic triangle. Meeting a customer's deadline for installation is critical for Alfa Laval's heat-exchanger business. Late delivery of the heat exchangers can delay the completion of other aspects of construction, causing considerable ill will and expense for the customer.

For Robins, timely introduction of new drugs is vital to ensure an adequate return on their research spending. Because of seasonal fluctuations in demand, Robins must plan carefully to have adequate supplies of cold and flu medicines available for the winter flu season. The cost systems of both companies must help them understand how delays affect their costs and profits.

When you are finished with this module, you will

- Appreciate the strategic importance of cost measurement systems.

- Recognize that organizations use different cost measurement systems because they produce different types of outputs using different production methods.

- Learn about key design issues such as the selection of cost objects, accounts used to track cost flows, and allocation procedures used to trace costs to cost objects.

- Understand how a cost measurement system converts data on resources purchased into information on resources consumed by the cost objects (customers, activities, operations, products, processes) of interest to management.

- Understand how traditional department-focused cost measurement systems such as job order costing and process costing differ from contemporary cost measurement systems that focus on all activities and operations required to design, produce, and deliver a product or service to a customer.

- Understand the technical, behavioral, and cultural attributes of traditional and contemporary cost measurement systems.

■ NATURE OF A COST MEASUREMENT SYSTEM

The process of cost measurement is like a building process. The basic raw material is data on purchases of resources such as materials, equipment, or labor. A cost measurement system uses these data as basic building blocks, arranging them into a structure that provides managers with cost information for making strategic decisions and managing costs. Exhibit 1 depicts this view of a cost measurement system.

Exhibit 1
Cost Measurement System as a Building Process

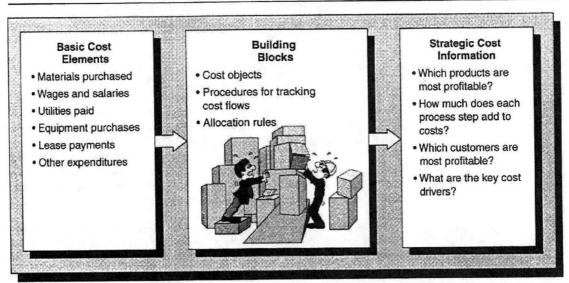

The reason we need to go through this building process is that most accounting systems initially capture data on resources *purchased*, whereas managers need to know how resources are *used* to meet strategic objectives. For example, the accounting system records events such as the purchase of $100,000 worth of materials; payment of $300,000 in salary and wages (recorded in the payroll account); and purchase of $50,000 worth of new equipment. However, managers want to know how much of the $100,000 in materials; $300,000 in salaries; and $50,000 in equipment was used to produce products, how much to deliver them, and how much to support them. More important is the question: Were the revenues generated greater than the resources used in generating these revenues? This type of information is critical in determining whether a firm is producing outputs that meet or exceed customer expectations and generate profits.

The cost measurement system provides this type of managerially relevant information by creating a structure whose primary building blocks are

- ■ *A set of cost objects*, processes, products, activities, customers, and so on that serve as the focus of cost accumulation and analysis.
- ■ *Procedures for tracking the flow of costs* through various accounts.
- ■ *Methods of allocating resources* shared by more than one cost object.

49

Cost Object Selection.

Most organizations use many different types of **cost objects.** Products, services, departments, activities, product lines, and customer groups are some examples of commonly used cost objects. In a well-designed cost measurement system, cost objects correspond to management's strategic decision needs. For example, to decide which market segment to focus on, Alfa Laval's management must know which of its customers are most profitable. This factor explains why individual customer jobs are an important cost object for Alfa Laval.

Cost objects must be selected with care. Inappropriate selection of cost objects can seriously impair the usefulness of a cost measurement system. For example, until recently most organizations did not use activities as cost objects and, therefore, did not have cost data that could be used for managing critical business processes. Even today many companies use cost objects that are relevant for external financial reporting and irrelevant or misleading for internal management decision making. Measuring inventory at "full product cost" is one example of this tendency.[2]

Selecting the right cost object is particularly difficult in service industries because their output is hard to define. For example, the output of a hospital can be measured in a variety of ways. The cost measurement system might report cost per patient, per patient day, or per bed. In the early 1980s the Medicare system implemented a new reimbursement plan, based on diagnosis-related groups (DRG). The DRG system classifies each patient into one of 470 DRGs based on the nature and severity of the patient's ailment. Medicare reimburses hospitals a standard amount for each patient treated in each DRG, regardless of the actual costs the hospital incurs to treat a patient. Today many hospitals use DRGs as a major cost object for accumulating and reporting costs.[3]

What is the cost object your university or college uses to measure the cost of educating students?[4]

THINK ALONG

Procedures for Tracking Cost Flows.

A cost measurement system provides the means of tracking costs through various accounts and intermediate cost objects to the final cost objects of interest to management. Traditional cost systems use functional areas or departments to flow and track costs to cost objects. Contemporary cost systems use activities and operations to accumulate the cost and then charge these costs to final cost objects.

Cost Allocation.

The **allocation** of costs that are common or shared is a critical part of the design of any cost system. Allocation rules can be quite complex. In a well-designed system the allocation scheme will reflect how costs are caused by or incurred to benefit the selected cost objects.

---

[2] The *Theory of Constraints and Throughput Accounting* module in this series develops in greater detail the difference between inventory measures for external financial reporting versus managing operations.

[3] For additional detail on hospital cost measurement systems, see Carol M. Lawrence, "The Effect of Ownership Structure and Accounting System Type on Hospital Costs," *Research in Governmental and Nonprofit Accounting*, Vol. 6, 1990, pp. 35–60.

[4] Colleges use full-time equivalent student hours. See discussion later in this module.

An Example.

Let us consider a simple example to illustrate the three steps in measuring costs. Assume a hospital uses a traditional department-based cost system and wants to know the cost of treating patients who are classified in disease group 215 (i.e., the cost object is DRG 215). The first step, if the hospital uses a traditional system, is to track costs to departments. Assume we have three departments: clinic, laboratory, and administration. Further assume that for this period the total materials, supplies, salaries, and other costs traced to the three departments and their other selected statistics are as follows:

Department	Costs	Other Statistics
Clinic	$1,000,000	16,000 physician hours
Laboratory	300,000	10,000 tests
Administration	700,000	
Total	$2,000,000	

The next step is to reallocate the administration cost to the clinic and the laboratory. Let us assume that, based on a predetermined formula, these costs are split $600,000 to the clinic and $100,000 to the laboratory. The new totals are clinic $1,600,000 and laboratory $400,000. Assume that physicians spent 100 hours treating 50 patients in DRG 215 and that these patients received 150 tests. Then the cost per patient in DRG 215 can be calculated as follows:

Exam cost:	[($1,600,000 ÷ 16,000 physician hours) × 100 hours]	= $10,000
Lab cost:	[($400,000 ÷ 10,000 tests) × 150 tests]	= $ 6,000
Total cost for DRG 215		= $16,000
Cost per patient in DRG 215 (divided by 50 patients)		= $ 320

THINK ALONG

> How would the hospital determine the cost of this DRG if it used activities rather than departments to collect cost?

An activity-based system would trace the $2,000,000 costs to specific activities that support treating a patient in DRG 215. The hospital in our example would have to compute the cost of admitting patients, keeping records, conducting a physical exam, performing each type of test (blood, EKG, etc.), filling prescriptions, and so on. The cost would be assigned to DRG 215 based on activities consumed by patients in this DRG. Later in the module we describe this process in greater detail.

■ INFLUENCES ON COST MEASUREMENT SYSTEMS

Before we look at the different methods organizations use in practice to track and flow costs to final cost objects, we need to consider the reasons behind these differences. This diversity of cost systems reflects the differences in the *type of output* organizations produce and the *production methods* they use.

51

Type of Outputs.

Cost systems differ because each type of output requires different cost elements and a different cost management strategy. For example, in the construction industry a single major building can be a cost object and costs can be traced to it. In rice farming it does not make sense to trace costs to each grain. In automobiles the cost of purchased parts and assembling them is critical. In oil exploration the product does not require any assembled parts.

In general, organizations provide one of five types of outputs:

Extracted products are removed or drawn out of the earth by special effort or force. Oil refining, natural gas production, and coal mining are examples of extractive industries.

Processed goods are obtained by converting raw materials through substantial additional processing. Agricultural products, such as milk, cheese, butter, and ice cream, are good examples. Other examples include chemicals, paint, and cement. Robins's output (bottles of Robitussin cough syrup) fits into this category.

Assembled products are those in which numerous parts and subcomponents are put together to form a final product. Examples include cars, televisions, radios, computers, airplanes, and ships.

Fabricated products are a hybrid between processed and assembled goods. A major raw material is typically processed and then a few parts are assembled to create the final product. Examples of this group include semiconductors; machine tools and dyes; plastic toys; and paper products such as cups, stationery, and packaging. The heat exchangers produced by Alfa Laval are fabricated products.

Personal services involve the performance of duties or work for another person. Services require skilled processing or work performed by professional or service specialists. The work product of accountants, lawyers, doctors, photographers, gardeners, insurance adjusters, and waiters falls in the personal services category.

Production Methods.

Cost systems also reflect the type of production environment in which they are used. Three types of production methods have dominated the 20th century.

Craft production, universally observed prior to the Industrial Revolution, is still used for one-of-kind products produced in very small quantities. Examples are artistic works such as paintings, sculpture, and animated movies. In craft production, analysis of past costs is of limited usefulness as a guide to predicting future costs because each unit produced may be unique.

Mass production techniques have been the dominant method of manufacturing products during the 20th century. Mass production firms produce large volumes of products with little product variety. They typically use inflexible equipment and specialized labor, have long manufacturing cycles, and rely on inventories to buffer their systems from uncertainty.

Lean and **"agile"** production, developed by Japanese firms such as Toyota, is fast becoming a popular method of production in the last part of the 20th century.[5] A lean or agile manufacturing system emphasizes flexibility and quick response. Such a system produces

---

[5] For a detailed discussion of differences between craft, mass, and lean production, see James P. Womack, Daniel T. Jones, and Daniel Roos, *The Machine That Changed the World.* Accounting implications of lean production methods are described in detail in the module *Management Accounting in the Age of Lean Production* in this series.

small volumes of products quickly and can provide a great deal of product variety. These systems typically rely on computer-aided manufacturing and use just-in-time manufacturing.

Some service industries, such as banks or insurance companies, handle large volumes of similar transactions and have characteristics of mass production. Other service industries, such as consulting, auditing, or legal services, more closely resemble a custom-order situation.

> How do the type of output produced and the production methods used influence the design of a cost system?

Influence on Cost Measurement Systems.

While the nature of output often dictates the choice of production methods, it is not a universally fixed relationship. For example, many products today, such as automobiles, machine parts, and electronic goods, are produced using both mass and lean manufacturing methods. The choice influences the design of a cost measurement system in three major ways.

First, companies that use mass production systems have substantial inventories of raw materials, work-in-process, and finished goods. Cost measurement systems in such environments focus heavily on *inventory measurement*. In addition, because historically financial-reporting standards have dominated management reporting, manufacturing costs are often equated with product cost; only costs that can be "matched" with revenues.[6]

Second, mass production systems use unskilled labor and emphasize functional specialization. The use of unskilled labor vests all authority and responsibility with functional area managers. Managerial accounting systems reflect this orientation by using *responsibility accounting* systems. In a responsibility accounting system, managers are held responsible for managing costs within the administrative department or organizational subunit under their control. The cost centers typically are organized functionally and are referred to as *responsibility centers*. Responsibility accounting systems track costs by the person or entity responsible for costs rather than the work that gives rise to a cost. For example, assume that the warehouse in a retail department receives goods and stocks the goods on shelves. A responsibility accounting system will track all costs incurred in the warehouse—the responsibility center. However, this system will not routinely report the cost of the activities "receiving goods" and "stocking goods."

Finally, mass production systems have low product variety (few products) and large volume. Lean production systems are the opposite. They have large variety and low volumes. Mass production systems, therefore, tend to use a simple single allocation base such as labor hours and machine hours to allocate common costs to products. Lean production systems tend to use systems that use multiple allocation bases, one for each major cost pool, to allocate common costs.

■ TRADITIONAL COST MEASUREMENT SYSTEMS

Traditional cost measurement systems reflect the influence of mass production and are characterized by excessive focus on inventory measurement, use of responsibility centers

---

[6] This is called the "matching principle." It has long governed financial reporting, and it asserts that inventory or product costs should include only costs that can be matched with revenues generated. In practice, therefore, only production costs are part of product costs, since they are easy to match with revenues.

for cost tracking, and a single base for allocating indirect or common costs. Many organizations use some variant of two popular forms of traditional cost measurement systems: job-order costing and process costing. In practice most cost systems are hybrid and combine features of both job-order and process costing. To understand their differences, however, we will illustrate job-order and process costing in their pure forms.

Increasingly, organizations are modifying or redesigning their systems to match changes in their production systems or to meet the changing needs of their competitive environment. We will use the two firms from our opening story (Alfa Laval and A.H. Robins) to describe traditional cost measurement systems and their operation and then show how these firms might design contemporary cost measurement systems.

Job-Order Costing—Alfa Laval.

In a job-cost system, the primary cost object is a customer job. Job costs provide the information necessary to compute unit product costs.

Alfa Laval is a classic example of a firm that would use job-order costing.[7] One of its products is a heat exchanger used in industrial processes that must change the temperature of liquids during processing. Each customer job is unique and starts with the development of detailed product specifications based on a customer's special requirements. The *engineering* department performs this function.

The production of a heat exchanger involves three manufacturing processes. First, sheet metal is stamped into plates. These plates are then moved from the *stamping* department to the *assembly* department where the plates, frames, and cover are assembled. Next, the *testing* department runs reliability tests on the assembled units. Alfa Laval's *customer support* department installs the units at the customer's site and trains customer personnel in the operation and maintenance of the units. We will illustrate a traditional cost measurement system for Alfa Laval by discussing two orders: eight units for a wastewater-treatment plant in Sweden and six units for a sugar mill in Zimbabwe. The Zimbabwe job is complete, but the heat exchangers for the Sweden job are still in process.

As stated earlier, traditional job-order costing defines *product costs* as costs that can be carried on the balance sheet as the asset inventory. Therefore, *only manufacturing costs are considered part of the product cost* for valuing inventory and calculating the cost of goods sold. All other costs are referred to as "period costs." Also, all costs are traced to functions and departments and from there to customer jobs and units produced. Exhibit 2 graphically depicts the cost tracking that occurs in a traditional job-cost system.

How can Alfa Laval determine the manufacturing cost of the heat exchangers for the two jobs?

THINK ALONG

As the box at the far left of Exhibit 2 shows, cost tracking starts when resources (materials, labor, machinery, buildings, etc.) are acquired by an organization. Resources purchased are originally recorded in the accounting records by cost elements (materials, wages, etc.).

---

[7] We use Alfa Laval and Robins for illustrative purposes only. All numbers are fictitious. The description here has been adapted for pedagogical purposes. We do not claim, nor are we attempting, to provide a detailed and accurate description of their cost systems. No criticism of their systems is implied by this illustration.

Exhibit 2
Cost Flows in Traditional Job-Order Costing

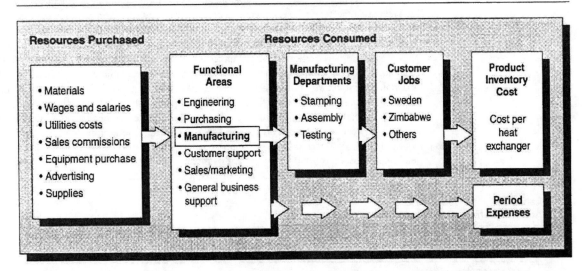

The cost system then traces these costs to the intermediate building blocks of functional areas, departments, and jobs. In traditional systems only resources consumed in manufacturing a heat exchanger are part of the job cost and unit product cost. Other cost elements, such as sales and marketing and general business support, are called period costs and are not traced to jobs or products. Instead, they are treated as expenses on the income statement.

The first step, therefore, is to identify those resources that are used by the manufacturing function. In addition, the logic of responsibility accounting requires that resources consumed within manufacturing be traced to the specific responsibility unit that uses these resources. The responsibility units are often called cost centers. Often a cost center also represents an organizational department headed by a manager who is responsible for managing costs in that cost center. As Exhibit 3 shows, Alfa Laval's manufacturing function has three cost centers: stamping, assembly, and testing. All resources consumed by these cost centers are broken into those that can be uniquely traced to particular customer jobs (direct materials and direct labor) and those that are common (manufacturing overhead costs) and must be allocated to jobs.

Exhibit 3
Analysis of Manufacturing Costs by Departments and Cost Categories.

	Stamping	Assembly	Testing	Totals
Direct materials issued	$3,200,000	$1,200,000	$300,000	$4,700,000
Direct labor	250,000	750,000	150,000	1,150,000
Manufacturing overhead	1,625,000	4,875,000	975,000	7,475,000
Total costs	$5,075,000	$6,825,000	$1,425,000	$13,325,000

From production departments Alfa Laval's system traces costs to individual customer jobs. This step requires the use of job numbers. Assume that the Sweden job is assigned the number WE-046-12-061-97 (WE signifies western Europe, 046 is the country code for Sweden, 12 is the sales territory within Sweden, 061 is the customer number, and 97 is the year the job started). The Zimbabwe job number is SA-263-15-026-97.

55

Job numbers serve both as authorization codes and as the means of tracing costs to jobs. When materials are requisitioned, the requisition slips indicate the department and the job that requested the materials. Engineers record the time they spend on each job on their time sheets. Machine operators and workers pass machine-readable bar codes on their identification badges through a bar code reader each time they change from one job to another.

Manufacturing overhead costs are indirect with respect to individual jobs. These costs are allocated to the two jobs using any one of several common allocation methods. For the example in Exhibit 4, we have assumed that manufacturing overhead is charged to jobs using machine hours in the stamping and testing departments and direct labor hours in the assembly department. A predetermined rate is used to charge overhead to jobs, and the difference between actual overhead incurred in a period and the amount charged to jobs is charged to the cost of good sold account. A full explanation of the allocation of common and shared costs is beyond the scope of this module. It is the subject of two separate modules in this series.[8] Exhibit 4 shows the results of this process.

Exhibit 4
Analysis of Manufacturing Costs by Jobs

	Sweden Job WE-046-12-061-97	Zimbabwe Job SA-263-15-026-97	Other Jobs	Totals
Direct materials				
Stamping	$384,000	$192,000	$2,624,000	$3,200,000
Assembly	108,000	72,000	1,020,000	1,200,000
Testing	54,000	18,000	228,000	300,000
Direct labor				
Stamping	5,000	3,000	242,000	250,000
Assembly	5,000	26,250	718,750	750,000
Testing	24,000	16,500	109,500	150,000
Manufacturing overhead*				
Stamping	48,750	32,500	1,543,750	1,625,000
Assembly	292,500	146,250	4,436,250	4,875,000
Testing	97,500	29,250	848,250	975,000
Total job cost	$1,018,750	$535,750	$11,770,500	$13,325,000
Number of units	8	6	86	
Current status	In process	Complete		
Cost per unit	$127,344	$89,292		

* Allocated on the basis of direct labor hours and machine hours used by each job.

Note that the total cost assigned to jobs in Exhibit 4 ($13,325,000) is the same as the total manufacturing cost shown in Exhibit 3. Also note that the cost per heat exchanger in Exhibit 4 is $127,344 for the Sweden job and $89,292 for Zimbabwe job. Finally, the cost per unit is different for the two jobs. Alfa Laval has already spent $127,344 per unit ($1,018,750/8) for Sweden's incomplete job as compared to $89,292 (535,750/6) for the fully completed units for the Zimbabwe job. This is because they use different materials and have different work specifications.

The basic mechanism for tracking costs is the *chart of accounts*. A chart of accounts is a list of accounts, each with a unique code to allow easy recording and tracking of costs in a computerized database. Account codes provide the capability to distinguish manufacturing

---

[8] See the modules *Indirect Costs* and *Manufacturing Overhead Allocation—Traditional versus Activity Based* in this series.

costs from other functional costs (see box 2 in Exhibit 2). The chart of accounts and codes also allow costs to be traced to individual departments within the manufacturing function (box 3 of Exhibit 2) and to individual jobs and units produced (boxes 4 and 5 in Exhibit 2). The design of the chart of accounts is a key activity in the development of a cost measurement system. The Appendix discusses the logic of account codes and shows the flow of costs between accounts in greater detail.

THINK ALONG

How would our costing approach change if the heat exchangers in all jobs had identical specifications?

Process Costing at Robins.

If all jobs had identical specifications, there would be no reason for Alfa Laval to separately track the costs of each individual job. The cost per unit could be computed simply by dividing the total cost in each department by the total number of units produced in that department. For example, the total cost in stamping is $5,075,000 (see Exhibit 3). The total number of units worked on in stamping is 100 (8 + 6 + 86 as shown in Exhibit 4). Because all 100 units are identical and assuming they have all been stamped and transferred to assembly, the stamping cost per unit for the heat exchanger is $50,750 ($5,075,000 ÷ 100 units). The total cost per heat exchanger would be the sum of the cost expended in all three operations.

This averaging of cost across processes is essentially what happens in our second example firm, A.H. Robins. Robins's production runs are much larger than Alfa Laval's and all units in a run are identical. A single production run may produce 2,500,000 tablets or 150,000,000 bottles of cough syrup, each exactly like the others in the batch. The processing time for various products ranges from two days to five months. The major processing steps are mixing, bottling, and packaging. Exhibit 5 below graphically represents the flow of costs in a traditional process costing system.

Exhibit 5
Cost Flows in Process Costing

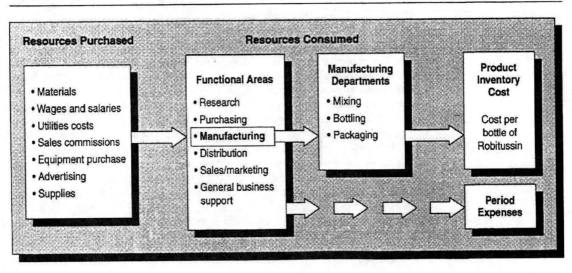

Compare Exhibit 5 with Exhibit 2, which portrays Alfa Laval's job-order costing system. In both Alfa Laval's job-costing system and Robins's process costing system, the first two steps are the same—costs are traced to functional areas of the firm and then to departments within these areas. Unlike Alfa Laval's customers, however, the individuals who purchase Robins's products expect no custom features, and Robins uses identical ingredients and processes for every bottle of cough syrup.[9] Therefore, the cost per unit does not vary from customer to customer, as was the case for Alfa Laval's heat exchangers, and Robins's cost measurement system can omit the step of tracing costs to individual customers or jobs. This situation greatly simplifies the design of the cost measurement system because fewer levels of building blocks are needed. Exhibit 6 shows the cost tracking for Robins. Note that Exhibit 6 is exactly the same as Exhibit 3 for Alfa Laval, except that for Robins the processing departments are mixing, bottling, and packaging.

Exhibit 6
Product Cost in Process Costing—Robitussin Cough Syrup

	Mixing	Bottling	Packaging	Totals
Direct materials	$1,200,000	$340,000	$700,000	$2,240,000
Direct labor	50,000	40,000	80,000	170,000
Manufacturing overhead	780,000	520,000	510,000	1,810,000
Total cost	**$2,030,000**	**$900,000**	**$1,290,000**	**$4,220,000**

Assume that the total processing costs of $4,220,000 is for producing 5,000,000 bottles of Robitussin cough syrup. Because all bottles are identical, we can obtain the cost per bottle of Robitussin by dividing $4,220,000 by 5,000,000 bottles to get $ 0.844 per bottle for this batch of the cough syrup. In addition, if we assume no spoilage or shrinkage, we can divide the cost of each processing center by 5,000,000 to obtain the processing cost per bottle in each processing center. You may recall from the opening story of the module that Robins's management was concerned that the cost per bottle was increasing in the mixing department. You can see that the computed cost of $0.406 per bottle in mixing ($2,030,000 ÷ 5,000,000) is the basis for this concern.

Inventory Issues in Traditional Cost Systems.

Product cost calculations in a traditional system rarely are as simple as those described for Robins, particularly in mass production environments. Long production cycle times and inventory buffers are two key characteristics of mass production systems. Accordingly, traditional systems have large amounts of raw materials, work-in-process, and finished-goods inventories. *Work-in-process* (WIP) means that there will always be some partially completed units in each process at the end of a period. That is, some cough syrup will be boiling, some will be bottled, and some will be packaged at the end of an accounting period.

Traditional job and process costing systems deal with this problem of work-in-process inventories by computing what are called **equivalent units of output**. An equivalent unit is a way of equating partially completed and fully completed units. Assume for example that Alfa Laval had four heat exchangers that were started at the beginning of the period and that no heat exchangers were in process at the beginning. At the end of the period, two exchangers are finished, and two are half finished. We can treat the two half-finished units as one finished unit

---

[9] In fact, once the Food and Drug Administration approves a product recipe, Robins *may not* alter the formulation.

and add them to the two fully completed units. Now we can say that Alfa Laval has three equivalent finished units. Because two out of three equivalent units are complete, two-thirds of the total cost for the period represents finished goods and one-third represents the cost of work-in-process.

THINK ALONG

> What does *half-finished* mean? How did we determine that the heat exchanger is half-finished? How do we test whether the cost calculation makes sense?

The concept of equivalent units is based on costs to completion and not time or physical completion. A 50 percent complete unit means that one-half of the costs have been incurred. It does not mean that the unit is physically half-complete or that 50 percent of the time to completion remains. These concepts of completion are important, but they are not the way accountants use the term *equivalent units*. Although these other concepts of completion may be related to cost, this is not always the case. For example, in home construction the most expensive items are finishing items (plumbing fixtures, electrical fixtures, appliances, doors, cabinets, etc.). They represent more than 35 percent of the cost but take up only 20 percent of the construction time.

To check the logic of equivalent units, let us return to the Alfa Laval example of the four heat exchangers. Assume that the total cost incurred on these heat exchangers is $450,000. Because we computed the output to be three equivalent units [2 + 2 (.5)], the cost per equivalent unit is $450,000 ÷ 3 = $150,000. Also, we know that two units are complete and have been transferred to the finished goods inventory. The transfer cost was $300,000 (2 × $150,000) and, therefore, work-in-process is $150,000. Because the $150,000 represents two (50 percent complete) units, each unit has a cost of $75,000. Completing these half-finished units, by definition, should require another $75,000 each. Thus when complete, all four heat exchangers will have the same per unit cost of $150,000.

In Robins's case, departments will have units in process from the last period (beginning work-in-process) and units in process at the end (ending work-in-process). Assume that during the current period, the mixing department started work on 5,300,000 bottles. In addition, it had 300,000 units in beginning work-in-process that were 40 percent completed last period. During the period, mixing transferred out 5,200,000 units to bottling. The remaining 400,000 units (300,000 + 5,300,000 − 5,200,000) in ending work-in-process are 70 percent complete. Exhibit 7 summarizes this data for the mixing department at Robins.

NOTE PAD

> Compute the cost per bottle transferred from mixing to bottling.

Exhibit 7
Equivalent Units Processed by Mixing Department

	Units Produced	Completion Stage
Bottles in process at beginning of period	300,000	40% complete
Bottles started this period	5,300,000	
Number of bottles transferred to next department	5,200,000	
Bottles in process at end of period	400,000	70% complete

Exhibit 8
Equivalent Units of Output for the Mixing Department

Bottles	Equivalent Units— FIFO		Equivalent Units— Weighted Average	
Beginning WIP	180,000	(300,000 × (1− .6)	300,000	
Started and finished (5,300,000 − 400,000)	4,900,000		4,900,000	
Ending WIP	280,000	(400,000 × .7)	280,000	(400,000 × .7)
Total	**5,360,000**		**5,480,000**	

The mixing department had 300,000 bottles on which 40 percent of the cost had been incurred. This period, to complete these bottles, they incurred the other 60 percent or the equivalent of 180,000 bottles. The department started another 5,300,000 bottles, bringing the total to 5,600,000. At the end mixing has 400,000 bottles still in process that are 70 percent complete. Therefore, 4,900,000 were started and completed during the period (5,200,000 − 300,000), and the equivalent of another 280,000 complete bottles (400,000 × .70) are still in process. The mixing department, therefore, completed work on 5,360,000 equivalent bottles this period. This procedure, which separates the percentage of completion of both beginning and ending work-in-process, is called the *first-in-first-out (FIFO)* method.

A more common method for dealing with percentage of completion is called the *weighted-average method*. This method ignores the percentage of completion of the beginning work-in-process. These units are combined with the units started and completed this period. The 70 percent completed ending work is added to the 5,200,000 units transferred to yield 5,480,000 equivalent units. Exhibit 8 shows the computation of equivalent units of output for the mixing department under the two methods.

Assuming the use of the weighted-average method, the information on equivalent units can be combined with the cost information from Exhibit 6 to determine the cost per equivalent unit for each cost element, as shown in Exhibit 9.

Exhibit 9
Calculation of Cost per Equivalent Unit

Cost Element	Amount	Equivalent Units Produced	Cost per Equivalent Unit
Direct materials	$1,200,000	5,480,000	$0.219
Direct labor	50,000	5,480,000	0.009
Manufacturing overhead	780,000	5,480,000	0.142
Total	**$2,030,000**		**$0.370**

NOTE PAD

Test your understanding of the concept of equivalent units of production by calculating the equivalent units for the bottling department. Assume the following: Beginning work-in-process inventory is 245,000 units, 30 percent complete; and ending work-in-process inventory is 240,000 units, 60 percent complete. During the current period bottling started work on another 5,200,000 units and completed and transferred 5,205,000 to packaging. (The answer is provided at the end of the module.)

The concept of equivalent units has wide applicability. In addition to manufacturing, equivalent-unit computation is relevant to service industries that have long production cycles. As college students you have may have completed two out of your four years toward a bachelor's degree at this point. From a cost perspective you are now a 50 percent equivalent finished student. Similarly, some students in your class may be full-time students, and others may be part-time students. Colleges compute their student load by adding these students through a unit called the "full-time equivalent" (FTE). Since 15 credit hours is a full-time load, two students, one with 9 credit hours and the other with 6 credit hours, will be counted as one full-time-equivalent student. In a class, however, the one equivalent student occupies two physical seats. Similarly, two students starting their junior year do not add up to one college degree. Ten half-completed planes, with only one wing attached, may be equal to five equivalent planes, but none of the planes can fly!

An equivalent unit is simply a way to account for two physically dissimilar units by adding together their common denominator, costs. It should not be confused with physical completion.

KEY POINT

Weaknesses in Traditional Job-Cost Systems.

Do the job- and process-cost calculations provide the information that managers at Alfa Laval and Robins need to better manage resources and to service their customers?

THINK ALONG

The costs traced to the two jobs in Exhibits 2, 3, and 4, and the cost per bottle in Exhibit 9 provide limited management insight for two main reasons.

First, total job cost and the per unit product cost of $1,018,750 and $127,344 respectively, for the Sweden job and $535,750 and $89,292 for the Zimbabwe job are neither the total cost of serving these customers nor do they represent total product cost. They are only manufacturing costs. Substantial costs incurred in other areas, such as marketing, distribution, and business support, are not included as part of the job cost. Hence the job cost calculated in this way is not the total cost of servicing a customer. The same is true for the cost per bottle of $0.37 for Robins.

Second, indirect costs account for a significant portion of the production costs in the two companies. For Alfa Laval manufacturing overhead costs account for 56 percent of total manufacturing costs (manufacturing overhead of $7,475,000/13,325,000 = .56). Single-driver allocation systems (direct labor or machine hours) used by many traditional systems to allocate indirect costs can provide a very misleading view of product cost and profitability. In addition, such single-allocation systems do not provide any information about cost drivers—that is, those factors that explain what causes costs to change. Thus management has very little information to assess whether the amount of resources consumed by a customer is excessive and how to better manage these costs.

Remember how the managers in our opening story lamented the lack of information to manage costs proactively and strategically. You can begin to see why.

■ CONTEMPORARY COST MEASUREMENT SYSTEMS

Traditional cost systems are not suited to the needs of today's competitive business environment. In particular, the advent of lean manufacturing systems, the use of Total Quality Management (TQM) techniques, and increasingly intense competition has greatly reduced the usefulness of traditional cost measurement systems.

Lean manufacturing systems use just-in-time systems and have little or no inventory. This system diminishes the usefulness of inventory valuation as a function of the cost measurement system and greatly simplifies the accounting part of the costing function because there are no work-in-process inventories and equivalent units to track.

TQM emphasizes cross-functional management of processes rather than department-based management systems. It reduces the need for responsibility accounting by departments and emphasizes instead cost management through redesign of products and processes. Cost tracking by departments does not help process management.

Finally, the competitive environment requires managers to think more strategically about how cost measurement systems can help an organization to compete effectively and to achieve its strategic goals.[10] This environment requires understanding cost drivers so costs can be managed proactively rather than reactively.

Contemporary cost measurement systems, therefore, emphasize the measurement of all costs and not just manufacturing (inventory) costs. Consistent with the process focus, contemporary cost systems use activities and operations as critical cost objects in building a cost measurement system. They also provide better information to help managers understand what drives the costs of each step in the process of developing, producing, and delivering products to customers. By analyzing costs at the detailed level of activities and operations involved in the cross-functional flow of work, these newer systems make visible how activities in one processing step may affect costs at other processing steps, thus enhancing the visibility of cost-driver relationships.

There are four important differences between traditional and contemporary approaches to cost measurement. A contemporary system:

- ■ Provides comprehensive product cost information by including in product cost not only manufacturing costs but the costs of all activities and operations that create, produce, deliver, and support the product or service. This includes both preproduction (upstream) costs and postproduction (downstream) costs.
- ■ Emphasizes management of the activities and operations that make up the process rather than the department that performs the work.
- ■ Allocates indirect costs to activities/operations and from there to products rather than from responsibility centers to products.
- ■ Supports strategic cost management by making cost-driver relationships visible as opposed to emphasizing external financial reporting.

One of the more important types of contemporary cost measurement systems is an activity/operations costing system. The focus of this system is on the total product cost (not just manufacturing costs). Its key building blocks are activities and operations that constitute the major cross-functional processes.[11]

---

[10] This is one of the fourteen principles of Total Quality enunciated by W. Edwards Deming, the leader of the quality movement.

[11] An *activity* is a series of related tasks performed by a person. An *operation* is a series of tasks performed by a piece of machinery. The distinction is not always clear, and the boundary between the two is somewhat fuzzy.

How will Alfa Laval or Robins need to modify its cost measurement systems to adopt this new approach?

Alfa Laval—An Activity and Operations-Costing View.

To convert Alfa Laval's traditional job costing system into an activity/operations costing system, we must start by developing a *process map*, which is a graphic representation of the sequence of activities/operations that must be performed to produce a heat exchanger. The heat exchangers in the two customer jobs examined earlier go through many activities and manufacturing operations. These activities involve all functional areas of the organization. Exhibit 10 is an abbreviated process map of some of the major activities/operations required by the two customer jobs.

Exhibit 11 identifies the functional area that has primary responsibility for each activity. Note that the various activities and operations involve all the functional areas and departments at Alfa Laval. Although we have kept this example simple, in practice many of the activities also cut across functional boundaries and involve several functions. A good example is drafting a contract. The legal, sales, engineering, and manufacturing departments all participate in this activity.

Each activity/operation consumes resources. The cost differences across jobs result from the fact that the various jobs require different activities and therefore consume different amounts of resources. To compute the cost of the two customer jobs, we must perform the following steps:

1. Identify activities and operations used by each job.[12]
2. Compute the costs of these activities and operations (including both direct and indirect costs).
3. Determine the cost drivers for each activity/operation.
4. Combine costs of activities that have common drivers into cost pools.
5. Assign costs to jobs based on the drivers each job consumes.
6. Determine unit product cost.

We can illustrate this six-step process using a sample of the activities identified in Exhibits 10 and 11.

1. Identify activities/operations used by jobs.
Notice that the completion of this job requires activities and operations in many areas of the organization. Substantial resources are required to support the activities performed by marketing personnel in visiting the prospective customer, by engineering personnel in developing product specifications, and by customer support personnel in the installation at the customer site. These activities are essential to complete the process of providing a heat exchanger to a customer, but traditional job-order costing systems do not treat these as part of the cost of heat exchangers. Costs of these activities must be included, however, to understand the full cost of the job. To understand why the cost of the Sweden job differs from the cost of other jobs, management needs to analyze which activities are unique to this job.

---

[12] Methods of documenting activities and computing their costs are discussed in detail in the modules *Activity-Based Management* and *Manufacturing Overhead Allocation: Traditional versus Activity Based* in this series.

Exhibit 10
Abbreviated Process Map for Alfa Laval's Customer Jobs

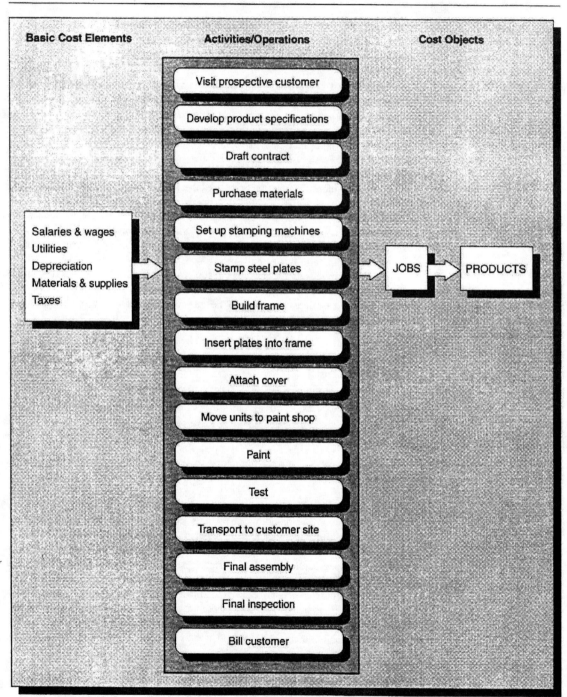

Basic Cost Elements	Activities/Operations	Cost Objects

Basic Cost Elements:
- Salaries & wages
- Utilities
- Depreciation
- Materials & supplies
- Taxes

Activities/Operations:
- Visit prospective customer
- Develop product specifications
- Draft contract
- Purchase materials
- Set up stamping machines
- Stamp steel plates
- Build frame
- Insert plates into frame
- Attach cover
- Move units to paint shop
- Paint
- Test
- Transport to customer site
- Final assembly
- Final inspection
- Bill customer

Cost Objects:
- JOBS
- PRODUCTS

Exhibit 11
Activities/Operations for Alfa Laval's Customer Jobs

Activity or Operation in the Process	Functional Area with Primary Responsibility
Visit prospective customer	Sales and marketing
Develop product specifications	Engineering
Draft contract	Legal
Purchase materials	Purchasing
Set up stamping machines	Stamping
Stamp steel plates	Stamping
Build frame	Assembly
Insert plates into frames	Assembly
Attach cover	Assembly
Move units to paint shop	Assembly
Paint	Assembly
Test	Testing
Transport to customer site	Customer support
Final assembly	Customer support
Final inspection	Customer support
Bill customer	General administration
Other activities	Various

2. Compute the costs of the activities and operations.

Each activity uses resources such as people, materials, factory space, and other cost items. Some cost items, such as operator salaries and supplies, are traceable to particular activities and operations. Other costs, such as property taxes on buildings, are indirect and have to be allocated to activities/operations based on *resource-usage drivers* such as square feet of space required by an activity. Exhibit 12 shows the results of this analysis for Alfa Laval.[13]

Exhibit 12
Activity Costs for Heat Exchangers

Activity or Operation	Cost
Visit prospective customer	$83,600
Develop product specifications	608,000
Draft contract	270,000
Purchase materials	288,000
Set up stamping machines	1,176,000
Stamp steel plates	3,952,000
Build frame	756,000
Insert plates into frames	5,040,000
Attach cover	126,000
Move unit to paint shop	9,000
Paint	480,000
Test	770,000
Transport to customer site	910,000
Final assembly	702,000
Final inspection	504,000
Bill customer	8,400
Other activities	87,000
Total activities cost	**$15,770,000**

[13] How to document and obtain the cost of activities is discussed in detail in the *Activity-Based Management* module in this series.

Exhibit 13
Activity Cost per Unit of Cost Driver

Activity or Operation	Cost	Driver	Units of Driver	Cost per Unit of Driver
Visit prospective customer	$ 83,600	Number of trips	22	$3,800
Develop product specifications	608,000	Engineering hours	3,800	160
Draft contract	270,000	Legal staff hours	1,800	150
Purchase materials	288,000	Per purchase order	2,400	120
Set up stamping machines	1,176,000	Per production run	120	9,800
Stamp steel plates	3,952,000	Per machine hour	520	7,600
Build frame	756,000	Per component	420	1,800
Insert plates in frames	5,040,000	Per plate	6,300	800
Attach cover	126,000	Attachment points	2,100	60
Move to paint shop	9,000	Per unit	120	75
Paint	480,000	Surface area, sq. ft.	32,000	15
Test	770,000	Per test	275	2,800
Transport to customer site	910,000	Per trip	140	6,500
Final assembly	702,000	Per unit	120	5,850
Final inspection	504,000	Per unit	120	4,200
Bill customer	8,400	Per bill	28	300
Other activities	87,000			
Total activities cost	**$15,770,000**			

3. Determine cost drivers for each activity and operation.

The accountant must work closely with personnel in other areas of the organization to determine what causal factors increase or decrease the cost of an activity. These causal factors are referred to as "cost drivers." Identifying the cost driver for the activity "developing product specifications," for example, may require talking to design engineers, sales people, manufacturing engineers, machine operators, quality assurance, installers, service engineers, and cost analysts. The analysis may reveal that the number of engineering hours consumed is the cost driver for this activity. The next step is to divide the cost of the activity by the number of engineering hours consumed to determine the activity/operation cost per unit of the driver. This analysis is shown in Exhibit 13.

Although this type of first-level cost driver is sufficient for assigning activity costs to heat exchangers, Alfa Laval may find it useful to conduct additional levels of analysis for cost management purposes. Exhibit 13 shows that using one more engineering hour for developing product specifications increases cost by $160. To manage engineering costs, however, they need to know what causes engineering hours to go up. For example, the heat exchangers being produced for Sweden must withstand severe winter weather and operate under various climatic conditions in the plant. Accordingly, engineering personnel have to spend additional time researching how to make existing components operate under different environmental conditions. Engineering hours, therefore, are being driven by the "variety of operating conditions" under which the heat exchanger must perform.

KEY POINT

To manage the cost of engineering hours consumed, Alfa Laval must go beyond the obvious cost drivers and understand the deeper levels of cost drivers.

4. Create cost pools for common cost drivers.

Some cost drivers may be common to several activities. Consider, for example, the activities "final assembly" and "final inspection." The cost driver for both activities is "number

Exhibit 14
Alfa Laval—Costs Assigned to Jobs

Activity	Sweden Job WE-046-12-061-97 Units of Cost Driver	Cost Assigned	Zimbabwe Job SA-263-15-026-97 Units of Cost Driver	Cost Assigned
Visit prospective customer	4	$15,200	1	$3,800
Develop product specifications	1,400	224,000	300	48,000
Draft contract	18	2,700	4	600
Purchase materials	240	28,800	90	10,800
Set up stamping machines	11	107,800	3	29,400
Stamp steel plates	22	167,200	8	60,800
Build frame	38	68,400	25	45,000
Insert plates into frames	280	224,000	95	76,000
Attach cover	122	7,320	90	5,400
Move unit to paint shop	14	1,050	6	450
Paint	3,800	57,000	825	12,375
Test	18	50,400	6	16,800
Transport to customer site	0	0	2	13,000
Final assembly	0	0	6	35,100
Final inspection	0	0	6	25,200
Bill customer	0	0	1	300
Total activities cost		**$953,870**		**$383,025**

of units." To simplify calculations, the costs associated with these two activities can be combined and treated as a single cost pool for allocation purposes. Aggregating costs by common cost drivers highlight those cost drivers that account for a significant portion of costs and thus helps to focus cost management efforts on the correct variables.

5. Assign costs based on drivers.
The next step is to assign costs to jobs based on the drivers consumed. Exhibit 14 shows this analysis as well as the calculation of cost per unit for each job.

6. Determine unit product cost.
The determination of unit product cost requires adding the cost of specific materials issued for each job to the cost of each activity or operation consumed by that job and dividing by the number of equivalent completed units in that job. Exhibit 15 shows this analysis and compares it to the traditional cost analysis for these same jobs.

Exhibit 15
Comparison of Job Cost

	Sweden Total Job Cost	Cost per Unit	Zimbabwe Total Job Cost	Cost per Unit
Activity/operations view				
Materials cost	$546,000	$68,250	$282,000	$47,000
Activities cost	953,870	119,234	383,025	63,838
Total cost	$1,499,870	$187,484	$665,025	$110,838
Traditional view				
Direct materials	$546,000	$68,250	$282,000	$47,000
Direct labor	34,000	4,250	45,750	7,625
Manufacturing overhead	438,750	54,844	208,000	34,667
Total cost	$1,018,750	$127,344	$535,750	$89,292

67

Notice that the activity/operations costs for the two jobs ($1,499,870 for Sweden; $665,025 for Zimbabwe) is substantially greater than that derived by Alfa Laval's traditional job order system ($1,018,750 for Sweden; $535,750 for Zimbabwe).

> Why is the cost per unit from the contemporary cost measurement system shown here different from the cost per unit determined by the traditional job-order costing system?

You may recall that the traditional cost measurement system described in Exhibits 3 and 4 includes only manufacturing costs. A contemporary activity/operations cost system traces all costs from other functional areas, such as engineering and customer support, and assigns these costs to jobs based on the usage of these activities.

Robins—An Activity and Operations-Costing View.

Like Alfa Laval, Robins can use the six steps described above to make their cost system more consistent with the contemporary activity/operations-based approach. Because all the steps, with the exception of tracing costs to jobs, are the same as for Alfa Laval, we will not illustrate them again in detail. Exhibit 16 provides an example of the final numbers that Robins's contemporary cost system might produce.[14]

> The mixing cost of a bottle of Robitussin as calculated by the activity-based analysis is $0.28. Why is this value different from the mixing cost per bottle of $0.37 shown in Exhibit 9?

The main difference between the costs shown in Exhibit 9 and those shown below (Exhibit 16) is due to the allocation of manufacturing overhead costs. In a traditional system all manufacturing overhead is first charged to the three processing centers and then to products. In an activity-based system, the overhead costs are charged first to activities and then to products.[15]

Also note that Robins's new cost system shown in Exhibit 16, provides an analysis of costs by traditional categories as well as by activities/operations and by cost drivers. This "kaleidoscopic view" of costs allows Robins to see the $2.05 cost per bottle of Robitussin cough syrup in many ways. The first is by type of resources consumed—that is, materials, wages, supplies, utilities, equipment, and so on. Next it also shows cost by activities. Finally, Robins can also see costs by drivers.

---

[14] Exhibit 16 has been adapted from an article on Teva Pharmaceutical Industries Ltd., which describes its experience in developing an activity-based cost system. The article supports our hypothetical example by showing how in the real world a company in the same business as Robins can use an activity/operations costing system. See Robert Kaplan, Dan Weiss, and Eyal Dinesh, "Transfer Pricing with ABC," *Management Accounting*, May 1997, pp. 20–28.

[15] For a detailed discussion of why differences in allocation systems result in different cost assignments, see the module *Manufacturing Overhead Allocation: Traditional versus Activity Based* in this series.

Exhibit 16
Sample Cost Breakdown for Robitussin Using a Contemporary Cost System

Classification	Cost	Classification	Cost
By Resources:		**By Activities:**	
Materials	$0.42	Develop customer relations	$.04
Labor	0.03	Process orders	.02
Manufacturing overhead		New product development	.34
Supplies	0.02	Purchase chemicals	.06
Utilities	0.06	Secure storage	.04
Wages	0.14	Issue chemicals to production	.02
Equipment	0.10	Print cartons	.09
Other	0.02	Mixing	.28
Subtotal	0.34	Bottling	.23
Other costs		Packaging	.35
Shipping supplies	0.04	Quality assurance	.06
Utilities	0.05	Equipment maintenance	.25
Salaries	0.90	Move to storage	.02
Equipment	0.07	Distribution	.03
Other	0.20	Billing	.22
Subtotal	1.26	**Total**	**$2.05**
Total	**$2.05**		
By Cost Drivers:			
Customer calls	$.07		
Purchase orders	.03		
Engineering hours	.31		
Material moves, secured	.11		
Material moves, unsecured	.02		
Production runs	.35		
Number of colors	.13		
Machine hours	.67		
Number of bottles	.33		
Number of bills	.03		
Total	**$2.05**		

Comparison of Traditional and Contemporary Cost Systems.

Traditional and contemporary cost measurement systems are built on fundamentally different conceptual foundations. A traditional cost system uses responsibility centers (commonly defined as departments or functional areas of the firm) as a key cost object in tracking cost flows. A contemporary cost system uses activities/operations as intermediate cost objects to trace costs to final cost objects. It assigns costs to final cost objects based on cost drivers and provides multiple views of costs—by resources consumed, by activities consumed, and by drivers consumed. The contemporary approach facilitates

69

Exhibit 17
Cost Flow Differences between Traditional (top) and Contemporary (bottom) Cost Systems

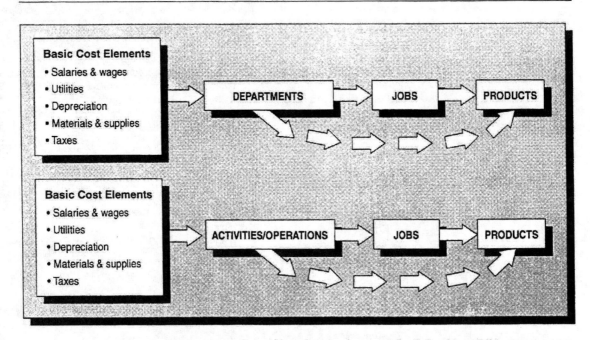

cost management by making these various causal relationships visible to managers. Exhibit 17 shows the differences in cost flows between these two approaches.

Another important difference is that the two systems define product costs differently. Exhibit 18 below shows this difference. A traditional system, the shaded portion of Exhibit 18, includes only manufacturing and manufacturing support costs in product costs. A contemporary system includes, in addition, the cost of all traceable activities in computing per unit product cost. Some costs, such as management training or the costs of operating corporate headquarters, are so distant from any specific product that both types of systems may choose not to trace them to products. However, by including these other costs, a contemporary cost system enhances the visibility of nonmanufacturing costs and provides a more comprehensive view of a job's profitability.

This difference between the two approaches represents the difference between generally accepted accounting principles (GAAP) and managerial use of accounting data. GAAP has a more restrictive definition of what can be included in product cost. An activity-based system allows many more costs to be directly identified with products. It is interesting to see whether GAAP rules will change to allow more costs to be part of product cost.[16]

A third difference between the two systems is that activity-based systems focus attention on the process of work rather than on who does the work. The contemporary system tells Alfa Laval's management that the most expensive activities are inserting plates in frames, and stamping steel plates.

---

[16] It is interesting to note that the income tax treatment is also different from GAAP. Many other costs, such as interest—treated as an expense by GAAP—must be capitalized in determining product costs for tax reporting.

Exhibit 18
Product Cost Buildup—Traditional and Contemporary

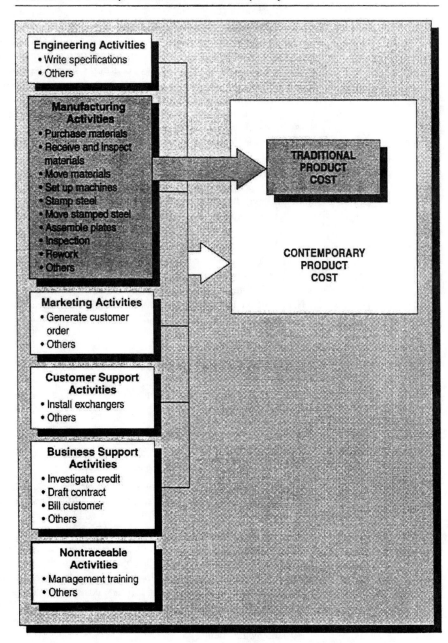

Finally, the contemporary system provides comprehensive product cost information by functions, resources, activities, and cost drivers. The information on cost drivers is particularly useful in managing and redesigning work processes. For example, the data in

Exhibit 16 facilitates effective cost management in several ways. The resource breakdown shows Robins that its single largest cost category is general and administrative salaries, which total roughly 44 percent of the total product cost of $2.05. The activity analysis shows packaging and new-product development are the two costliest activities. Finally, analysis of costs by drivers shows machine hours and production runs are the most significant cost drivers for Robins, accounting for 65 percent of the product cost for Robitussin. The cost management strategy for Robins should be to reduce materials price and usage, search for ways to better perform new product development and packaging activities, and reduce the number of machine hours used if possible.

Although the contemporary cost measurement system expands the definition of costs, it is still not a complete picture of all costs incurred to serve a customer. What a customer pays for Robitussin includes costs incurred by firms that provide or receive services from Robins. They are part of the value chain of suppliers and dealers that enable the cough syrup to get to the final consumer. Few cost measurement systems in use today track such costs, partly because of the practical problems associated with analyzing costs incurred by different organizations. However, a large part of the reason is a lack of trust that makes organizations reluctant to share cost information with others.

KEY POINT

> Although many costs are traceable to products, under current GAAP many such costs cannot be included as inventory cost on the balance sheet. In an activity/operations costing system, each discrete *activity* and each *manufacturing operation* become cost objects. The product cost includes many activities and operations that are traceable to products.

■ ATTRIBUTES OF A COST MEASUREMENT SYSTEM

A well-designed cost measurement system must have desirable technical, behavioral, and cultural attributes.

Technical Attributes.

A cost measurement system should improve the quality of management decisions and enhance their process understanding to facilitate process management.

Decision relevance.
For a cost system to provide information relevant to management's decisions, cost objects must be related to the strategic objectives of quality, cost, and time. For example, cost measurement systems must help managers understand the costs associated with providing existing levels of quality and estimate costs of adding features desired by their customers. The following quote from a manager at Hewlett-Packard's circuit board assembly plant in Palo Alto, California, reflects the expectations of managers with regard to their cost measurement systems.

> We expect our cost system to do more than just allocate costs and produce reports.
> We need to know what drives these costs. We want the cost system to talk to our design engineers so they can carry their understanding of costs into product designs that are cost-effective to produce.

Note that at Hewlett-Packard the test of a good system is its ability to improve product design decisions. The cost system aids engineers in designing better products by showing them how design decisions drive product costs. We have seen in this module that traditional systems are of little help in proactively managing costs, since they focus on departments and not on cost drivers. The contemporary approach's focus on cost drivers improves decisions about where to spend managerial time and what areas to focus on.

Process understanding.

A good cost measurement system must help managers to understand their work processes and the economic impact of activities or operations that reduce quality, increase cost, or cause delays. This feature is a major strength of the contemporary cost systems. Their primary focus is work operations and activities. As we have seen, their starting point is a process map (Exhibit 10). Contemporary systems can readily extend the analysis to include all value chain activities, thereby providing a more comprehensive process view than a system constrained by the departmental boundaries of a single organization. Finally, the cost impact of manufacturing and innovation cycle time are not made visible by traditional systems. By emphasizing costs across all steps in a process, a contemporary cost measurement system can reveal which activities or operations cause delays and thus cause cost increases.

Behavioral Attributes.

Cost measurement systems can affect behavior of people in organizations in many ways. The selection of cost objects can be a particularly important means of changing behavior in organizations because a cost object makes the selected variable *visible*, *focuses attention*, and *communicates* managerial intent. When selected carelessly, the cost system can lead to dysfunctional behaviors.

Consider the use of DRGs as cost objects by hospitals. Many industry observers claim that this shift has made hospitals play games to provide proper health care to patients. Hospitals sometimes discharge and then readmit patients under a different DRG to complete the treatment for a single episode or ailment when a patient's length of stays exceeds that permitted by a DRG. Similarly, state colleges measure costs based on equivalent full-time students. Some critics charge that this method of measuring and funding state colleges has led to overcrowding in the classroom.

Another way in which cost measurement systems can change behaviors is through highlighting cost drivers. Cost driver analysis can focus attention on managing the right variables and can also help to communicate efficient and better design rules and practices. As the Hewlett-Packard quote points out, many world-class organizations use their cost measurement system to communicate with design engineers about how to develop better and more cost-effective product and process designs.[17] They do this by penalizing designs that consume more of critical cost drivers. This approach forces designers to explicitly consider cost as an important variable in putting features and functions into products and in choosing the processes to produce and deliver these products.[18]

---

[17] For example, see D. Berlant, R. Browning, and G. Foster, "How Hewlett-Packard Gets Numbers It Can Trust," *Harvard Business Review*, Jan–Feb 1990, pp. 178–183 and T. Hiromoto, " Another Hidden Edge—Japanese Management Accounting," *Harvard Business Review*, July–Aug 1988, pp. 22–26.

[18] The *Target Costing* module in this series discusses cost management in the product design phase in greater detail.

73

A well-designed cost measurement system uses the selection of cost objects and cost measurement rules as an opportunity to reinforce behaviors that lead to the accomplishment of strategic objectives. When properly selected, that cost object will make visible customer requirements throughout the organization, reduce product costs, and decrease cycle time for manufacturing, innovation, or delivery.

Cultural Attributes.

A cost measurement system both reflects and reinforces an organization's culture. In an organization where finding fault and laying blaming are a pervasive *mind-set*, the cost measurement system becomes a tool toward that end. Traditional systems, in general, are more susceptible to this because they are responsibility-focused, and therefore encourage the tendency to assign blame. They reinforce the role of the accountant as a corporate cop. On the other hand, activity systems have a process focus. They encourage improving processes by looking for underlying causes of changes in costs. By focusing on cost drivers and cross-functional processes, activity-based cost measurement systems transform the role of an accountant from a cop to a business advisor.[19] Management accountants become symbols and actors that help to create and foster a healthy organization culture.

The selection of cost objects can send symbolic messages in an organization. An organization that uses cost objects related solely to profitability and efficiency sends a message that it cares only for its own well-being. A corporation that measures costs for cost objects such as the environment, social activities, and human resource development can use these cost objects as powerful symbols to say that it is socially responsible and cares about its people and the environment.

■ LESSONS LEARNED

- ■ A cost measurement system is part of a strategic management accounting system that helps an organization to meet its strategic objectives of quality, cost, and time.
- ■ A cost measurement system is like a building process that transforms raw data about resource purchases into useful information about resources consumed.
- ■ The design of a cost measurement system involves selecting the right cost objects, establishing a chart of accounts and codes to track cost flows, and establishing rules for allocating the cost of shared resources.
- ■ The type of cost measurement system an organization uses typically reflects the nature of products or services it produces and the production methods it uses.
- ■ Firms that fabricate, assemble products from parts, or provide personal services using mass production techniques typically use job-order or batch costing. Firms using mass production methods in extractive and process industries typically use process costing.
- ■ Traditional job and process cost systems trace costs first to departments (responsibility units) and from there to units produced.

---

[19] For an extended discussion of these two roles of accountants, see *The Organizational Role of the Management Accountants* module in this series.

- Firms using lean production methods typically use activity/operations costing systems. These contemporary cost systems trace costs first to activities and operations and then to units produced.
- An activity/operations costing system provides more comprehensive product cost data and makes cost drivers visible to managers.
- A well-designed cost measurement system improves decisions and facilitates process management by providing data on the cost of outputs produced, the cost of the processes (activities) used, and the underlying causal relationships (drivers) that cause costs to change. A good cost system encourages behaviors consistent with strategic objectives and creates mindsets and values that create a healthy and positive organizational culture.

Solution to Note Pad problem
Equivalent Units in Bottling

Bottles	Equivalent Units— Weighted Average	Equivalent Units— FIFO
Beginning WIP	245,000	171,500 (245,000 × (1−.3)
Started and finished (5,205,000 − 245,000)	4,960,000	4,960,000
Ending WIP	144,000 (240,000 × .6)	144,000 (240,000 × .6)
Total	5,349,000	5,275,500

APPENDIX

■ COST TRACKING—TECHNICAL ISSUES

This appendix explains how a *chart of accounts* and *account codes* allow Alfa Laval to generate the job-cost data shown in Exhibits 3 and 4. Before you read on, it may be useful for you to review once more the job costs identified in these exhibits.

Cost Flows and the Chart of Accounts.

A *chart of accounts* is a series of general ledger accounts that record the resources acquired and the resources used by an organization. Consider the information in Exhibits 3 and 4. We know that during the current period, Alfa Laval used materials, labor, machinery, utilities, supplies, and so on to produce heat exchangers. We also know that some of the work was complete and was transferred to customers and some work is still in process. The resources used during the current period were acquired in prior periods (materials) or during the current period (employee wages).

To understand the flow of costs during the current period, we must gather and record data pertaining to resource acquisition and use. Exhibit 19 summarizes this data for Alfa Laval.

The data for Exhibit 19 comes from various source documents. For example, purchase orders, receipts, and invoices paid are documents generated when materials are purchased. A material requisition slip is the source document that identifies the type of material requested, who requested it, and for what job.

Exhibit 20 below uses T-accounts to show how Alfa Laval records the information from source documents into various accounts. The letters *a* to *l* correspond to the items listed in Exhibit 19.

Can you reconcile these numbers with the numbers shown in Exhibits 3 and 4 of the module?

NOTE PAD

The top part of Exhibit 20 shows the source documents. We know from looking at invoices that we purchased $12,800,000 of materials this period. The material requisition slips tell us that $4,700,000 worth of materials were issued to departments for specific jobs. The departmental amounts are the same as those in Exhibit 3. In addition, another $1,600,000 in materials was issued but could not be identified with specific jobs and is initially charged to the manufacturing overhead account. Alfa Laval started the period with a beginning materials inventory of $3,000,000; after the new purchases and uses, it has an ending inventory balance of $9,500,000.

In each department a work-in-process account combines the materials, labor, and other manufacturing costs for production during a period. Because not all work is completed within the accounting period, the work-in-process accounts also start with a beginning and ending balance. As work is completed, the cost of completed jobs is transferred from work-in-process of a preceding department to the work-in-process of the succeeding department. The last department, assembly, transfers its completed items to the Finished Goods Inventory account.[20] Finally, when goods are shipped to customers, we record the sales revenue and move the cost of that job from the Finished Goods Inventory account to

---

[20] Realistically, Alfa Laval will have little or no finished goods inventory, due to the nature of its product. The heat exchangers are all done to order, and final assembly occurs at the customer's location.

Exhibit 19
Alfa Laval—Data on Resources Purchased and Used

Item	Description
a.	Purchase of materials, $12,800,000.
b.	Direct materials requisitioned by production departments: stamping $3,200,000; assembly $1,200,000; testing $300,000.
c.	Indirect materials consumed, $1,600,000.
d.	Direct labor recorded: stamping $250,000; assembly $750,000; testing $150,000.
e.	Indirect labor recorded, $1,200,000.
f.	Actual manufacturing overhead costs incurred, including $400,000 in depreciation on manufacturing equipment and $4,400,000 in other items.
g.	Overhead applied to production departments at rate of $6.50 per direct labor dollar.
h.	Movement of jobs from stamping to assembly, $8,000,000.
i.	Movement of jobs from assembly to testing, $14,000,000.
j.	Completion of jobs, $18,000,000.
k.	Delivery of completed units to customer sites, cost of goods sold recorded.
l.	$19,500,000. Sales revenue and accounts receivable recorded, $28,000,000; general and administrative expenses recorded, $6,550,000.

Exhibit 20
Alfa Laval—Cost Flows and Source Documents

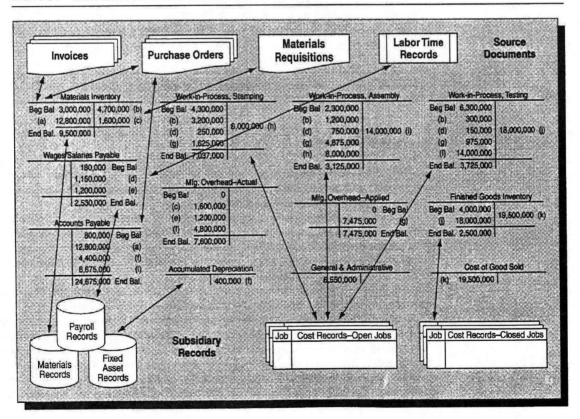

Cost of Goods Sold. General & Administrative expenses of $6,550,000 are not treated as part of product cost and are expensed at the end of the period when financial statements are prepared.

Before any department transfers out a job, it must allocate a portion of the indirect manufacturing costs to that job. In a traditional job-order costing system, the actual overhead costs are first traced to departments and then assigned to jobs using predetermined departmental or plantwide overhead rates. A predetermined rate is an estimate based on the total budgeted dollars of overhead for the year divided by a budgeted allocation base such as machine hours, labor hours, or labor dollars. Because a detailed discussion of overhead allocation is beyond the scope of this module, we will simply use a plantwide rate to illustrate the cost flows.

Assume that Alfa Laval's budget calls for total labor cost of $1,170,000 and estimated overhead costs of $7,600,000. At the beginning of the accounting period, the company would calculate an overhead application rate as follows:

$$\text{Overhead Rate} = \frac{7,600,000}{1,170,000} = \$6.50 \text{ (rounded) per direct labor dollar}$$

Notice in Exhibit 20 that the overhead cost assigned to each department is 6.5 times the direct labor cost for that department. At the end of any given period, there is a difference between overhead costs incurred and overhead costs charged to jobs. This difference is called *under-* or *overapplied overhead* and is charged to the Cost of Goods Sold account at the end of the period.

Finally, note that the bottom part of Exhibit 20 shows the subsidiary records that support the cost tracking. For instance, payroll records for employees support labor cost tracking. Individual job cost sheets allow separation of material, labor, and overhead costs by jobs.

THINK ALONG

> How would the accounts used be different in a contemporary cost measurement system?

Account Codes.

For a firm to benefit from an activity-based approach, the accounting system must capture costs not just by departments and jobs but also by activities and operations. These systems require a new set of accounts and account codes.

Account codes are the technical mechanism that permits organizations to track costs in a variety of ways. An account code is a number assigned to an account. Each number codes a particular field of data that is of interest to the users of the system. For example, Exhibit 3 tells us that during the current period the three manufacturing departments used $4,700,000 in direct manufacturing materials. Also, we know that of this amount $3,200,000 went to the stamping department. Exhibit 4 tells us that the stamping department used $384,000 out of the $3,200,000 in materials on the Swedish job.

Clearly, Alfa Laval's accounting system must be capable of tracking all expenditures by type, function, cost center, and job. In addition, because materials purchased exceed materials used, any remaining materials have to be shown on the balance sheet as an asset. Therefore, the system must also distinguish between expenditures that create assets and categorize the asset as current or noncurrent. In database terminology the five items of interest about the expenditure for materials (type, function, cost center, job, and balance sheet classification) are called "fields." In an accounting database, the fields are coded with a single- or double-digit number. For example, direct materials may be account number 1152137. The explanation for each digit is as follows: 1 = asset, 1 = current asset, 5 = materials, 2 = manufacturing, 1 = stamping department, and 37 = Swedish job. If we want to know the total cost in stamping, the database needs to add all expenditures charged to accounts that have 21 as the fourth and fifth digit. Similarly, to get the cost of the Sweden job, we must sort all expenditures that have a 37 as their sixth and seventh digits.

In practice, account codes and the database programs that handle cost tracking are quite complex. The account codes must be flexible enough to allow for both future expansion and any special analysis management may request. Many organizations do not think far enough ahead when they establish their chart of accounts and find that their computer systems cannot code data by certain cost objects because they "have run out of digits." This problem is not trivial if you consider that the so-called millennium bug (the inability of computer programs to handle the two-digit year change from year 1999 to 2000) has cost billions of dollars to fix.

Because most traditional accounting systems track costs by responsibility centers or departments, these systems do not easily provide activity/operations costs. Firms seeking to obtain activity costs often resort to one-time special cost studies to obtain this data. We believe that in the long run, this approach is costly. If possible, the system should be modified to provide an additional field for activity/operations coding of raw data.

One solution, for organizations that can afford it, is to use software packages called enterprise resource planning (ERP) programs to track cost flows.[21] These packages can track resources in various ways. For example, sorting all employees by a certain field will tell us the salary cost for a functional area such as manufacturing or engineering. Most of these software packages are adding modules that allow organizations to organize and sort data by activities and operations. This feature will make it easier for organizations to move from traditional to contemporary cost systems in the future.

---

[21] Some major ERP software packages/providers are BANYAN, PEOPLESOFT, ORACLE, and SAP.

■ PROBLEMS AND CASES—INTRODUCTORY LEVEL

1. Self-test Questions.

a. What are the four components of a strategic management accounting system?

b. What are the three primary building blocks of a cost measurement system?

c. How should an organization determine what cost objects it needs?

d. What is cost allocation?

e. How does responsibility accounting differ from more modern cost measurement systems?

f. How is *product cost* defined for financial-reporting purposes?

g. Give examples of some cost items that are not part of product cost using the financial-reporting definition, but which would be included in product cost in a modern cost measurement system.

h. Give several examples of cost items that would be classified as period costs in a traditional cost measurement system.

i. Give several examples of firms that would use job-order costing.

j. What level of building blocks does a job-order costing system use that would not be found in a process costing system?

k. Describe the journal entries that are used to record manufacturing costs in a traditional job-order costing system.

l. Give several examples of firms that would use process costing.

m. What is an equivalent unit of production?

n. Why is inventory valuation less important in the cost measurement systems of firms that use modern manufacturing techniques?

o. Explain in your own words the three major differences between modern and traditional cost measurement systems.

p. What is a process map?

q. Name and explain the six steps involved in determining product cost in a modern cost measurement system.

r. What is a cost driver?

s. Exhibit 17 of the module shows some activity costs that are not traced to products. Why is this?

t. Explain why a modern cost measurement system provides superior process understanding.

u. Give an example of the behavioral impact of different definitions of cost objects.

v. What mindset does traditional responsibility accounting foster?

Exercises, Problems, and Cases.

2. For each of the firms described below, identify a strategic decision related to each leg of the strategic triangle (quality, cost, time). For each decision identified, what cost objects should be defined in the firm's CMS?

a. Heartthrob, Inc., which manufactures two kinds of heart monitors, including one for fitness enthusiasts to wear while working out and another for people at risk for heart attacks.

b. Mug Shots, Inc., produces insulated coffee mugs for Starbucks Coffee and Barnes & Noble Bookstores, and also produces a line of mugs with company logos on special order for organizations to use for promotional purposes.

c. TrashMasters, Inc., makes plastic trash bags using a process that includes the steps of mixing the plastic compounds, extruding sheets of plastic, and forming the sheets into bags.

d. Provident Beneficial Insurance Co. sells life insurance, homeowners' insurance, and car insurance to individuals and corporations.

3. You are conducting a continuing education course for financial managers. At the first session you presented the diagrams shown in Exhibits 2, 5, and 17 of the module, and described the basic differences between traditional job order and process costing and contemporary cost measurement systems. Two financial managers from a local hospital are debating whether the hospital should use job-order costing or process costing. A third individual comments that because hospitals are labor-intensive service organizations, the only kind of cost measurement system they should consider is an activity-based system. How will you (diplomatically) resolve this issue? (Hint: Consider the technical, behavioral, and cultural attributes of the cost measurement systems.)

4. Consider the following list of cost items:

- Production workers' wages.
- Salaries of product design engineers.
- The salary of an accountant at corporate headquarters.
- The president's salary.
- Salaries of customer sales representatives.
- Utilities for the factory.
- Commissions paid to sales staff.
- Supplies and salaries related to maintaining records for a major customer who orders parts just-in-time and is billed monthly.

Required:
a. For each item, indicate whether it would be considered part of product cost by a traditional cost measurement system.
b. For each item, indicate whether it would be considered part of product cost by a contemporary cost measurement system.

5. Fragonard Perfume Company in Paris produces two lines of perfumes. One is a generic brand sold to tourists. The other product line is sold to exclusive name-brand retail outlets at a high markup. The resources consumed by the firm include space in Paris for a production facility and sales room, employees and equipment there, and farming costs for fields of flowers and other ingredients grown in the south of France. Among the Paris employees is a blender, referred to in the trade as a "nose," who custom blends the ingredients at a large pigeonhole desk called the "organ." A major cost item is insurance on the "nose," since only 30 individuals in the world are qualified to perform this function.

Required:
a. Prepare a listing of the main cost elements Fragonard will record and indicate how each would be classified in a traditional cost measurement system (direct materials, direct labor, indirect manufacturing costs [overhead], or nonmanufacturing costs).

81

b. Develop a set of account codes that Fragonard could use to record these costs. Design your codes to allow the firm to analyze costs by the nature of the resources consumed and by activities performed.

c. Of the cost elements your account codes will track, which might differ across the two types of perfume? *production? field operations?*

6. The University of Southern Iowa encourages faculty to submit proposals for research grants to various external foundations and government agencies. The university's Office of Grants and Research assists faculty in preparing and submitting proposals, and Campus Computing Services provides data entry and analysis support. Some faculty members in the chemistry department are preparing a proposal for a research project. They estimate that the direct costs associated with the project will be as follows:

Cost Item	Amount
Faculty summer support	$8,000
Graduate student stipend	4,500
Travel	1,500
Total	$14,000

The university requires that researchers include in their grant budgets a request for funding to recover the cost of operating the Office of Grants and Research. Each year the university calculates an indirect cost rate based on budgeted expenses for the department and the total dollar of grants it expects faculty will receive during the year. For this year the total departmental budget is $3,600,000. This amount includes $2,400,000 in general operating expenses and $1,200,000 for data entry services. Faculty members are expected to receive grants totaling $8,000,000 during the year. The university uses a traditional job-order costing system that charges indirect costs to jobs based on a predetermined rate.

Required:

a. Based on this year's budget, what will be the indirect cost rate?

b. What amount of indirect costs will be charged to the research proposal? What is the total amount the researchers must request?

c. The researchers have learned that the agency to which they plan to submit the grant proposal will reimburse indirect costs only in amounts up to 35 percent of a project's direct costs. Assume you are the university's finance director, and the chemistry professors have come to you for help. How can you help them?

d. If the researchers are not able to recover all of the indirect costs from the grant, how will these costs be covered? What cultural values are relevant to this situation?

7. A small print shop currently has two jobs in process—an elementary school textbook and a children's craft book. Both books sell for $9 per unit, and both jobs are for 2,000 books. The production of a book involves several steps. After the material is received from the author, the design department performs the preliminary activities of copyediting and typesetting. Next the book goes to printing and finally to the assembly department, which completes the process of assembling the book and attaching the binding. The two books are similar in the resources they require for design and printing. Compiling the book is considerably more complex because of special design features and the need to withstand hard use. Materials requisitions and payroll records provide the following information about costs incurred on the two jobs.

	Textbook	Craftbook
Design		
Materials	800	800
Labor	144	144
Printing		
Materials	440	440
Labor	80	80
Assembly		
Materials	275	280
Labor	1,440	1,680

Labor time cards indicate that the highly skilled workers who compiled the craft book were paid, on average, $12 per hour rather than the normal wage of $8 per hour paid to all other workers. The company applies manufacturing overhead to jobs based on a predetermined overhead rate, calculated at the beginning of the year based on budgeted spending for labor and overhead. This year's budget called for 20,000 direct labor hours, at a total cost of $180,000. Budgeted spending for overhead items was $450,000.

Required:
a. Assume the firm uses direct labor hours to apply overhead. Calculate the overhead rate and the amount of overhead applied to each job.

b. Assume the firm uses direct labor dollars as the basis for assigning overhead. Calculate the overhead rate and the amount of overhead applied to each job.

c. For each job, calculate the cost per book and the total cost for the job using each of the two overhead allocations you calculated in questions (a) and (b). Which job is more profitable?

d. Based on your calculations, what behavioral problems might arise due to the choice of an overhead allocation basis?

e. How can the choice of an overhead allocation rate affect the firm's pursuit of its strategic goals?

8. Gloria Lauren, Inc., is a couture dress company. It has three production departments—design, cutting, and sewing. The accounting system provides the following balances in the company's general ledger as of May 1.

Account No.	Description	Beginning Balance
18000	Fabric	$6,000
12000	Supplies Inventory	380
14300	Work-in-Process—Design	8,500
14500	Work-in-Process—Cutting	7,200
14700	Work-in-Process—Sewing	9,400
15000	Overhead—Applied	0
16000	Overhead—Actual	0
18000	Finished Goods Inventory	11,500
42000	Cost of Goods Sold	0
45000	General and Administrative Expenses	0
50000	Sales Revenue	0
19000	Accounts Receivable	6,500
21000	Wages and Salaries Payable	3,500

Required:

a. Set up T-accounts and show how Gloria would record the following transactions/ events for the month of May. Be sure to show the beginning and ending balance for each T-account.

    i. Fabric was purchased at a cost of $1,300.

    ii. The cutting department began work on job number 98-5-761 and requisitioned fabric costing $450.

    iii. Payroll records show the following amounts were paid to employees during the month: designers, $15,000; cutters, $4,200; sewers, $6,500. The production supervisor was paid $3,000. Marketing department salaries for the month totaled $8,200; the president was paid $12,000; and the bookkeeper was paid $2,300

    iv. Supplies consumed during May, $220.

    v. Other expenses during the month were miscellaneous overhead items, $13,500, and various general and administrative expenses of $5,500.

    vi. Overhead was applied to each department at a rate of $.60 per direct labor dollar.

    vii. Jobs with $2,800 in costs were transferred from the cutting department to the sewing department.

    viii. The sewing department completed jobs with costs of $3,800. These were moved to the finished goods storage area.

    ix. Jobs with costs of $9,000 were shipped to customers. The customers were billed $23,000.

b. Determine the amount of costs that Gloria should classify as direct materials, direct labor, indirect materials, overhead, and nonmanufacturing costs.

c. A student from a local college has been hired as a summer intern. As you are explaining the account codes, the intern suggests that, since all account numbers have zeros in the last two places, it would make sense to shorten the codes, to speed up data entry and reduce the potential for errors. How do you respond to this suggestion?

9. Jack Biddle and Jeff Greene have started a business assembling disk drives. During their first month of operation, they incurred costs of $4,365 and completely assembled 85 units. In addition, they had 40 units partially assembled at the end of the month.

Required:
Assuming the ending inventory is 30 percent assembled, what is the cost per equivalent unit for the month?

10. Jen and Mary's is a small firm that produces flavored ice tea and similar drinks using only environmentally friendly ingredients and processes. The production process has two departments, processing and bottling. Tea is bottled after it is completely processed. There was no beginning or ending inventory in the bottling activity this year.

At the beginning of 1997, Jen and Mary had 22,000 gallons of kiwi-pomegranate tea in processing at a total cost of $4,611 using the weighted average method of inventory valuation. Jen estimates this beginning inventory was 60 percent complete at that time for this activity. During the year processing started on 148,500 additional gallons. By the end of the year, 152,000 gallons were completely through processing. Jen believes the tea in the processing activity at the end of the year was 30 percent complete.

Jen and Mary incurred the following production costs during the year:

Cost Item	Amount
Juices and teas	$7,500
Purified water	5,000
Bottles and cases	15,200
Processing labor	24,000
Bottling labor	18,000
Depreciation and other equipment costs—processing	27,000
Depreciation and other equipment costs—bottling	10,000
Occupancy cost of plant	15,000

Processing uses 3,000 square feet of the plant space; bottling uses 1,500 square feet. In addition to these costs, Jen and Mary also incurred marketing expenses of $30,400 and administrative expenses of $45,000.

Required:

a. How many equivalent units of product were processed this year?

b. What was the cost per equivalent gallon of tea processed this year?

c. How much total cost was incurred in bottling this period?

d. How many equivalent units of product did bottling produce this period?

e. What is the cost per equivalent unit for bottling this period?

f. Based on the definition of product cost used by traditional cost measurement systems (direct materials, direct labor, manufacturing overhead) what is the cost per equivalent unit of tea completed this period?

g. Based on the broader definition of product cost used by contemporary cost measurement systems, what is the full cost of a gallon of tea this period considering production, administrative, and marketing costs?

h. What are the behavioral implications of the two different product cost calculations you have done in parts (f) and (g) of this problem?

11. The American Association of University Women (AAUW) provides college scholarships for economically disadvantaged high school graduates. The AAUW grants scholarships based on applications filed by students. The following table shows the activities involved in evaluating an application and the approximate percentage of total processing effort consumed by each activity.

Activity	Percent of Total Processing
Receive and log application	10%
Enter into computer evaluation template	10
Send letters of verification	20
Update file and print evaluation score	10
Rank applicants and grant scholarships	40
Notify and disburse funds	10

In the first year of the program, the scholarship committee received 800 applications. Of these the committee completely processed 650 during the first year. The remaining applications had been received and logged, but no additional processing steps had been performed at the end of year 1. In the second year the committee received 900 additional applications. At the end of year 2, one hundred applications were partially processed. One-half of these had been received and logged; the other half had letters of verification sent.

Required:

a. On an equivalent units basis, how many scholarship applications did the committee process during year 1?

b. On an equivalent units basis, how many scholarship applications did the committee process during year 2?

c. From the perspective of the scholarship applicant, what constitutes quality in the process of granting scholarships?

d. What quality measures might you suggest that the committee track?

e. What is the time required for the scholarship application process? (Think in terms of the customer's perspective of time.)

12. Refer to the previous problem. Assume you work for University of the South. One of your jobs is to prepare advertising materials and supervise application processing for AAUW. You are also responsible for managing the costs of its operations. The work you do for AAUW uses about 20 percent of your time, and AAUW reimburses your university for 20 percent of your salary. AAUW receives free space for this operation from University of the South, and faculty members donated old computers, file cabinets, desks, and other office equipment. Your major cost item is payroll. You don't have any permanent employees, but students serve as temporary employees when processing has to be performed. In addition, you have supplies, telephone, and advertising expenses. The costs incurred in years 1 and 2 are as follows:

Expenditure Item	Year 1	Year 2	Comments
Salaries	$7,000	$10,275	Part-time wages of college students.
Telephone	600	750	Monthly charge of $50 levied by the university plus extra service features installed.
Supplies	875	1,283	Used on each application.
Advertising	1,500	2,000	The AAUW committee approved a higher budget in year 2.
Manager's salary	7,000	7,210	Twenty percent of manager's salary and benefits.

Required:

a. What was the cost per application processed in year 1?

b. What was the cost per application processed in year 2?

c. How well is the manager managing the cost of the operation? (Hint: Think about how costs would behave as the volume of applications change.)

d. The industry norm for processing applications is about $15 per application. Given the cost structure that exists for this operation, how many applications must AAUW process to achieve the industry norm?

Writing Assignments

13. You have been hired as project manager for financial systems at an old-line *Fortune* 500 manufacturing firm and want to get approval for an activity/operation costing project. However, your boss, who has been with the firm for 37 years, argues that the firm has been profitable for 50 years without this "new-fangled accounting" and there is no need for a new system. Write a memo to persuade the boss. Remember, she does your performance evaluation, so you must be very tactful.

14. Explain two ways in which financial reporting principles have influenced the focus of traditional cost measurement systems.

Team Projects

15. Visit a local business. Determine what its key strategic decisions are, define relevant cost objects for each, and design a set of account codes for its cost measurement system.

16. Identify a *Fortune* 500 firm that you would expect to use job-order costing. Visit its website or obtain a copy of its annual report to see whether you can deduce what kinds of jobs it would need to account for. What cost items should it trace to jobs? Are there any costs the firm should not trace to jobs?

17. Visit a local firm and draw a process map of its production process similar to that shown in Exhibit 10 of the module. Describe activities and operations the firm must perform to produce its product or provide its service to customers and define a set of account codes to track costs to each.

■ PROBLEMS AND CASES—ADVANCED LEVEL

18. The Boys Club of Boone County operates two programs designed to keep at-risk teenagers out of trouble—an after-school program and a summer camp. In addition, staff members conduct numerous fund-raising events during the year, such as open houses at the club and a family day of activities for children of donors. For financial reporting purposes, the Boys Club is classified as a voluntary health and welfare organization (VHWO) and is subject to the standards of the Governmental Accounting Standards Board (GASB). The GASB requires all VHWOs to prepare an annual Statement of Functional Expenses that shows spending separately by the broad categories of program spending and supporting services. Supporting services expenditures are further subdivided into management/general and fund-raising. The club's cost measurement system is designed to facilitate compliance with this reporting requirement as well as to provide information to help manage costs in these areas. Accordingly, the cost measurement system uses these four cost objects:

> Program spending, after-school program
> Program spending, summer camp
> Supporting services, management and general
> Supporting services, fund-raising

You have recently been hired as a part-time student intern to help with the club's accounting. From the club's records you have obtained the following information about resources consumed during the past year of operation.

Cost Elements	Amount
Direct labor	
Sports director	8,800
Art teacher	7,200
Camp counselors	9,000
Bus driver	14,000
Custodian	22,000
Other operating expenses	
Manager's salary	44,000
Travel	7,600
Van operating expenses	9,500
Printing and publicity	18,000
Rent	16,000
Utilities	3,500
Insurance	7,400
Phone	3,800
Supplies	4,200

The club's existing cost measurement system traces labor costs to cost objects on the basis of information provided by time sheets indicating the time spent on each program. For last year, the employee salaries traced to each program are as shown below.

Employee	After School	Camp	Management/ General	Fund-raising
Sports director	5,250	1,600	700	1,250
Art teacher	4,520	1,464	678	538
Camp counselors	0	9,000	0	0
Bus driver	8,400	4,900	0	700
Custodian	15,400	3,300	0	3,300

The club's existing cost measurement system assigns operating expenses (including the manager's salary) to the programs on the basis of direct labor costs. However, you have convinced the club manager to let you experiment with activity analysis and design a contemporary cost measurement system for the club. After much coaxing, you induce the manager to review his calendar and estimate how he spends his time. He determines that during the 42 weeks of the year when the after-school program is operating, he spends, on average, 15 hours per week in supervisory activities related to that program, 4 hours on developing programs for the summer camp, 11 hours on general management tasks, and 10 hours meeting with donors and other activities related to fund-raising. During the 8 weeks when the summer camp is operating, he spends, on average, 6 hours per week in various activities related to the after-school program, 20 hours on the summer camp, 10 hours on general management tasks, and 4 hours in activities related to fund-raising. The remaining 2 weeks of the year the club is closed.

You determine that travel expenses, van operating expenses, and printing and publicity costs can be traced directly to cost objects. Analysis of travel reimbursement records reveals that the travel costs are distributed as follows: after-school program, $750; camp, $800; management and general, $3,500; and fund-raising, $2,550. In discussions with the driver, you estimate that the van drove 15,000 miles for the after-school program; 9,000 miles for the camp; 600 miles on miscellaneous errands for management; and 400 miles for fund-raising events. Invoices show charges for printing and publicity of $4,500 for the after-school program; $3,600 for the camp; $2,700 for management; and $7,200 for fund-raising.

All other indirect costs will be combined into a single cost pool and assigned on the basis of square feet occupied. You and the manager estimate that roughly 50 percent of the space is used by the after-school program, 20 percent for camp-related activities and storage, and 25 percent by general and administrative activities. The rest is used for records storage related to fund-raising.

A local corporation has offered to provide a major grant to help the club cover operating expenses. The company's bylaws stipulate that it may donate only to nonprofit organizations whose expenditures for items other than program services are less than 20 percent of their total budget.

Required:

a. Based on the club's existing cost measurement system, determine the cost of the after-school program, the summer camp, management/general expenditures, and fund-raising. Calculate the total cost for the two categories of program spending and supporting services. Calculate the percentage of the club's total expenditures in each category.

b. Determine the total cost of the after-school program, the summer camp, management/ general expenditures, and fund-raising as defined by the contemporary cost measurement system suggested earlier. Calculate the total cost for the two categories of program spending and supporting services. Calculate the percentage of the club's total expenditures in each category.

c. Which system better helps management understand the resources consumed by the various programs?

d. The club's bookkeeper has suggested that rather than combine facilities costs (rent, utilities, insurance) with supplies and phone in a single cost pool, the system should use 2 cost pools, with the facilities cost allocated on the basis of square feet and the phone and supplies allocated on the basis of salaries. What is your response to this suggestion?

e. The manager rejects the new system because the new cost assignment means that the club will not qualify for the gift. The manager justifies this action by saying, "Allocations are all arbitrary, and there's no way to prove that one is any better than another." Write a memo to the club director, who has no accounting background, explaining your position on which system the club should use.

f. Comment on the behavioral and cultural issues raised by this situation.

19. A.P. Brown Industries (APB) is a small firm that produces five-speed transmissions for sale to specialty automakers such as Porsche and Lamborghini. The accountant is preparing a cost of production report for 1997. During 1997 the firm incurred $301,000 in materials costs and $129,000 in conversion costs. At the beginning of the year, it was working on 65 transmissions that were approximately 20 percent completed at that time. During the year work began on 180 transmissions. At the end of the year, the firm had 80 partly completed transmissions on the shop floor. The production supervisor believes these units are 30 percent complete.

Last year's cost per equivalent unit for transmissions was $2,400. The production manager receives a year-end bonus based on cost control. If this year's cost per equivalent unit is higher than last year's, he will receive no bonus. He is pressuring the supervisor to report a higher percentage of completion for the ending inventory in order to reduce the calculated cost per equivalent unit. The company uses the FIFO method of inventory valuation.

Required:

a. What is this year's cost per equivalent unit?

b. What must the percentage of completion of the year-end work-in-process be for the manager to qualify for a bonus?

c. How could the manager's performance be evaluated to avoid this adverse behavioral impact?

20. Reider Processing, Inc. manufactures food products, primarily vegetable oils. Its main customers are restaurant chains and grocery stores. Various crude oils (corn, soybean, palm) are purchased on long-term contracts. Because of the fluctuating prices in commodities markets, speculative buying of raw materials is key to maintaining profitability. Trading specialists monitor commodities markets continually, locking in long-term contracts when prices are favorable. Contracts specify price and delivery date, but Reider does not actually take delivery until the oils are needed.

All oils go through four processing steps: refining, bleaching, deodorizing, and hydrogenization. Oils for industrial customers such as Frito Lay are piped directly into tank trucks for delivery. Oils for restaurant chains such as Arby's and McDonald's are packaged in 35-gallon barrels.

Reider uses a traditional process costing system for its main production. At the beginning of the year, 125,000,000 gallons of vegetable oil were in process. These were approximately 40 percent processed. Costs incurred in the prior period on the oil in beginning work-in-process include $24,375,000 in materials and $5,900,000 in conversion costs. During the year, 400,000,000 gallons of oil were placed into production. At the end of the year, the firm had 90,000,000 gallons in work-in-process. These were about 55 percent processed. Accounting records show that Reider spent $88,000,000 for materials and $55,890,000 for conversion costs during the year.

Required:

a. Assume that all materials are added at the beginning of the process. Determine the cost per equivalent unit (gallon) for materials using the FIFO cost flow assumption. (Round your answers to four decimal places.)

b. Assume that conversion costs are incurred evenly throughout the process. Determine the cost per equivalent unit (gallon) for conversion costs using the FIFO cost flow assumption. (Round your answers to four decimal places.)

21. Although Reider (refer to previous question) is tiny, it has been able to compete successfully with such giant food processors as Cargill and Archer Daniels Midland by providing quick turnaround on special orders. For pricing special orders Reider uses a job-order costing system with costs assigned to jobs on the basis of activities performed to complete the job. Records provide the following information about activity costs, cost drivers, and units of the cost drivers.

Activities	Cost	Cost Driver	Units of Cost Driver
Commodities trades	$988,000	Time, hours	3,800
Receiving	1,128,000	Incoming shipments	1,200
Materials management	23,760,000	Materials cost	88,000,000
Refining	12,960,000	Batch	180
Bleaching	11,700,000	Batch	180
Deodorizing	19,800,000	Batch	180
Hydrogenization	6,300,000	Batch	180
Lab tests	3,510,000	No. of tests	3,600
Finished goods storage	15,229,000	No. of barrels	2,600,000
Delivery	10,625,000	Truckloads	3,400

During a recent flood in the Midwest, Cargill asked Reider for 15,000,000 gallons of oil because Cargill's plants were flooded and it was unable to meet commitments to its customers. Michelle Reider, the president of the firm, estimates that traders will need about 4 hours to locate and purchase the necessary oils on the spot market. The crude oil can be shipped to Reider in three shipments. Production personnel indicate the order will be processed in five batches. Because of Cargill's strict quality requirements eight lab tests will be needed to ensure adequate quality control. Because the oil will be piped directly from the production vats to the delivery truck, no finished goods storage is needed. The order will be delivered to Cargill in two truckloads. The cost of ingredients for the order is estimated to be $3,300,000.

Required:

a. Determine the total cost of all activities necessary to fill the Cargill order.

b. Use the activity cost analysis and estimated materials cost to determine the total cost per gallon of the oil produced for Cargill.

c. Why is the cost per gallon for the Cargill order different from the cost per gallon you calculated in (b)?

d. What factors other than cost should Reider use in deciding whether to accept the Cargill order?

e. Based on your answers to these two problems, should Reider accept the Cargill order? Why or why not?

Case 1: Yamazoo Waverunner Manufacturers.

Yamazoo manufactures two models of waverunners in its Kalamazoo, Michigan, plant: the Stingray and the Shark. The Shark has a larger engine and is generally more costly than the Stingray. Yamazoo's income statement for the year 1997 is shown in Exhibit 21. In 1997 it sold 2,000 Stingrays and 975 Sharks to waverunner dealers. These units were sold to dealers at approximately 200 percent of Yamazoo's manufacturing or product cost.

Dealers sell the waverunners to customers and perform warranty repairs for Yamazoo, during the one-year warranty period, using parts obtained from Yamazoo. Yamazoo pays dealers for labor and overhead at standard rates established for each type of repair performed. During the warranty period, an average of $75 is paid to dealers for warranty repairs for Stingrays and an average of $90 is paid for Sharks.

Internally, Yamazoo is divided into three production areas: engine assembly, final assembly, and special finishing. Each engine assembly cell is staffed by three highly trained, flexible employees who fully assemble and inspect engines. Shark engines spend approximately twice the time in engine assembly as Stingrays. Final assembly is a production line operation with lesser skilled employees who routinely perform the same assembly step on each waverunner. Both waverunner models receive the same processing and parts in this area. Stingrays are complete after final assembly; they do not receive special finishing. Sharks go through both assembly areas and also through special finishing. Stingrays and Sharks have different direct materials as well. The costing system captured the following information about production during 1997:

Description	Job Order 101	Job Order 102
Number and model of waverunner	1,000 sharks	2,000 Stingrays
Direct materials:		
Engine parts	$300,000	$220,000
Waverunner parts other than engines	200,000	300,000

In addition, engine assembly, final assembly, and special finishing incurred $300,000; $450,000; and $50,000; respectively, in other costs. During this period, special finishing was the only area with work-in-process inventory. It started the period with no inventory, and it completed only 975 units. The other remaining waverunners were 50 percent complete with respect to special finishing.

In addition to the manufacturing process, Yamazoo has an internal administrative office that performs normal personnel, accounting, and other administrative functions. Auditing, tax planning and preparation, and legal services are handled by outside contractors. The president of Yamazoo also contracts all product design and marketing services to outside agencies.

During this past year an external product design firm worked extensively with the Shark. It had engine problems that were corrected in the 1997 model. The design firm estimated that 80 percent of its effort was devoted to Sharks and that the remaining 20 percent went to developing the 1997 Stingray.

About 50 percent of all marketing costs were for the benefit of both products last year. Of the remaining 50 percent, the marketing firm spent 300 hours developing new manuals for the redesigned 1997 Shark and 150 hours reviewing and refreshing literature for the 1997 Stingray model.

Exhibit 21

Income Statement		
Sales Revenue		$3,599,450
Cost of Goods Sold		
Materials	$1,020,000	
Direct Labor	105,000	
Indirect Labor	163,000	
Factory Depreciation	232,500	
Rent & Utilities	150,000	
Tools & Supplies	99,500	
Insurance	50,000	1,820,000
Gross Profit		1,779,450
Warranty Expenses		$237,750
Marketing		150,000
Design Charges		100,000
Outside Accounting		50,000
Legal Services		25,000
Common Carrier (delivery charges)		150,000
Administrative Office Costs:		
Office Rent	48,000	
Salaries	250,000	
Depreciation, Office Equipment	16,000	
Utilities	16,000	
Insurance	30,000	
Supplies	50,000	
Telephone	40,000	450,000	$1,162,750
		637,336
Taxes		254,934
Profit after tax		$382,402

Required:

a. What is the conversion cost in engine assembly for a Shark engine? What is the cost for a Stingray engine?

b. What is the conversion cost per unit in final assembly if both Sharks and Stingrays require the same time, effort, and cost factors?

c. How many equivalent units of Sharks are complete with respect to special finishing?

d. What is the cost per unit in special finishing?

e. What is the product cost of a Shark and a Stingray?

f. How much marketing cost would you allocate to each product line? Why?

g. How would you suggest that common carrier cost should be allocated to each product? Why?

h. Using units of production to allocate all indirect costs that do not have a clear allocation base suggested in the problem, determine the full cost of a Shark and a Stingray. Considering this cost, what is the return on sales from selling one of each?

Case 2: Logic Conductors.©

> The semiconductor business is extremely competitive and rapidly changing. We need to choose our products and processes carefully. We are under extreme cost pressures and always welcome opportunities to reduce or manage our costs better. If we are not cost competitive, we will not last very long in this business. We need a good operations cost system not only to tell us what our products cost, but also to help us understand how each step in our production process contributes to that cost.

This is how the chief manufacturing engineer of Logic Conductors, Bangkok, Thailand, described the nature of the firm's business. Logic Conductors is an international manufacturer of electronic components such as circuit boards, semiconductors, cables, and connectors. It has manufacturing facilities throughout the United States, Asia, and Europe. Its Asian manufacturing operations are in Thailand, Malaysia, Hong Kong, and Singapore. Corporate offices are located in the United States. Regional headquarters make the sales and then assign production to plants based on their location and manufacturing capability. The company's current sales exceed $5,000,000,000 and it employs more than 30,000 people. Half of its sales are from North America. The other half is split evenly between Europe and Asia.

Products.

Semiconductors, or chips in common parlance, are integrated circuits usually made out of silicon. High-precision chips, though, use other materials such as gallium arsenide. Semiconductor chips vary in sophistication from simple "merchant" semiconductors to sophisticated application-specific integrated circuits (ASICs). Merchant semiconductors are integrated circuits used in simple electronic applications such as telephones, kitchen appliances, and sophisticated children's toys. They are typically mass produced in large batches. Next in terms of complexity and sophistication are dynamic random access memory (DRAM) chips used in personal computers and peripherals. ASICs are dedicated to specific applications and, therefore, are produced in smaller lot sizes. Logic produces mostly sophisticated DRAM memory chips and ASICs in its wafer-fabrication facility in Bangkok.

Fabrication Process.

The fabrication process for the various types of chips reflects their level of sophistication. Typically, the fabrication process is defined by the distance between the number of transistors packed on a chip. For example, Intel's Pentium II chip introduced in 1997 has several million more transistors than the Pentium introduced in 1995. The distance between each transistor on the Pentium was .35 microns. The Pentium II has been fabricated on a new process that packs the chips at .25 microns or much closer together.

©Copyright Shahid Ansari and Jan Bell, 1997. This case is based on fieldwork done in connection with a CAM-I supported project titled *Strategy Deployment*. We have disguised the name of the organization at its request.

Given the nature of its product line, the company produces a large variety of integrated circuits in small lot sizes. Its design facility in California does the basic design and lithography of the chips. In the lithography process a blank wafer coated with light-sensitive material is exposed to the circuit pattern. A laser-etching machine transfers the circuit design onto a "wafer," which is then doped with solvents and stripped away until the circuit design is etched on the wafer. The etched wafer, which contains several dies, is the basic raw material for the Bangkok plant whose process starts with the receipt and storage of wafers. Exhibit 22 shows a simplified schematic diagram of the most important manufacturing operations.

The first step in the manufacturing process is to cut each die on the wafers with a diamond saw. A resin bonds the good dies to a backing in the cavity of the ceramic package. The dies are then mounted on a frame and a threading machine attaches metal wires (aluminum, silver, or gold) that act as the inserts that connect the chip to the external electrical connection in the end product. The cutting operation, which is next, cuts the wires to the exact size called out in the product specification. The stamping operation puts an ink stamp on each chip that identifies the type of chip and its manufacturing location. The last step is a test to ensure that all connections are functioning; this step also burns in the chips in electronic ovens to ensure stability in the operating environment for that application. The special ovens typically take batches of 200 chips at any one time.

Exhibit 22
Manufacturing Layout for Bangkok Plant

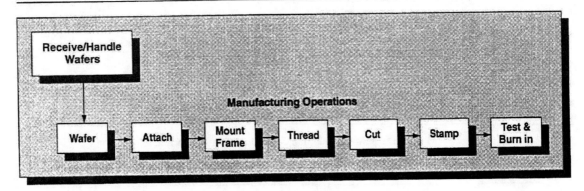

Each manufacturing operation has one machine operator. One supervisor and one manufacturing engineer oversee the entire manufacturing operation.

At each stage of the manufacturing process, the yields are different. Of the wafers introduced in the production process, only 90 to 92 percent reach the resin-attachment operation. Another 5 to 6 percent of the chips are lost between resin attachment and stamping. Finally, the test stage usually uncovers another 1 percent defective so that the final yield is typically much lower than the number of wafers put into process during any given period.

95

Cost Data.

In the early 1990s, responding to increased competition on both price and quality in the electronics industry, Logic Conductors instituted a TQM program. The program was well received and cascaded training was used to get the message to every level in the organization. Within two years a quality focus had emerged, but costs were still not under control.

The company's cost system was typical of most traditional job-order costing systems. It identified materials cost based on requisitions. Labor time tickets were used to assign labor costs. For manufacturing overhead costs the system traced them first to departments and then assigned them to customer jobs using predetermined rates. While all manufacturing operations were in one department, the manufacturing overhead was divided into two cost pools. The first pool included materials handling and supervision. These costs were allocated to jobs based on direct labor hours. The other pool included the remaining costs, and machine hours were the base for allocating these costs. There was a growing feeling that the system was not providing the type of cost data needed for cost management.

To solve this problem the company began to implement an activity-based cost system to determine cost of the products and cost of each manufacturing operation (activity). The new system traced all resources to activities and manufacturing operations. Next the system identified a resource and cost driver for each activity and operation. The cost drivers were used to assign costs to products. The last step was to create cost pools based on common drivers.

This last year the total manufacturing cost was $540,500 broken down as follows:

Cost Item	Total
Machine operator salaries	$88,000
Supervisor salaries—material handling	12,000
Supervisor salaries—manufacturing	35,000
Machine depreciation	370,000
Occupancy	28,000
Supplies	4,800
Furniture/fixtures	2,700
Total cost	$540,500

The following additional information is also available.

1. Operator salaries and machine depreciation for each operation are as follows:

	Material Handling	Saw	Resin	Frame	Wire	Cut	Stamp	Test	Total
Salaries	$10,500	12,500	10,500	12,500	13,000	11,400	9,600	8,000	88,000
Machine depreciation		55,000	65,000	35,000	50,000	24,000	16,000	125,000	370,000

2. The manufacturing supervisors spend equal time on all operations.

3. Space occupied by the equipment in each operation is as follows:

	Material Handling	Saw	Resin	Frame	Wire	Cut	Stamp	Test	Total
Percentage of total space	14%	11	11	10	15	11	9	19	100

4. All activities and operations have roughly the same use of supplies.

5. Each employee is provided with furniture and fixtures. The cost is approximately 2 percent of their salary.

6. The following table provides cost drivers for each activity and operation. Also available are total amount of each driver consumed and the amount consumed by two of the many jobs done this last year. Job 1 produced video dynamic random access memory (VDRAM) chips for a manufacturer of PC video cards. Job 2 is a digital signal processor (DSP) chip for use in a cellular telephone/beeper combination device.

Activity/Manufacturing Operation	Cost Driver	Drivers Consumed by All Jobs	Drivers Consumed By	
			Job 1 VDRAM	Job 2 DSP
Material handling	# of units	300,000	20,000	28,000
Saw cut	# of saw cuts	1,750,000	2	3
Resin	# of wafers	250,000	18,000	26,000
Frame	# of framing hours	6,750	1 minute	2 minutes
Wire	# of inserts	5,000,000	12	8
Cut	# of wire cuts	750,000	4	2
Stamp	# of items stamped	230,000	17,000	25,000
Test	# of hours	7,245	75 min	120 min

7. The raw material cost of the wafer for the two jobs was

Chip job 1	$11.45 per wafer
Chip job 2	14.56 per wafer

8. Both jobs were complete at the end of the period.

Required:

a. Compute the total cost of each manufacturing operation at Logic Conductors. Do you think there might be better ways of tracing resources to operations?

b. Do you think it is appropriate for the new system to lump labor with the other manufacturing support costs and assign it to products as a single number?

c. Which management insight does this calculation provide? How might you use this information for cost management?

d. For each manufacturing operation, compute a cost per driver.

e. Which management insight does this calculation provide? How might you use this information for cost management?

f. Compute the unit product cost for the two jobs. What is the impact of "yield" rate on unit product cost?

97

MODULE

Manufacturing Overhead Allocation: Traditional Versus Activity-Based

VERSION

1.2

AUTHORS:

Jan Bell and Shahid Ansari
California State University Northridge

SERIES CONCEPT DEVELOPED BY:

Shahid Ansari • Jan Bell • Thomas Klammer • Carol Lawrence

Manufacturing Overhead Allocation: Traditional Versus Activity-Based

RINGING UP WRONG NUMBERS AT TELECO

"I never thought I'd being saying this, but it's depressing being the product manager for our traditional products these days." Pete Malloy, product manager for Standard phones at Teleco, commented over lunch to Renee Pappas, manager of the product cost analyst group. "Our sales group works harder and harder to compete against overseas producers who are selling phones at prices close to our costs. Through lots of work we've managed to achieve our budgeted sales volume, yet the report I received this morning shows that our traditional, standard model phones hardly make a profit! I personally don't see how that could be. All the cash that's generated in this company is flowing into our newer products, and I see the time and attention those product lines get from engineering, purchasing, scheduling, and the plant manager. I'm no accountant, but I think something is wrong! I think we're paying the bills for the other product lines, and they're showing our profits!"

"Pete," began Renee, "you know that older established product lines are always cash cows used to support new products. They pay the bills."

"Yes," Pete interrupted, "but they show profits, and our line isn't. It's depressing, and I feel cheated. I think something is wrong with the way costs are figured around here. We're subsidizing the new lines. I'm sure of it! You can't make phones with all those added features and not think they cost more than these reports show."

"Pete," Renee continued, "I can see that you're upset by this report, but you're making a valuable contribution to the company. Our group analyzes product costs, and you know that a sophisticated cost system was put into place when we expanded our product lines. It tracks costs by departments and cost pools, and product lines are costed based on how much machine time products require for plastic extrusion as well as the labor time they require to assemble."

"Well," Pete grumbled, "I know you're doing your job carefully, but I tell you those new products cost more to produce than the reports show. I was in production for fifteen years before this job. If your product costing system is so good, can you tell me why we didn't earn the profits that were budgeted? Every product line met its budgeted sales volume."

"We're having cost problems in our support and service departments, that's why," replied Renee. "We're trying to get to the bottom of it and correct the problems."

"Or those fancy new products cost more to make than your system shows," retorted Pete.

■ STRATEGIC IMPLICATIONS OF OVERHEAD COST ALLOCATIONS

For students of management accounting this story about Teleco raises several important strategic issues.

- ■ **Quality.** Management decisions about adding features to a product or increasing its level of reliability often lead to increases in manufacturing overhead costs. A good manufacturing overhead allocation system provides information about the

101

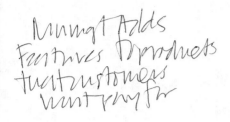

costs of features and reliability. If these costs are not assigned to the product with the enhanced feature or reliability, management can add features to products that customers are not willing to pay for.

■ **Cost.** Manufacturing overhead is a substantial part of a product's cost. Good product cost data is critical for strategic market positioning. Organizations, relying on an inappropriate cost allocation system, may surrender profitable portions of a market to competitors and may continue to sell in market segments that are unprofitable.

■ **Time.** To compete effectively on time, a company must manage its production and shipment schedules. Altering schedules or using alternative processes increases costs. A good allocation system distributes the cost of altering these factors to products in a manner that reflects the way resource use changes when schedules are changed.

■ PURPOSE OF THIS MODULE

The purpose of this module is to describe the nature and types of manufacturing overhead costs and to compare and contrast the two major methods of allocating such costs to products—the traditional volume-based and the more recent activity-based cost allocation methods. We discuss when each method is appropriate for determining manufacturing costs of products and consider the technical, behavioral, and cultural attributes of these methods in making a choice between them. After reading this module you should understand:

■ The nature and components of manufacturing overhead costs.

■ The basics of allocating manufacturing overhead costs.

■ The traditional volume-based overhead allocations methods.

■ The more recent activity-based allocation methods.

■ A comparison of the traditional volume and activity-based allocation methods.

■ Desirable technical, behavioral, and cultural properties of an allocation scheme.

■ NATURE AND COMPONENTS OF MANUFACTURING OVERHEAD COSTS

Manufacturing overhead costs include all costs incurred to manufacture a product that cannot be uniquely or economically traced to that product. Other names for these costs are indirect manufacturing costs, manufacturing burden, factory overhead, or factory expenses. Manufacturing overhead includes the cost of support activities performed to produce a product or a service.[1] These include purchasing; storing; and issuing materials; maintaining machinery; supervising line workers; cleaning supplies for machines or plant facility; planning and scheduling production; recordkeeping; and providing utilities; janitorial services; gardening and parking lot cleaning for the manufacturing facility.

---

[1] This module focuses on manufacturing overhead. However, students should remember that manufacturing is only one kind of production situation. The problem of allocating indirect costs also holds for service activities. We use the terms *manufacturing* and *product* only as substitutes for the more general phrases "production function" and "cost objects."

Exhibit 1
Classification of Factory Costs for an Ice-cream Manufacturer

Cost Item	Account Classification
Milk, sugar, flavoring	Direct raw materials
Fruit pulp	Direct raw materials
Machine operator salaries	Direct labor
Production supervisor salary	Manufacturing overhead—indirect labor
Maintenance engineer salary	Manufacturing overhead—indirect labor
Electricity, water, gas, and phone	Manufacturing overhead—factory utilities
Janitorial supplies	Manufacturing overhead—indirect materials
Janitorial salaries	Manufacturing overhead—indirect labor
Factory manager salary	Manufacturing overhead—indirect labor
Factory payroll clerk	Manufacturing overhead—indirect labor
Depreciation on machinery	Manufacturing overhead—equipment depreciation
Property taxes on factory building	Manufacturing overhead—factory taxes

Raw materials and labor that can be traced directly to products comprise the other major category of manufacturing costs. These are often referred to as *direct or prime costs.* In a Pepsi bottling plant, for example, carbonated water and syrup become a part of the Pepsi during manufacturing, and their costs are direct materials. The cost of laborers who physically work on bottling or on other machines that manufacture Pepsi, is classified as direct labor cost. The remaining costs collectively are called manufacturing overhead costs. They are indirect costs.

Indirect manufacturing costs include many cost elements and have a large material and labor component. For example, packing supplies, stationery, forms, cleaning products, and lubricants are referred to as indirect materials. Salaries for personnel such as plant managers, supervisors, schedulers, accountants, inspectors, materials handlers, janitors, and engineers are part of indirect manufacturing costs. These are often referred to as indirect labor. In addition costs for items such as training programs, safety programs, and environmental programs are part of manufacturing overhead costs.

A recent study of 32 plants in the electronics, machinery, and automobile components industries shows that direct materials, direct labor, and manufacturing overhead average 65, 9, and 26 percent of manufacturing costs.[2] This means that indirect manufacturing costs are a very large and important component of product costs. Exhibit 1 shows a typical set of cost items included in the three categories for an ice-cream manufacturer. These items are classified as either direct costs or as (indirect) manufacturing overhead.

■ BASICS OF OVERHEAD ALLOCATION

Because manufacturing overhead costs are not or cannot be traced to individual products, they must be assigned or shared among products that benefit from these costs. *The process of assigning or sharing manufacturing overhead is called* **allocation.**

To understand the allocation process, let us begin with a very simple situation. Assume that Teleco assembles two types of telephones—a Standard desk model and a Designer

---

[2] R.D. Banker, G. Potter, and R.G. Schroeder, "An Empirical Study of Manufacturing Overhead Cost Drivers," *Journal of Accounting and Economics,* January 1995, pp. 115–138.

Exhibit 2
Teleco's Estimated Overhead Costs

Overhead Cost Item	Amount
Indirect materials, supplies & tools	$ 1,134,000
Indirect labor	3,090,000
Administrative salaries	4,410,000
Utilities	2,240,000
Depreciation	6,250,000
Property taxes	1,200,000
Total	**$18,324,000**

trimline model. Both telephones are assembled by hand using very simple parts that are purchased from outside vendors. Both telephones have roughly the same number of parts and require the same number of production runs per year in the same batch size. These simplifying assumptions will be relaxed later.

Allocating manufacturing overhead to the two telephones in this situation is a three-step process.

Step 1. Estimate the manufacturing overhead for the coming year.

This process is shown in Exhibit 2. The total is $18,324,000 for the six major components of manufacturing overhead costs in Teleco.

Step 2. Select and estimate an appropriate physical measure of work to allocate the cost to the products.

The physical measure used to assign manufacturing overhead to products is called an *allocation base* or a *driver*. An *allocation base* is a general term that describes any measure that is used to assign overhead. The number of direct labor hours, the number of machine hours, or the pounds of materials processed are often used as allocation bases. When possible, an allocation base is selected that varies as manufacturing overhead costs vary. This means that a statistical relationship usually exists between an allocation base and manufacturing overhead costs. The term *driver* is used for a special kind of allocation base. A driver *causes* a manufacturing overhead cost to be incurred. A driver is used as an allocation base when a work process is well understood, that is, when the factors that cause work and its related costs have been identified.

THINK ALONG

What allocation base or driver do you think Teleco should use?

The manufacturing overhead costs listed in Exhibit 2 will vary by the amount of work required to produce each telephone. Because of our simplifying assumptions that both phone types are similar on dimensions such as number of parts, batch sizes, number of inspections, and so on, the overhead costs will vary directly with the number of units produced for each type of telephone. The telephone with more units produced will consume more indirect material and labor, require more work space, use more utilities, and need more supervisory personnel.

Exhibit 3
Per Unit Manufacturing Overhead for Teleco

Style (1)	Labor Hrs. per Unit (2)	Units Produced (3)	Total Labor Hours (4)	Allocation Overhead (5)
Standard	.50	2,440,000	1,220,000	.50 LH × $9.00* × 2,440,000 = $10,980,000
Designer	.80	1,020,000	816,000	.80 LH × $9.00* × 1,020,000 = $7,344,000
Totals		3,460,000	2,036,000	$18,324,000

* $9.00 = $18,324,000/2,036,000

Since the production process is labor intensive, a good estimate of the volume of work is the direct labor hours used. Therefore, the two types of phones will consume manufacturing overhead costs in direct proportion to the number of direct labor hours used in producing them.

KEY POINT

> Traditional allocation systems assign or allocate indirect manufacturing costs to products using measures of production volume such as direct labor hours or machine hours worked. These volume measures are used instead of counting products because most companies produce more than one product. A volume measure that is common to all products is selected.

Step 3. Develop an overhead rate and apply it to products.

An overhead rate results from dividing total overhead cost by the selected allocation base. An overhead rate is also called a *burden rate*, a *charge rate*, or an *application rate*.

Assume that the Standard model takes 0.5 hours to assemble and that the Designer model takes 0.8 hours to assemble. In the next year Teleco expects to produce 2,440,000 units of the Standard phone and 1,020,000 of units of the Designer phone. This level of production will require a total of (2,440,000 × .5 + 1,020,000 × .8) 2,036,000 direct labor hours. The overhead rate for Teleco is $9.00 per direct labor hour ($18,324,000 manufacturing overhead cost ÷ 2,036,000 direct labor hours = $9 per direct labor hour).

Exhibit 3 shows the overhead costs allocated to total production.

As Exhibit 3 shows, the cost of each style of telephone will include manufacturing overhead based on the number of direct labor hours it requires multiplied by the overhead rate of $9. This rate is used to assign all the manufacturing facility's overhead to products. It is called a *plantwide overhead rate*, because it includes all the manufacturing plant's overhead.

On a per unit basis, a standard telephone would be assigned $4.50 of manufacturing overhead cost ($9.00 overhead rate * .50 labor hours), while a designer telephone would be assigned $7.20 ($9.00 overhead rate * .80 labor hours).

Note that an overhead rate is typically developed in advance of production. This rate is called a *predetermined overhead rate*. Developing a predetermined overhead rate requires the use of estimated or budgeted manufacturing costs and production volume. Using the predetermined rates, products are charged for overhead as they are produced. This process is called *overhead application* or *overhead absorption*.

105

Behaviorally, the use of a predetermined overhead rate places cost pressure on production personnel. They understand that output will only contain predetermined amounts of overhead costs and that overhead costs incurred beyond normal monthly amounts will result in negative performance evaluation. Fearing unfavorable performance evaluation, they may avoid incurring costs such as preventive maintenance on machinery during periods when high overhead costs are being incurred. Such behavior can lead to dysfunctional results.

Why do firms use a predetermined rather than an actual overhead rate to assign manufacturing overhead costs to products?

THINK ALONG

A predetermined overhead rate is used for two reasons. First, it speeds up and simplifies internal record keeping. Product costs can be determined without waiting for all actual indirect cost bills to be received and for all production to be finished for a time period. If actual indirect cost was applied to actual production, then both of these would have to be known before the actual costing could be done. Second, many costs are not incurred evenly. For instance, factory heating costs are higher in winter, repairs may be done during off-peak season, and so forth. To charge products produced in winter for higher heating costs penalizes them for production scheduling when there is no basic variation in the fundamental cost factors.

What happens if there are many different products that require different types of production activities many of which are not affected by the production volume? Can a single plantwide overhead rate using one volume measure give good product cost data?

THINK ALONG

■ DEPARTMENT-BASED OVERHEAD ALLOCATION

In the previous section we saw that if both telephones require a similar production process, then Teleco's manufacturing overhead will vary by the number of units produced. This simplicity of the production environment makes it possible to collect all costs into one *plantwide cost pool* and then assign it to products using a single *volume based* measure such as direct labor hours.

Manufacturing environments are seldom this simple. Teleco does not make two telephones. It makes a whole line of standard and designer phones. The lines combine various features such as caller ID, automatic redial, speaker, hold button, and so forth. In addition, the designer line offers different styles such as character phones in the shape of Mickey Mouse, Minnie Mouse, Donald Duck, Daffy Duck, Tasmanian Devil, Tweetie, Sylvester, and Yosemite Sam. These products require many different work activities, which makes the production process more complex than depicted in the previous section.

One way in which firms handle the complexity created by many products and activities is to assign manufacturing overhead to products using departmental overhead rates. Departments are headed by supervisors or managers who are responsible for coordinating work activities. They are responsible for procuring, safeguarding, and accounting for the resources they need to perform work in their respective units. A departmental view of Teleco's operations is provided in Exhibit 4.

Exhibit 4
Departmental View of Teleco's Factory

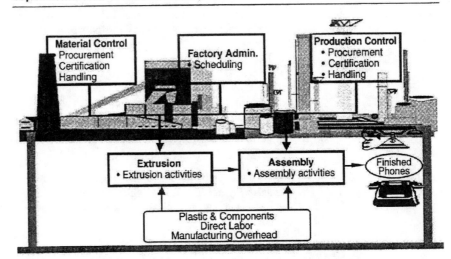

As shown in Exhibit 4, Teleco's factory has five departments or responsibility units.

The Materials Control Department performs activities such as vendor certification, procuring materials, receiving, warehousing, and coordinating the arrival of all subcomponents into assembly at the proper time (materials handling). The primary costs in this area are salaries, supplies, and space.

The Factory Administration Department schedules machines, processes factory payroll, and supervises production. The primary costs of the department are clerical and supervisory salaries.

The Production Control Department is responsible for engineering design, quality assurance, and machine setups. The primary cost in production control is salaries.

The Extruding Department has plastic extrusion machines that form the outer plastic body for the telephones. Direct materials and direct labor costs are incurred in this department. The primary indirect costs in this department are associated with equipment depreciation, maintenance, and operating supplies.

The Assembly Department uses direct laborers and robots to assemble phones from various components and parts that are accounted for as direct materials. The primary indirect costs of the assembly department are indirect labor, materials, depreciation, and supplies.

There are three important things to note about Teleco's departments.

First, Extruding and Assembly Departments work on manufacturing the telephones. These departments are called *production centers.* The remaining departments exist to provide service and support to the production departments. They are called *service* or *support centers.*

Second, each department performs many different types of activities. For example, the Materials Control Department performs vendor certification, materials procurement, and materials handling. Performance of many varied activities is common since departments are created to utilize managers and employees fully and economically. Housing multiple activities within a single department reduces employee idle time and saves on supervisory and managerial salaries.[3] Exhibit 4 lists only some of the activities performed within these departments.

Finally, products may not draw upon the activities of all departments equally. For example, a Mickey Mouse telephone that has caller ID, automatic redial, and a hold button will require greater production coordination, more quality inspection, and materials handling than a standard push-button desk telephone.

A departmental system of manufacturing overhead cost allocation has two *purposes:*

- To hold departments *accountable* for resources entrusted to them.
- To determine unit product *costs*.

We listed accountability first because a departmental system is based on the key concept of *responsibility accounting*. Its primary focus is on controlling costs through the management structure by measuring the services and support that departments receive from each other.

KEY POINT

Note that accountability is based on who consumes resources, not on who acquired the resources.

This sometimes leads to political and behavioral problems because managers perceive that they are being assigned costs that they have no control over. The assignment is done to reduce overconsumption of services and resources. Culturally, it is desirable for managers to perceive this accountability system as fair and equitable and reflective of the services each uses.[4]

To determine *product costs*, the departmental allocation method traces costs to departments and then assign those costs to products. Since service departments and factorywide cost pools do not work on products, a departmental system allocates all service department and common pool costs to production departments prior to allocating them to products.

Illustration of Traditional Volume-Based Allocation Systems.

Allocation of manufacturing overhead costs using a departmental system requires six steps.

Step 1: Estimate manufacturing overhead costs by different cost categories.

This was done previously in Exhibit 2, and the total amount is $18,324,000.

---

[3] Economists refer to the utilization of common assets to perform related operations cost effectively as "economies of scope."
[4] For an interesting article on fairness, see "Figuring Fairness by the Numbers," *The Los Angeles Times, Column One,* April 26, 1996.

Exhibit 5
Manufacturing Overhead Classified by Departments and Cost Pools

	Plantwide	Materials Control	Factory Admin.	Production Control	Extruding	Assembly	Totals
Overhead Costs							
Indirect materials/supplies	$20,000	134,000	86,000	110,000	450,000	334,000	$1,134,000
Indirect labor	25,000	10,000	15,000	137,000	1,242,000	1,661,000	3,090,000
Administrative salaries	1,440,000	1,520,000	1,208,000	242,000			4,410,000
Utilities	2,240,000						2,240,000
Depreciation	3,500,000	137,000	85,000	115,000	2,035,000	378,000	6,250,000
Property Taxes	1,200,000						1,200,000
Totals	$8,425,000	1,801,000	1,394,000	604,000	3,727,000	2,373,000	$18,324,000

Exhibit 6
Selected Volume-Based Drivers for Departments and Plantwide Cost Pool

	Plantwide	Materials Control	Factory Admin.	Production Control	Extruding	Assembly	Totals
Square feet	14,000	12,000	3,000	6,000	9,000	6,000	50,000
Number of requisitions		70	250	180	5,000	10,500	16,000
Number of employees	15	35	90	45	55	590	830
Maintenance/ planning hours					90,000	50,000	140,000
Machine hours					1,435,000		1,435,000
Direct labor hours						2,036,000	2,036,000

Step 2: Assign overhead costs to production and support centers and any remaining costs to a central cost pool.

Exhibit 5 shows the reassignment of the $18,324,000 in manufacturing overhead costs to the various production and support departments. In addition to these five departments, Teleco also has a group of costs that are common to the entire manufacturing facility. These costs include utilities, depreciation, and property taxes. Teleco grouped these costs into one cost pool labeled *plantwide costs*.

Step 3: Choose an allocation base for each department.

The choice of an allocation base to charge departmental costs to user departments should reflect what causes costs to vary. This process typically requires estimating the relationship between operating statistics that provide measures of volume and the behavior of costs in a department. Exhibit 6 shows some of the bases or drivers available for allocation purposes.

109

Exhibit 7
Allocation of Service and Central Support Costs to Production Departments

	Plantwide	Materials Control	Factory Admin.	Production Control	Extruding	Assembly
Before allocation totals (from E 5)	$8,425,000	1,801,000	1,394,000	604,000	3,727,000	$2,373,000
Allocation antwide costs	(8,425,000)				5,055,000	3,370,000
Materials Control		(1,801,000)			580,968	1,220,032
Factory Admin.			(1,394,000)		118,868	1,275,132
Production Control				(604,000)	388,286	215,714
After allocation totals	0	0	0	0	$9,870,122	$8,453,878

THINK ALONG

> Which base is the most appropriate for each department?

Reviewing the statistics and costs in the various departments, it appears reasonable to use the following bases.[5] Since plantwide costs are related to space occupancy, the best measure seems to be square feet occupied. Number of purchase requisitions appears to be the most reasonable measure of work volume in the Materials Control Department. The Factory Administration Department's costs are related to the volume of administrative work, which in turn depends upon the number of employees in the other departments. Production Control provides engineering, production planning, and scheduling. Its work can be best measured by the number of planning hours. For production departments, number of machine hours best measures the activity and cost consumption in Extruding, and direct labor hours measures the activity within Assembly.

Step 4: Allocate all central and service department costs to production centers.

In practice, there are three methods for assigning service department overhead to production departments: the direct method, the step-down method, and the simultaneous method. Only the direct method is presented here. The other two are discussed in an appendix to this module.

The direct method allocates the cost of service and support departments and cost pools directly to production departments. It ignores any services that service departments provide to each other. The advantage of the direct method is its simplicity. Of all the departmental methods, it requires the fewest calculations and the least data. Starting with any cost pool,[6] the costs of all pools and service centers are allocated to the two production centers based on service use.

Exhibit 7 provides the results of the direct method of allocation using Teleco's data from Exhibits 5 and 6.

---

[5] In practice this might be decided on the basis of statistical analysis of cost behavior.
[6] Since no allocations are made to other service departments, the starting point does not matter in this method of allocation.

Explanation of Allocations[7]

(1) **Plantwide cost:** Allocation base is space as measured by square feet.

Extruding square feet	9,000	60% × $8,425,000	$5,055,000
Assembly square feet	6,000	40% × $8,425,000	$3,370,000
Total production	15,000	100%	$8,425,000

(2) **Materials control cost:** Allocation base is number of requisitions.

Extruding requisitions	5,000	32.25% × $1,801,000	$580,968
Assembly requisitions	10,500	67.74% × $1,801,000	$1,220,032
Total	15,500	100%	$1,801,000

(3) **Factory Administration:** Allocation base is number of employees.

Extruding employees	55	8.52% × $1,394,000	$118,868
Assembly employees	590	91.47% × $1,394,000	$1,275,132
Total production	645	100%	$1,394,000

(4) **Production Control:** Allocation base is number of planning hours.

Extruding planning hours	90,000	64.28% × $604,000	$388,286
Assembly planning hours	50,000	35.72% × $604,000	$215,714
Total production	140,000	100%	$604,000

Step 5: Develop a departmental overhead rate for each production center.

The revised costs, after all allocations, for the Extruding and Assembly Departments can be used to develop departmental overhead allocation rates. The Extruding Department's overhead rate is determined by taking the new departmental total costs and dividing by the number of machine hours. The Assembly Department's overhead rate is determined by taking the new departmental total costs and dividing by the number of labor hours. Exhibit 8 shows the two rates.

---

[7] There are slight rounding differences from the numbers shown in Exhibit 7 due to calculator versus spreadsheet calculations.

Exhibit 8
Overhead Rates Determined by Direct Departmental Allocation

Description	Extruding	Assembly	Total
Total overhead after allocations	$ 9,870,122	$ 8,453,878	$18,324,000
Total machine hours	1,435,000		
Total labor hours		2,036,000	
Overhead rate per machine hour	$6.8781		
Overhead rate per direct labor hour		$4.1522	

Exhibit 9
Overhead Allocation to Products Using the Direct Method

Model ⇒	Standard	Designer	Total
1. Machine hours/unit	0.40	0.45	
2. Direct labor hours/unit	0.50	0.80	
3. Extruding Department Overhead	$ 2.7512 ($6.878 ×.40)	$3.0952 ($6.878 ×.45)	
4. Assembly Department Overhead	$2.0762 ($4.15 × .5)	$ 3.3217 ($4.15 ×.80)	
5. Manufacturing overhead, per unit	$4.8274	$6.4169	
6. Planned Production	2,440,000	1,020,000	
7. Total manufacturing overhead (Row 5 × 6)	$11,778,742	$6,545,258	$18,324,000

Step 6: Assign overhead to products as they pass through the production center.

As each product passes through the two departments, it is assigned overhead costs based on the rates shown in Exhibit 8. To do so we need to know the amount of machine hours that each phone receives in Extruding. (Recall that we previously stated the number of labor hours in Assembly as .5 and .8 for Standard and Designer phones respectively.) Assume that the Standard phone uses .4 machine hours and the Designer model uses .45 machine hours in Extrusion. The overhead cost allocated to the two telephones is shown in Exhibit 9.

NOTE PAD

> Compare the overhead costs assigned to the products in Exhibit 3 using a plantwide rate with the overhead assigned to products using the departmental rates in Exhibit 9. Why do the two methods yield different manufacturing overhead costs for the products? Which one is better?

Based on rates in Exhibit 3, standard telephones are assigned $4.50 of overhead ($9 plantwide rate * .50 labor hours) and designer telephones are assigned $7.20 of overhead ($9 plantwide rate * .80 labor hours). In Exhibit 9 these same telephones are assigned

approximately $4.83 and $6.42 of overhead costs, respectively. The small differences are caused because departmental assignments use *both* direct labor hours and machine hours. Since both products have similar machine hours, the overhead assigned to product using the departmental method will be more similar ($4.83 for standard and $6.42 for designer) than in the plantwide method where direct labor alone is used as an assignment base ($4.50 for standard and $7.20 designer).

■ ACTIVITY-BASED OVERHEAD ALLOCATION

An **activity-based cost (ABC) allocation system** *focuses on work activities instead of on departments and assigns indirect manufacturing costs to products according to the activities that are performed on them.*[8] It represents a work process focus rather than the responsibility focus used by departmental allocation systems.

Products are produced by performing a sequence of ordered and coordinated activities. Activities consist of many tasks. For example, an activity such as extrusion *setup,* which is needed when a new product is placed into production, includes tasks such as resetting dials, installing new molds or dyes, testing, calibrating machinery, changing colors and materials, coordinating material deliveries to machine requirements, and adjusting the flow of production line items.

While some activities reside within the formal boundaries of a department, many activities cut across departmental lines. As we saw in Exhibit 4, departments typically undertake many different types of work activities.

THINK ALONG

> What happens if two products draw on activities in the same department differentially?

Examples of typical activities in a manufacturing facility are: ordering materials, receiving materials, scheduling production, inspecting quality, setting up machines, handling materials, shipping finished goods, cleaning the plant facility, processing payroll, and so on. Work activities consume material and personnel time, which explains the logic of an activity-based cost allocation system.

KEY POINT

> Products consume activities and activities consume resources; therefore, costs should be assigned to products in the proportion in which they consume activities.

Two products that use different amounts of an activity receive different cost allocations in an ABC system.

ABC systems use five key steps in assigning manufacturing overhead to product costs.

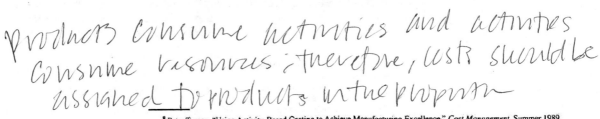

[8] Peter Turney, "Using Activity-Based Costing to Achieve Manufacturing Excellence," *Cost Management,* Summer 1989.

Step 1: Identify activities used by products and determine their cost drivers.

Activity-based allocation starts by identifying the *activities* in the production process.[9] Instead of activities varying as production volume varies, they are generally described as varying at four levels:[10]

Unit-level activities are performed each time a unit is produced. For example, assembly activities that consume supplies and indirect labor are performed for each unit of product produced.

Batch-level activities are performed each time a batch of products is placed into production. For example, each batch of products requires scheduling, material handling, and machinery setup activities.

Product-level activities are performed to support a product or product line. For example, each product line (not each unit) requires engineering activities such as design, modification, documentation, instruction manual preparation, and technical support.

Facility-level activities are performed to support and provide space to the entire production facility. Items such as insurance, property taxes, general maintenance of the plant and parking lots, and the employee cafeteria are included in the facility-level category. Facility-level activities are very similar to central cost pools used in departmental allocations (see step 2 of departmental allocations).

We assume that Teleco has performed an activity analysis. Hundreds of activities could be identified in Teleco's manufacturing process, but this is not practical for costing purposes. A 1995 CAM-I study of best practices showed that around 32 percent of best practice companies identify between 101 and 250 activities, about 25 percent identify between 26 and 100, and around 18 percent identify less than 25 activities.[11] After an activity is identified we determine the causes or drivers of the cost of this activity. This is called a *cost driver*.

To keep our illustration simple we identify only nine major activities for Teleco's manufacturing operation. Our purpose is to illustrate the mechanics of cost allocation, and not to provide a complete representation of Teleco's manufacturing process.

Vendor certification includes tasks involved in identifying and approving vendors. It also includes inspecting samples of delivered items and tracking on-time delivery to maintain statistics on vendor performance. These tasks are performed for each unique part used in a telephone; therefore, the more unique parts a telephone contains, the higher the cost for that model. This activity is driven by the number of parts in a product (further, this activity is classified as a product-level activity).

Materials procurement includes the costs of placing orders and arranging transportation and storage. These activities have to be performed each time a purchase order is placed. Orders are placed for each part within a product. Accordingly, this activity is driven by purchase transactions, which is measured by the parts in a product times the quantity

---

[9] The Activity Based Management (ABM) module in this series demonstrates how to perform activity analysis, how to cost activities, and how to improve them.

[10] Robin Cooper, "Cost Classification in Unit-Based and Activity Based-Manufacturing Cost Systems," *Journal of Cost Management* 4, No. 3 (Fall 1990), p. 6.

[11] George Foster, J. Miller, and D. Swenson, "Activity-Based Management Consortium Study," Consortium of Advanced Management-International (CAM-I), 1995, p. 17.

produced divided by the purchase order size. (Again, this activity is classified as a product-level activity).

Engineering support includes work performed to modify existing products because of customers' requests, raw material changes, or problems during production. Usually an engineering modification benefits a particular product and can be traced to that product when made. Since the number of engineering hours spent on each product is routinely tracked, *engineering support is no longer an indirect cost that has to be allocated. It should be reclassified as a direct cost, and engineering hours is the cost driver for this activity.*

Materials handling includes moving materials from the receiving area, within production areas, and to packing areas. Each product line has pre-established material moves. The number of material moves required is the cost driver for the materials-handling activity. (Again, this activity is classified as a product-level activity).

Quality assurance comprises all the tests performed on products. The more tests a product requires, the more Teleco spends on quality assurance. The number of inspections or tests required for each product is the cost driver for this activity. (This activity is also classified as a product-level activity.)

Extrusion activities use plastic molding machines and workers to mold plastic, which is a direct cost of the product, into the outer shell of telephones. Extrusion activities consume indirect costs such as machinery, tools, software, indirect materials, as well as labor time spent cleaning or adjusting machinery. For this activity, indirect costs vary with the pounds of plastic extruded. Accordingly, allocation base for extrusion stations is pounds of plastic. (This activity is performed on each unit of product and is thus classified as a unit-level activity.)

Assembly activities use a small number of skilled laborers and robots to combine the various pieces of telephones into completed units. The number of assembly operations required for a telephone causes costs and time to increase. Assembly operations are a function of both the parts in a product and the quantity of products produced. Number of assembly operations (parts in a product times quantity produced) is the cost driver for this activity. (This is also a unit-level activity.)

Production scheduling tasks assure that proper extrusion machines are available, raw materials arrive on time, assembly operators with proper tools and skills will be available when extruding is finished, and that work load is smoothly averaged to avoid idle machine time or overtime while meeting customers' required shipment dates. These tasks are required every time a batch of products is put into production. The cost driver for scheduling is the number of batches of product started. (This activity is classified as a batch-level activity.)

Setup activity involves installing proper molds to produce telephone shells, calibrating extruding machinery for proper plastic shell thickness and for smooth edges, and color testing plastics against prototypes for each product. The cost driver for these activities is the number of setups that have to be performed, which is the same as the number of batches started. (This activity is also a batch-level activity.)

115

Exhibit 10
Activity View of Teleco's Manufacturing Process

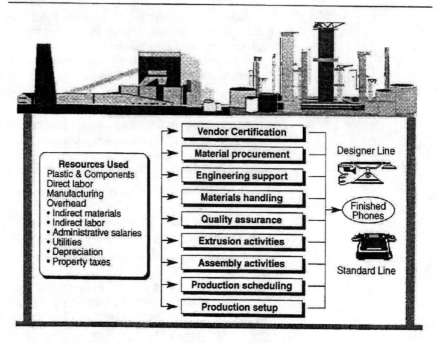

Exhibit 10 provides an activity view of Teleco's manufacturing process. Compare Exhibit 10 to Exhibit 4, which provided a departmental view.

Step 2: Trace costs to activities.

Activities consume resources such as indirect labor, materials and supplies, equipment, software, space, utilities, and so forth. Although most of these items can be traced to an activity or assigned based on a driver that reflects use of resources, some costs cannot be handled in this way. These costs are included in a cost pool and allocated to activities in a fair and equitable manner. At Teleco, the common activity cost pool contains items such as building depreciation, utilities, property taxes, accounting, and payroll that exist for the common good of the entire manufacturing facility. As previously discussed, these are referred to as *facility-level* costs. These costs support all activities and need to be allocated to activities. Because most of the costs are space related, square feet within each activity was selected for that allocation.

Exhibit 11 shows the costs in the common activity cost pool. Exhibit 12 shows the costs directly traced to each activity and the amount allocated from the common activity cost pool. In addition, Exhibit 12 shows the cost driver to be used for each activity (discussed in step 1 previously).

Notice that the total activity cost shown in Exhibit 12 is the same as the total indirect cost shown in Exhibit 5 ($18,324,000). The difference between the two exhibits is the way the data is organized. In Exhibit 5, costs are arrayed by departments and the type of expenditure, for example, indirect labor or materials. In Exhibit 12 those same costs have been organized according to work performed, or activities.

116

Exhibit 11
Common Activity Cost Pool

Depreciation on Building	$3,500,000
Property Taxes	1,200,000
Utilities	2,240,000
Total	$6,940,000

$\frac{4k}{36k} * 6 940,000$

Exhibit 12
Activities and Drivers

Activity	Costs Directly Traceable To Activities	Space Used in Square Feet	Allocation of Common Activity Costs	Total Activity Cost	Driver
Vendor certification	$3,383,384	4,000	$771,111	$4,154,495	# of parts
Materials procurement	386,367	4,000	771,111	1,157,478	# of purchase transactions
Engineering support	534,969	1,000	192,778	727,747	engineering hours
Materials handling	891,616	8,000	1,542,222	2,433,838	# of moves
Quality assurance	936,196	1,500	289,167	1,225,363	# of inspections
Extrusion stations	2,689,707	11,000	2,120,556	4,810,263	lbs. of plastic used
Assembly stations	386,367	4,000	771,110	1,157,477	# of parts × quantity
Machine setups	1,615,905	500	96,389	1,712,294	# of setups or batches
Production scheduling	559,489	2,000	385,556	945,045	# of setups or batches
Totals	**$11,384,000**	**36,000**	**$6,940,000**[1]	**$18,324,000**	

[1] The common cost pool of $6,940,000 is allocated according to the square feet used to support each activity. This value has to be measured or estimated. Each activity is charged costs based on its square feet divided by total square feet. For example, materials procurement: (4,000 square feet in procurement * 36,000 total square feet) × $6,940,000 = $771,111 (rounded).

Step 3: Reclassify and combine activity costs.

In practice an allocation worksheet like Exhibit 12 will contain several hundred activities.

THINK ALONG

> If several hundred activities exist with different cost drivers, how can managers deal with the technical complexity of an ABC system?

If several hundred drivers were used for cost allocation purposes, the system would be far too complex, detailed, and costly to be useful. When many activities have a common driver, a better approach is to group costs of activities together into larger groupings. This method not only makes the system more manageable, but also focuses attention on key cost drivers. This information is very useful for cost planning.

Activities with the same driver, therefore, are combined into a single cost pool. This reduced set of cost pools and drivers is used for product costing. The CAM-I best practices

117

Exhibit 13
Combination of Activities with Common Drivers

Activity or Cost Pool	Total Activity Cost	Driver
Vendor certification	$4,154,495	# of parts
Materials procurement	1,157,478	# of purchase transactions
Engineering support	727,747	engineering hours
Materials handling	2,433,838	# of moves
Quality assurance	1,225,363	# of inspections
Extrusion stations	4,810,263	pounds of plastic used
Assembly stations	1,157,477	# of assembly operations
Machine setups & production scheduling	2,657,339	# of setups
Totals	$18,324,000	

study reports that about 25 percent of the companies use between six and ten drivers, and 20 percent use five or fewer drivers.[12]

In Teleco both machine setups and production scheduling share number of batches or setups as their driver. The costs of these activities are combined into a cost pool in Exhibit 13. This combination leaves eight drivers for allocating overhead costs to products. One of these, engineering hours, is not an allocation base. It is a driver for tracing direct costs to each product.

THINK ALONG

> Even in our simple example, eight cost drivers are used. How can an ABC system be managed cost effectively?

Firms might combine even more activities. Consider material procurement and assembly. Each part in a product must be procured and assembled. These two activities might be combined into one cost pool and assigned to products based on the number of parts in each. This not only simplifies the process, but it also encourages product engineers to redesign products with fewer parts.

Step 4: Collect data on the use of cost drivers for each activity and determine the overhead cost per driver.

KEY POINT

> To determine the cost of products, manufacturing overhead costs should be assigned to products in the proportion that they consume activities.

Statistics must be kept on total cost drivers consumed. These are maintained for each product and show how much each product normally requires of each activity.

Exhibit 14a contains product data required for ABC. It shows expected consumption of drivers for total planned production for the next time period. The data in Exhibit 14a is

---

[12] G. Foster, J. Miller and D. Swenson, "Activity-Based Management Consortium Study." Consortium of Advanced Management-International (CAM-I), 1995, p. 17.

Exhibit 14a
ABC Cost Drivers for Product Lines

ABC Cost Drivers (1)	Standard (2)	Designer (3)	Total (4)
Planned production in units	2,440,000	1,020,000	3,460,000
Pounds of plastic used	610,000	1,530,000	2,140,000
Engineering hours	3,460	6,500	9,960
Number of parts per product	98	145	243
Number of purchase transactions*	239,120	295,800	534,920
Number of quality inspections	14	18	32
Number of material moves	168	400	568
Number of assembly operations	239,120,000	147,900,000	387,020,000
Number of batches (setups)	30	110	140

*Each purchase order is assumed to be for 1,000 standard items and 500 designer items.

Exhibit 14b
Activity Cost per Unit of Driver

Activity or Cost Pool	Activity Cost/Driver	Driver
Vendor certification	$17,096.69	per unique part
Materials procurement	$2.16	per purchase transaction
Engineering support	$73.07	per engineering hour
Materials handling	$4,284.93	per material move
Quality assurance	$38,292.58	per inspection
Extrusion stations	$2.25	per pound of plastic used
Assembly stations	$0.0030	per assembly operation
Machine setups & production scheduling	$18,980.99	per setup

calculated by multiplying expected production by driver specifications for the two products. Exhibit 14b shows the per driver cost of each activity. It is obtained by dividing activity cost, shown in Exhibit 13, by the total use of cost drivers, shown in Exhibit 14a.

Step 5: Assign costs to products.

The manufacturing overhead cost of each product is calculated from the data in Exhibits 13 and 14. This calculation is a fairly simple and routine. Each product is assigned activity cost by multiplying the per unit activity cost (Exhibit 13 costs divided by Exhibit 14 column 4) by the drivers used by each product (Exhibit 14 column 2 or 3). For example, vendor certification has a total cost of $4,154,495 (Exhibit 13). There are 243 total parts which means that vendor certification costs $17,096.69 per part (Exhibit 14b). Because the standard phone has 98 parts, it is allocated a cost of $1,675,475 (98 × $17,096.69).[13] This

---

[13] If you are using a hand-held calculator to compute the numbers in Exhibits 15 and 16, you may be off from the numbers in the exhibits. We prepared the exhibits in a computer spreadsheet that does not round intermediate calculations. We strongly recommend that you build these calculations on a generic spreadsheet to reinforce your learning.

Exhibit 15
Activity Costs Incurred by Product Line Under ABC

	Standard	Designer	Total
Vendor certification	$1,675,475	$2,479,020	$4,154,495
Material procurement	517,416	640,062	1,157,478
Engineering support	252,812	474,935	727,747
Materials handling	719,868	1,713,971	2,433,838
Quality assurance	536,096	689,267	1,225,363
Extrusion stations	1,371,150	3,439,113	4,810,263
Assembly stations	715,147	442,331	1,157,478
Machine setups & production			
scheduling	569,430	2,087,909	2,657,339
GRAND TOTALS	**$6,357,393**	**$11,966,607**	**$18,324,000**

Exhibit 16
Manufacturing Overhead per Product Under ABC

Manufacturing Overhead	Standard	Designer
Vendor certification	$0.69	$2.43
Material procurement	0.21	0.63
Engineering support	0.10	0.47
Materials handling	0.30	1.68
Quality assurance	0.22	0.68
Extrusion stations	0.56	3.37
Assembly stations	0.29	.43
Machine setups & production		
scheduling	0.23	2.05
Total	**$2.61**	**$11.73**

value represents the vendor certification costs consumed by the Standard phone product line. Since Teleco plans to produce 2,440,000 Standard models, (Exhibit 14a) each Standard phone contains a 69 cent charge for using vendor certification activities ($1,675,475 ÷ 2,440,000 units).

Exhibit 15 shows the amount of overhead costs caused by and therefore allocated to each product line.

NOTE PAD

> Compute the total and the per unit activity cost allocated to the two phones for the other activities shown in Exhibits 15 and 16.

Step 6: Determine unit product costs.

To determine the unit cost of products, divide the budgeted activity cost assigned to products[14] (Exhibit 15), by the planned production of each product (Exhibit 14a). This results in a planned overhead cost per product (Exhibit 16). This is sometimes referred to as a *bill of activities* since it lists each activity required and its contribution to the cost per unit of product.

---

[14] While we demonstrate ABC determining the cost of a product, it is often used to determine the cost of jobs or processes.

Exhibit 17
An Overview of the ABC Allocation Process

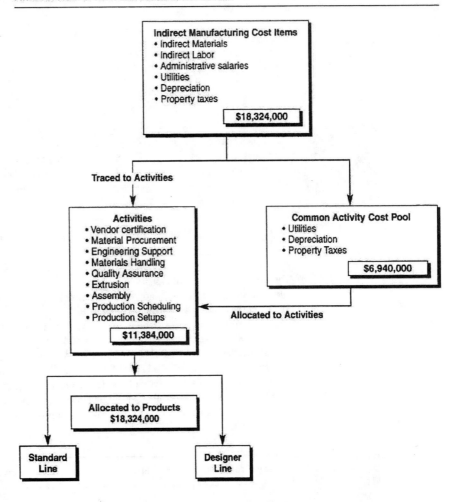

ABC assumes that costs are caused by many factors or cost drivers while traditional allocation assumes that costs are caused by volume.

KEY POINT

In ABC, many costs can be traced directly to activities and from there to products; yet, certain type of costs, for example, facility level costs, require allocations to activities and products. ABC does not eliminate allocations and does not provide a "true" product cost.

KEY POINT

Exhibit 17 graphically summarizes the entire ABC cost allocation process.

121

Exhibit 18
Comparison of Manufacturing Overhead Allocation Systems
Traditional versus ABC

	Standard	Designer	Difference
Traditional department-based (direct) allocation	$ 4.82	$ 6.42	33%
ABC overhead allocation	2.61	11.73	350%
Difference	2.21	(-5.31)	
	85%	-45%	

ABC has been described as yielding "true" and "accurate" product costs. This results because more costs are directly traced to products, or cost drivers are used to charge the cost of activities to products. Does ABC yield "true" and "accurate" product costs?

■ COMPARISON OF TRADITIONAL AND ABC OVERHEAD ALLOCATIONS

The two prior sections demonstrate how Teleco's manufacturing overhead costs would be allocated under traditional and ABC systems. Exhibit 18 presents a comparison of the manufacturing overhead allocations under the department-based and the ABC systems.

As Exhibit 18 shows, there is only a moderate cost difference (33 percent, ($6.42−4.82)/ 4.82) between the Standard and Designer phones in a traditional departmental overhead allocation system. Under an ABC system, however, the Designer phone is assigned nearly 350% (($11.73−$2.61)/$2.61) more cost than the Standard phone! (Remember Pete Malloy's complaint from the opening story.) The traditional system reports the Standard model at a higher cost (85 percent or $2.22/$2.61) and the Designer model at a much lower cost (−45 percent or ($5.32)/$11.73) as compared to the ABC system.

Can you reconcile these cost differences to the cost allocation system?

Three key differences between the two allocation approaches explain the cost differences between the products. These are: (1) types of allocation bases used, (2) focus of costing system, and (3) steps in the allocation process.

Types of Cost Drivers Used.

A traditional system typically uses a volume-related allocation base. The basic logic is that costs change with number of units produced. A review of Exhibit 9 shows that the traditional method allocates overhead based on volume measured by machine and labor hours. Since the two phone styles use roughly the same amount of machine hours, there is little difference in their costs as far as the Extruding Department overhead is concerned. Their main difference is in the use of labor hours. Since the Designer phone uses more labor hours, it also gets more of the Assembly Department overhead costs.

Now review the statistics on ABC cost drivers in Exhibit 14a. Costs are distributed to the two products by pounds of plastic; engineering hours; and number of parts, assembly operations, inspections, material moves, and setups or batches. These drivers reflect differences in batch size and design characteristics between the products. The large differences that are revealed when comparing the drivers across product lines result in large cost differences. The standard models cost less than designer models under ABC because they have fewer parts, require fewer quality inspections, and for the volume of products sold, they have relatively few engineering hours, material moves, and batches put into process.

Focus of the Costing System.

A traditional department-based system primarily focuses on management responsibility for costs. Its cost allocation follows the logic of the formal organization structure. It assumes that within a department there is no variability in how products consume resources. Therefore, a single driver, such as machine hours, is sufficient to capture costs consumed by products in that department. Consider what happens to vendor certification costs. They are first merged with the total for the Material Control Department. From there they are charged to the Extruding Department based on number of requisitions and then allocated (almost equally) to the two products based on machine hours used. How much vendor certification each product requires is lost in this departmental focus.

ABC systems have a *process focus*. They capture and assign costs by how products consume work activities. Multiple drivers are commonly used to provide a more refined picture of resource consumption by products. Therefore, ABC traces vendor certification activities to each product and charges costs accordingly.

Steps in the Allocation Process.

Both systems use a two-step allocation process. However, the steps are different. A traditional system assigns overhead costs first to departments and second to products. Consequently, multiple and often diverse activities are combined and assigned using a single cost driver. Support department costs go through another step. They are allocated first to production departments and then to products.

In contrast, an ABC system assigns costs first to activities and then to products. The department or departments that perform these activities makes no difference to the cost allocation for product costing purposes. The direct relationship between products and activities is the base for allocation. Exhibit 19 presents this difference graphically.

THINK ALONG

> Which of these two methods do you think we should use?

■ EVALUATION OF ALLOCATION METHODS

To select an appropriate allocation system, we should consider the technical, behavioral, and cultural attributes of the two systems and use the one that has better properties in all three areas.

Exhibit 19
Comparison of ABC and Departmental Allocation Methods

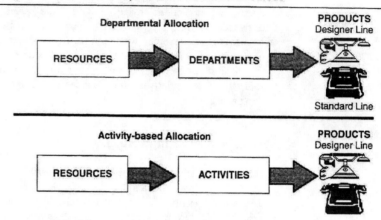

Technical Attributes.

A good cost allocation system provides *decision-relevant information* and enhances manager's *process understanding*.

Decision-relevance.

Many strategic decisions, such as what markets and customers to target, how to establish product prices and profitability plans, which products to promote, the level of quality or service to provide, and how to manage costs and allocate resources, require good product cost data. Without good assessments of product profitability, Teleco could easily be in the wrong market segment or provide features too costly for customers. In the opening story Pete Malloy's complaint that Teleco is under-emphasizing older products goes to the heart of this strategic issue. Whether the older products are indeed losing money, depends upon which cost allocation system we believe provides a better measure of resources consumed by a product.

The choice of an allocation scheme depends upon the nature of the production process. If Teleco were to use a traditional mass manufacturing process, *the two systems will most probably yield very similar cost allocations.* A typical mass production system produces relatively few homogenous products in large quantities.[15] Because they are produced in large quantities and are basically similar, there is little difference between products on variables such as the number of setups, engineering support, production planning, parts purchasing, and so on.

When product variety is large, the production process becomes more complex. Products now consume setups, quality inspections, production planning activities, parts purchasing, and so on differentially. *It is precisely because these factors represent the costs of variety and complexity that the ABC system chooses them to be the drivers for cost allocation.* Since Teleco produces a large variety of telephones, the ABC system will probably provide a better measure of overhead costs consumed by each product.[16]

---

[15] For a discussion of mass production environments, their cost structures, work processes, and environmental conditions, see *Management Accounting in the Age of Lean Production* in this modular series.

[16] The *Indirect Costs* module in this series discusses acceptable criteria for allocating indirect costs. Readers may recognize ABC as similar to the "who ate what" solution to the restaurant example in that module.

KEY POINT

Traditional and ABC allocations of manufacturing overhead costs will not be vastly different in mass production environments where product variety and process complexity are low. Traditional allocations work in such environments because products are homogenous enough so that overhead costs can be averaged across them.

THINK ALONG

Can ABC data provide any useful information in mass production environments?

Even if product costs show no variation across products, the "bill of activities" shown in Exhibits 14b and 16 provides valuable information for product design and cost management. These exhibits show that the cost of manufacturing telephones varies by parts used, pounds of materials consumed, batch sizes, engineering support, and other such activities. It also pinpoints how much cost each unit of driver consumes, which provides very useful information to product designers. They can determine how much will be saved by redesigning products so they use fewer parts, require less engineering support, have simpler setups, and so on. ABC creates a bank of cost data readily useable by product designers.

Process understanding.

ABC leads to better process understanding by documenting activities. It shows the relationship between costs incurred and work performed in an organization. It also pinpoints how actions taken by employees or how work performed in one activity causes work and cost in other activities. Understanding why work occurs and what drives costs are the first steps in process improvement. Traditional allocations simply tell us that lower production volume lowers overhead costs. This method does not provide useful information about how to manage overhead costs.

If ABC allocation yields better cost for decision-making purposes, does it follow that if a product is dropped or redesigned, then the amounts of overhead allocated by the ABC system will be avoided by the organization? ABC cost allocations contain some costs that are flexible and respond quickly to production stopping or product redesign. Many product and batch level costs are flexible and would be saved. ABC allocations also contain less flexible costs that must be proactively managed over a longer time frame to affect reductions. Many product level and facility level costs are committed, less flexible costs, that will not respond quickly to dropping a product from a line or from redesigning it. For these committed costs to change, they must be diverted to other productive ventures, or they must be discontinued. Discontinuing such costs generally requires a time frame that exceeds a year.

Behavioral Attributes.

ABC systems also have several desirable behavioral properties not present in traditional systems. Well-executed ABC systems can make a cost structure visible to decision makers, facilitate communication with operational personnel, and empower employees. When not executed well, ABC can lead to a sense of disappointment and detract from a customer focus.

Cost structure visibility.

In most organizations operating personnel create costs by the way they design and deliver products or services. For example, in manufacturing firms it is design and manufacturing engineers, in hospitals it is doctors and nurses, in universities it is faculty and administration who decide what will be offered and how it will be delivered. Cost management requires that the cost structure be visible to those whose decisions influence costs. Through the choice of cost drivers, management can make visible the organization's cost structure. For example, Teleco's ABC system, in Exhibit 13, shows that number of parts drives both vendor-certification and material-procurement costs. The behavioral message is to reduce the number of parts in the product. Since overhead costs will be allocated based on these drivers, design engineers will be motivated to reduce them. Many Japanese manufacturers have allocated overhead costs to products based on number of parts for this very reason. If cost drivers do cause costs, then in the long run, this visibility will help to reduce costs.

Facilitates communication with operating personnel.

Closely related to visibility is the need to communicate the cost structure to operating personnel. Cost management is possible only if operating personnel understand the financial implications of their decisions. Operating people speak operational language. They understand soldering circuit boards, performing blood tests, or designing curricula. If accountants want operating people to understand the financial implications of their actions, the accountants must learn to communicate in an operational language. This type of communication is not easy with traditional product cost information arrayed by type of expenditure, such as indirect materials or indirect labor, and by department. By reporting activity costs, accountants create a link between what people do and the financial impact of their actions on an organization. For example, Exhibit 15 shows that the work of certifying vendors is one of the most expensive work activities for Teleco costing $4,154,495 in total or $17,097 for each unique part certified.

Employee empowerment and motivation.

The departmental focus of traditional allocations is designed to assign responsibility to managers. It is a "fix blame" orientation in which managers are motivated to blame other departments for cost overruns or to take short-term measures, such as postponing needed maintenance, to cut costs. This orientation creates poor morale all around. ABC is a "process" orientation. It shows how work is interrelated and creates costs upstream or downstream. The focus shifts to how to work and not who to blame. Implementing ABC gets employees involved because their knowledge is required to understand activities, select cost drivers, and make operations more efficient. When improvements occur, they are attributed to employee participation. This response can reinforce a sense of empowerment and motivate employees further, since they can link their actions to tangible improvements.

Failed expectations.

In many organizations, ABC implementations have caused a sense of disappointment because ABC has been sold as a method for determining the "true" cost of a product. Many people assume that ABC does not entail allocation. This false assumption leads to disappointment during implementation when they discover that allocations still exist, and that people may classify activities differently, disagree on how to cost them, or disagree on what drives their cost. Further, allocations in traditional systems often are determined politically. People assume that such political behavior is eliminated with ABC. To the extent that fewer costs are allocated in an ABC system, political allocations may be lessened. Politically determined allocations are not eliminated by ABC. ABC does not determine true cost; it is an attempt to have product costs better reflect resource consumption patterns.

No link to customer.

ABC does not automatically provide a link to customers. It is an internally focused, cost-efficiency tool. Managers sometimes think that installing ABC will solve all their problems.[17] This belief is untrue. ABC needs to be combined with other cost management tools that have a strong customer orientation, such as target costing and total quality management (TQM). Without this tie, managers may focus exclusively on internal operations and efficiency and forget about quality and timelines, which are issues of importance to customers.

Cultural Attributes.

ABC promotes a functional organizational culture by encouraging a process orientation and encouraging cross-functional participation.

Process culture.

ABC reorients the organizational mindset to think in terms of activities, their drivers, and costs. Process improvement, not who to blame, becomes the dominant cultural value. Organizations lacking a process culture are placed at a relative disadvantage over world-class organizations that routinely analyze the way work is performed. Traditional allocations make matters worse by masking operational data behind responsibility and financial structures. Further, the order in which service and support center costs are allocated in departmental systems is often political. Traditional systems focus on who spent money and used services, instead of analyzing what activities are performed and what activities are strategically important.

Encourages cross-functional participation.

Activities cut across department lines. ABC restructures traditional cost reporting from departments to activities. This approach causes costs to be collected and analyzed across departmental lines. Reducing activity costs requires cross-departmental cooperation and reduces the functional isolation that typically occurs within organizations. To succeed in an ABC environment, employees must abandon their departmental and functional orientation and work together on activities. Traditional allocation systems reinforce this functional isolation by emphasizing departmental responsibility.

KEY POINT

> An ABC system has better technical, behavioral, and cultural properties compared to a traditional system of cost allocation. These properties are particularly important when operating in complex production environments that have high product variety.

---

[17] H. Tom Johnson, "It's Time to Stop Overselling Activity-Based Concepts," *Management Accounting*, September, 1992, reprinted in *Activity-Based Management in Action*, IMA, 1994, pp. 40–49.

■ LESSONS LEARNED

- ■ Indirect manufacturing overhead costs are typically allocated to products using either a traditional department-based or an activity-based cost systems (ABC).
- ■ The primary focus of a traditional department-based allocation system is to assign costs to responsibility units headed by management. The focus is *resource stewardship* and this same focus is used for product costing as well.
- ■ ABC systems are *process-focused*. They identify costs by activities and use them to assign costs to products. The logic is that activities consume resources and products consume activities.
- ■ The traditional departmental system of allocation is acceptable for product costing in a manufacturing environment that produces a *few* products in *large* quantities using a *simple* manufacturing process.
- ■ An ABC system is particularly suited for product costing in manufacturing environments that produce *many* products in *small* quantities using a *complex* manufacturing process. In these situations products draw differentially on production-related activities.
- ■ ABC systems are good cost-management tools because they highlight the drivers that cause cost and focus attention on how the way we work causes costs to be incurred.
- ■ A well-executed ABC system can empower and motivate employees and build a strong process-oriented management culture that values continuous work improvement instead of assigning blame.

■ APPENDIX—OTHER DEPARTMENTAL OVERHEAD ALLOCATION METHODS

In practice, two other variations of the departmental method are used to allocate manufacturing overhead costs. They are called the *step-down method* of allocation and the *simultaneous allocation method*. Both these methods recognize that service departments receive benefit from other service departments. For example, purchasing may order material used by production and factory administration. Similarly, the plant cafeteria will service all employees whether they work in production or service centers.

These methods add another step to the calculations. A cost pool or service department's costs are allocated first to *all* other departments, service or production, that receive services. They are then charged to production departments. The service department totals, however, include cost allocations from other service departments.

Step-Down Method.

The step-down method usually allocates the service department that is the largest or has provided the most service to other service centers first. Rules for step-down allocation specify that once a service department's costs have been allocated, that department cannot receive further allocations, even if it receives services from other departments. In some organizations this rule politicizes the selection of the order in which to allocate cost pools and service department costs. Hospitals are prime examples of organizations where the earlier a department's cost is allocated, the lower its total costs appear.

Exhibit 20
Overhead Allocation Using the Step-Down Method

	Plantwide	Materials Control	Factory Admin.	Production Control	Extruding	Assembly
Total Costs before allocation	8,425,000	1,801,000	1,394,000	604,000	3,727,000	2,373,000
Allocation of plantwide costs[1]	(8,425,000)	2,808,333	702,083	1,404,167	2,106,250	1,404,167
Revised total		4,609,333				
Materials Control[2]		(4,609,333)	72,337	52,083	1,446,746	3,038,167
Revised total			2,168,421			
Factory Admin.[3]			(2,168,421)	141,419	172,845	1,854,157
Revised total				2,201,668		
Production Control[4]				(2,201,668)	1,415,358	786,310
Revised total					8,868,199	9,455,801
Total machine hours					1,435,000	
Total labor hours						2,036,000
Rate per machine hour					$6.18	
Rate per labor hour						$4.64

[1] Plantwide cost is allocated based on square feet. Total square feet in all departments (excluding plantwide) is 36,000.

Material Controls: 12,000 square feet * ($8,425,000/36,000) = $2,808,333

[2] Materials Control total cost, $4,609,333, after the allocation of plantwide costs, is allocated based on the number of purchase requisitions issued for the remaining departments, 15,930 (16,000 total less 70 for Materials Control. For example:

Factory Administration: 250 requisitions * ($4,609,333/15,930) = $72,337.

[3] Factory Administration's total cost, $2,168,421 after previous departmental allocations is allocated based on number of employees in other departments. Excluding Plantwide, Materials Controls, and Factory Administration, employees total 690. This cost is allocated to Production Control for example as:

Production Control: 45 employees * ($2,168,421/690) = $141,419.

[4] Production Control's total cost after previous allocations, $2,201,668, is allocated based on total planning hours (140,000) performed for each of the remaining departments.

Extruding: 90,000 hours * ($2,201,668/140,000) = $1,415,358.

Step-down allocation for Teleco is illustrated in Exhibit 20. These allocation are based on information contained in Exhibit 6 in the module. Refer to that exhibit now.

Verify each of the allocations in Exhibit 20. Follow the notes to Exhibit 20, remembering to include statistics from unallocated service departments as well as production departments.

NOTE PAD

Step-down allocation yields a rate per machine hour of $6.18 for the Extruding Department instead of the $6.88 rate developed under the direct method. For the Assembly Department, the step-down method yields a rate of $4.64 compared to $4.15 under the direct method.

Simultaneous Allocation Method.

The simultaneous allocation method recognizes the mutual services provided by departments to each other. It therefore uses a series of linear equations, one for each production and service center, to allocate costs. Each department's equation specifies its direct cost and its percentage share of other department's cost. For example, the equation for Materials Control would be:

129

Materials Control Cost = $1,801,000 + (12,000/50,000) Plantwide Cost + (70/16,000) Materials Control Cost + (35/830) Factory Administration Costs

Because Teleco has six departments or cost pools, six simultaneous equations would be solved. This calculation typically would be done on a computer using matrix algebra. The results would yield slightly different overhead rates for the Extruding and Assembly Departments than the direct and the step-down methods yielded.

Although the simultaneous method improves the mathematical accuracy of the step-down method by recognizing mutual services provided and received, *it does not solve the basic problem of meaningful product cost allocations.* Both these methods suffer from the same problems (discussed previously) as the direct method when it comes to meaningful product cost allocations. Their use is particularly problematic in high variety, complex production environments. In fact, their mathematical precision may create an unwarranted illusion of precision.

■ PROBLEMS AND CASES—INTRODUCTORY LEVEL*

1. Self-test questions.

a. How can a good manufacturing allocation system help organizational members meet quality needs of customers?

b. Give three examples of how indirect cost allocations can be useful to cost management efforts.

c. How do indirect cost allocations impact the time taken to respond to customers' orders?

d. Define manufacturing overhead or indirect manufacturing cost.

e. How large is manufacturing overhead in electronics, machinery, and automobile components manufacturers?

f. Give some examples of costs included in the category, indirect labor.

g. Give some examples of items found in indirect materials and supplies.

h. What is overhead allocation? Why do organizations allocate overhead?

i. What is a plantwide overhead rate? Where or when is it useful?

j. What is the measure of output used to establish an overhead rate called?

k. What terms are used to describe an overhead rate?

l. Why is a predetermined overhead rate often established?

m. What information is required to develop a predetermined overhead rate?

n. Traditional volume based overhead allocation was developed for what type of manufacturing environment?

o. What kinds of items or activities are included in the indirect cost category, setup?

p. Why do traditional overhead allocation systems use volume measures as the denominator or allocation base for overhead cost allocations?

q. What measures of volume are commonly used in traditional allocation systems?

r. What happens if a plantwide rate is used when different production departments with different volume measures exist?

s. What are the three departmental methods of allocating indirect costs?

t. Why is the direct method of allocating overhead costs called direct? What does the term *direct* refer to?

u. How does step-down allocation differ from direct allocation of indirect cost?

v. In step-down allocation, what happens if a service or support department, such as maintenance, has been charged for costs of another service department, such as scheduling, but maintenance also provides service to the charging department, scheduling?

w. Where are activity-based costing systems appropriate for overhead allocation?

x. What is an ABC system?

y. What are "activities" as used in ABC systems?

z. What happens if ABC costing is used when costs vary with volume?

aa. Technically, which gives better product cost information, ABC or traditional systems?

---

*Some material for this section was contributed by Paul D. Dierks, Wake Forest University-MBA, Paul Juras, Wake Forest University, and Oksana Melamed, California State University-Northridge.

131

bb. How does ABC provide good technical information for product design?

cc. How does ABC assist cost-management efforts?

dd. What kind of work-process understanding does ABC provide?

ee. How does ABC information make strategic variables visible and lead to good behaviors?

ff. How does ABC lead to employee empowerment?

gg. Does ABC yield true, accurate product cost?

hh. How does ABC help instill a process-oriented culture in organizations?

ii. How does ABC help foster cross-functional participation in organizations?

Exercises, Problems, and Cases.

2. Mass producers expect economies of scale. What are the sources of economies of scale that cause volume to be such an important cost driver?

3. Printworks Co. produces various assembly parts for high-quality commercial printers including color ink cartridges. The cartridges are manufactured on a job-order basis. Most business is obtained through competitive bidding. To stay competitive and earn a desired profit, Printworks bids full cost plus a 20 percent markup. The company operates two producing departments and two service departments. The Equipment Repair Department provides service to all other departments. It is responsible for routine maintenance as well as repair of equipment malfunctions. The Quality Control Department inspects the quality of products at the end of each production activity, case construction, and ink filling. The quality of a cartridge case is evaluated using simple tools. In the Ink Filling Department, quality control personnel use fairly sophisticated equipment that is susceptible to frequent breakdowns because when defects occur in ink filling, the ink fouls the testing equipment.

The budgeted costs and the normal activity levels for each department are given below:

| | Service Departments | | Producing Departments | |
	Equipment Repair	Quality Control	Case Construction	Ink Filling
Overhead costs	$30,000	$30,000	$200,000	$100,000
Number of breakdowns	—	25	5	30
Quality control hours	—	—	70	10
Labor hours	—	—	5,000	1,000
Machine hours	—	—	2,000	6,000

Departmental overhead rates are used to assign costs to products. The Case Construction Department uses labor hours; the Ink Filling Department uses machine hours.

The Case Construction Department spends 2 labor hours to produce a cartridge case; the Ink Filling Department uses 0.15 labor hours and 0.5 machine hours to fill a cartridge.

Direct materials and direct labor costs for a cartridge are $157.

132

Required:
  a. Using direct labor hours, compute a plantwide overhead rate.
  b. Compute a bid price using the plantwide overhead rate.

4. Refer to the data in Exercise 3.

Required:
  a. Allocate the service costs to the producing departments using the direct method.
  b. Compute a bid price under the direct method.

5. Refer to the data in Exercise 3. While departmental methods of allocating overhead, such as step-down or simultaneous, are supposed to provide greater accuracy in product costing, complaints have emerged that they distort the assignment of cost items to products. Some organizations use the direct method because of this problem.

Required:
  a. Allocate the service costs to the producing departments using the step method. Assume that the direct costs of the Equipment Repair Department are allocated on the basis of the number of equipment breakdowns, while those of the Quality Control Department are allocated on the basis of quality controls hours.
  b. Compute a bid price under the step method.
  c. Do you think the step-down allocation method might cause a distortion in the cost of a cartridge? Explain how this could happen. (Hint: Carefully study the pattern of equipment breakdowns that occur.)

6. Newline produces two kinds of video game controller pads: a standard pad that normally is packaged with video game systems and a deluxe "warrior" pad that provides enhanced movements and is packaged with upgraded systems.
  Overhead costs have been assigned to various production activities:

Equipment Maintenance	Setups	Packing	Total Overhead Costs
$80,000	$100,000	$90,000	$270,000

  Routine maintenance of equipment has to be done after each 10,000 hours of continuous machine work. A maintenance worker lubricates and cleans the equipment. Setups are done every time a batch of materials has to be fed into a machine. Additionally, setups are performed when a machine has to be prepared to work on a different part of a product.
  The controller pads are packed into boxes and sent to the manufacturers of video games.
  The two products use resources as follows:

			Cost Drivers		
Product	Quantity (units)	Prime costs (DL + DM)	Machine Hours	Number of Setups	Number of Boxes
Standard	200,000	$800,000	30,000	100	40,000
Warrior	50,000	$250,000	10,000	80	25,000

133

a. What will be the unit cost of product if a traditional volume-base costing system is used?

b. What will be the unit cost of product if an activity-based costing system is used?

7. Classify the following activities as being incurred at the facility level, product level, batch, or unit level. Identify a cost driver for each activity.

a. Packing

b. Receiving

c. Purchasing

d. Planning and scheduling

e. Shipping

f. Setups

g. Maintaining machinery

h. Supervising line workers

i. Record keeping

j. Gardening

k. Material handling

l. Plant depreciation

m. Machinery depreciation

n. Product design

o.. Utilities

p. Product testing

q. Vendor certification

r. Quality inspection

8. Syracuse Graphics is noted for the quality of its graphic design and printing of advertising brochures. Producing brochures in bulk for national organizations has always been the greatest profit generator for the firm. However, the sales department has recently been able to capture a great deal of the low-volume, custom-design work.

At the weekly managers' meeting the sales manager was asked why the firm had won so many custom bids. He responded, "It really has not taken much effort at all. From what I hear, no one has been able to come close to our price. I guess we must be more efficient than the competition or the economies of scale of the bulk production work has made us the low-cost provider."

Brenda White, the CEO, interrupted, "I am glad you think we are so far ahead of our competition, but I don't think we hold an edge in terms of efficiency or economies of scale. I think I understand our processes fairly well and I know we run an efficient operation, but I also know the people over at Upstate Graphics have some new equipment that can produce product a heck of a lot faster than we can. I would like to review the bidding process to be sure we are not missing something."

Jim Crowder from accounting responded, "I can tell you that currently a bid is based on the cost of materials, graphic design hours, and an assignment of overhead using machine hours. We use machine hours because we run the machines for quite a while to produce those bulk-order brochures. The machines run for a lot less time when we print a custom job."

Chuck Driver from production chimed in, "The machines may not run as long on a custom job, but the machines are tied up for a long time because custom jobs normally have multiple colors rather than the two colors that most bulk orders have. That means we have to spend extra time setting the machines to handle each additional color."

Required:

a. Do you think the company is using an appropriate method to assign overhead when preparing a bid?

b. What change would you suggest they make in assigning overhead to determine a bid price?

9. Jason Helms, CFO, was considering a suggestion from Terri Sands, the corporate controller, to move from a traditional costing system to an activity-based system. Jason knew that the company was facing an increasingly competitive market and that if it could not get costs under control, projected financial results would be dismal.

"Perhaps the activity-based system would help," Helms said to himself, "but I wish I knew more about the basics of such a system." He decided to schedule a meeting with Terri to find out more about activity-based systems. As part of her preparation for the meeting, Sands asked her assistant to prepare a 15-minute presentation on the following aspects of an activity-based system:

- ■ The objectives of an ABC system and how they affect where management should focus their attention.
- ■ Who should be involved in the ABC implementation process.
- ■ The two main phases to ABC: costing activities and products.
- ■ The pitfalls or obstacles might be encountered in implementing or adopting ABC.

Required:

Take the role of the controller's assistant and prepare an outline for the presentation. (This assignment could be done on presentation software so the outline would then become the basis for computer-based slides.)

Advanced:

10. Era Company produces two kinds of women's handbags: a designer label bag and a private label bag. Price competition in the private label market is very strong. Therefore it is very important to accurately allocate overhead costs between designer label products and private label products. To achieve that goal Era uses activity-based costing.

The information about Era's products is as follows:

	Designer Bag	Private Label Bag
Quantity produced	5,000	10,000
Material handling (# of moves)	12,000	13,000
Engineering hours	5,000	2,000
Setups	40	20
Maintenance (hours used)	1,000	1,000
Inspection hours	2,000	500

The overhead costs associated with the activities are given below:

Activities	Overhead costs
Material handling	$30,000
Engineering	140,000
Setups	72,000
Maintenance	26,000
Inspection	40,000
Total	$308,000

a. Allocate all overhead costs to the two products using activity-based costing.
b. Compute the unit cost of each type of bag.
c. List types of organizations in which ABC may be more/less likely to succeed. Why might there be resistance to adopting an ABC allocation approach?

11. Chestnut Furniture Company manufactures a full line of hardwood dining room chairs. While the most popular product is the standard armless chair, Chesnut is also known for its custom-work captain's chairs. The company produced 10,000 standard chairs and 2,000 custom chairs last year. Total overhead was $250,000 for the year. Analysis showed that the overhead could be evenly attributed to labor and machine use. The following table summaries of the production results for last year.

	Materials	Labor	Labor Hours	Machine Hours
Armless	$500,000	$100,000	10,000	20,000
Captain's Chairs	$120,000	$60,000	6,000	7,000

Required:
a. Determine the cost per unit for each type of chair using direct labor hours as the allocation base.
b. Determine the cost per unit for each type of chair using machine hours as the allocation base.
c. The analysis revealed that the overhead costs should be evenly assigned to two cost pools. Determine the cost per unit for each type of chair using two cost pools.
d. The three approaches to assigning overhead used above resulted in different unit costs. Which of these three methods would you suggest the company adopt and what criteria would you use to select?

12. Deacon Corp. is a forms distribution company that captured market share by offering to store a client's forms and then will pick, pack, and ship requested forms on demand. Clients are charged for the direct cost of the forms and an overhead charge based on square footage of storage space used during the year. Overhead is budgeted at $200,000 per year.

In order to get a better understanding of the cost of servicing clients, an ABC system was proposed. After interviewing a number of production personnel, the ABC project manager identified the following activities and drivers for the coming year:

Activity	Budgeted Cost	Driver	Available Capacity
Processing orders received	$ 30,000	# of orders	1,000 orders
Picking orders	$ 50,000	picking hours	4,000 hours
Forms storage	$120,000	square feet	5,000 sq. ft.

The activity profiles of two clients for the past year were also prepared to determine whether or not the extra effort to compute the more detailed cost analysis would result in any differences in cost assignment.

Item	Customer 1	Customer 2
Direct cost of forms	$3,000	$5,000
Number of orders	50	12
Picking hours	250	18
Square feet used	100	150

Required:

a. Calculate the cost of servicing each customer using square footage as the overhead allocation base.

b. Calculate the cost of servicing each customer using the proposed ABC system.

c. What accounts for the difference in the cost per customer between the two overhead assignment methods?

■ PROBLEMS AND CASES—ADVANCED LEVEL

Case 1: Blue Ridge Manufacturing.

Blue Ridge Manufacturing produces knit apparel in a modern plant located in the Blue Ridge Mountain region of North Carolina. Overall, the company is profitable, as the performance report below indicates.

The company sells three product lines, which differ in the amount of customization. The sports line is a v- or crew-neck sweater customized for school color and yarn type (bulky versus fine gauge). Each sweater order requires an artistic development of the school's logo. After development, the logo is either knitted into the sweater or sewn on it (like athletic letters). The children's line is a collection of infant sweater and pull-on pants. These are standard and vary only by color and size. The designer line contains a variety of standard products, redesigned each season, and is sold to department stores. These lines vary in sales volume, with the designer line selling most, the children's line selling a close second and the sports line having the smallest sales.

	Total	Designer	Children's	Sports
Sales	$8,451,112	$3,464,915	$3,246,687	$1,739,510
Variable product costs	4,944,487	1,829,464	1,977,798	1,137,225
Commissions	640,013	236,805	256,006	147,202
Contribution margin	$2,866,512	$1,398,646	$1,012,783	$455,083
Indirect expenses	1,409,232	687,601	497,903	223,728
Income	$1,457,280	$711,045	$514,880	$231,355

Recently, sales of the sports line have increased, although the nature of the products has not changed. Management cannot account for the increasing market share and wants more information before devoting an even greater share of production resources to this market segment.

The cost accounting system is fairly sophisticated with respect to variable product costs, but thus far indirect costs have been allocated to products based on their contribution margin. Management has concern that indirect manufacturing expenses may be affected by which product line is produced.

During a review of the issue, management realized that many general overhead items represented resources consumed in proportions different than the relative gross profit of the product line. Management decided to use ABC to determine product-line profitability. The following table contains the results of management's analysis.

Cost	Amount	Driver	Designer	Children	Sports
Designer pay	$488,260	Work Hours	10,105	3,857	14,760
Supervisory pay	163,176	Work Hours	76,411	82,606	47,498
Samples	218,711	# Items	2,223	2,224	1,229
Setup costs	76,220	# setups	15,806	15,807	11,290
Travel for design	47,266	hours/line	3,985	2,213	6,476
Scheduling	67,142	# orders	246	1,870	11,990
Customer service	13,369	# calls	118	882	13,580
Design office costs	7,925	Sq. Ft.	900	811	1,004
Supervisory, setup and schedulers office costs	66,665	Sq. Ft.	1,800	1,622	2,008
Inspection	13,501	# of inspections	1,897	1,297	7,113
Purchasing	175,356	# of unique items	1,870	246	11,990
Materials handling	71,641	# of material moves	118	882	13,580
Total	$1,409,232				

Required:

a. What amount of overhead is attributable to each product line? (Use a spreadsheet software for this assignment.)

b. Using sales and variable costs given originally and your findings from part one, determine the profitability of each product line. (Use spreadsheet software.)

c. What issues are raised by the results of question (b)?

Case 2: Piedmont Siding.**

It all started one hot day in July 1993. Duane Smith, president of Piedmont Siding, slammed down the phone and asked his secretary to have Bill Johnson, the CFO, come to his office. A few minutes later, Bill walked in asking, "What's up, Duane?"

**This case is adapted from a case prepared by Paul E. Juras of Wake Forest University and is intended to be used as a basis for class discussion rather than to illustrate either effective or ineffective handling of the situation. The names of the organizations, individuals, and financial information have been disguised to preserve the organizations' desire for anonymity. The original case was presented to and accepted by the refereed Society for Case Research. All rights reserved to the author and the SCR. Copyright © 1994 by Paul E. Juras. Reprinted by permission of Paul Juras.

Duane responded, "I just received a call from our majority shareholder Thompson Jeffries. He wants to talk about the financial results for the first half of the year. He thinks our profit margin is too low and wants to meet with us to discuss a plan for next year. He will be here this afternoon."

Later that day, Thompson Jeffries, Duane Smith, and Bill Johnson were in a meeting, Thompson Jeffries was speaking. "Duane, you have done an excellent job cultivating a customer base of reputable building contractors. While you have built Piedmont Siding into a $2,000,000 company in four years, I just don't think you can continue to run this operation by the seat of your pants any longer. You need a plan for action."

Duane responded, "I have a plan! My plan is to expand the replacement vinyl market. We both know that there is a large number of older homes in need of updating. I think we can get quite a few people to put siding on instead of repainting. I even hired a salesman to build volume in this market."

"I know that is your plan, I just question whether we should be in the replacement vinyl market at all. I would like Bill to do an analysis of the profitability of each of our major markets," said Thompson.

"I know how to bid a job to make it profitable. I also know that, while the replacement vinyl business offers a less than 10% margin on each job, with a high enough volume we can build a healthy bottom line." Duane continued, "Besides, Bill is already so overworked with all the time he spends on reconciling receivables, verifying payables for materials, and calculating the amount due to each of the installation crews that he doesn't have time to do this type of detailed analysis. Why should Bill waste his time on it?"

"Duane, I think you just answered your own question," Thompson said. "I'll tell you what. Have Bill break the income statement results for the past six months into five columns, one for each of our four major markets, and a column for the totals. That chore should not take long, and it may provide some insights to both of us."

With that last statement, Thompson got up to leave. "I expect that revised income statement to be ready when I come back on Monday morning," he said as he walked out the door.

Background and Financial Information.

Over the following weekend Duane Smith's thoughts turned back to that day in 1989 when he landed the first vinyl siding installation contract for his newly formed company. Times were simpler then. As the sole shareholder of his company, he had called all the shots. He used to be the one ordering the materials from vinyl siding manufacturers and doing all the installation. And as long as he had money in the bank, he knew he was making a profit. However, even back then he knew that his fifteen years of experience in construction did not prepare him to handle the paperwork and other operational details involved with running a business. In early 1991 Duane could afford to hire someone to handle the day-to-day operations of the business. That person was Bill Johnson.

In the following years the company grew rapidly. While Duane was still heavily involved with bringing in business, the company was now contracting with new home builders to install the vinyl siding as well as continuing to put siding on older homes (replacement vinyl). Piedmont Siding still purchased all the materials, but now the company hired crews to do the installation. The company served an area known as the Piedmont Triad, which had been experiencing a growth in new home construction.

The company's growth caused cash flow problems, and by the end of 1992, Duane needed cash to keep his business out of bankruptcy. Thompson Jeffries provided the necessary cash in exchange for a majority interest in the company. All Thompson wanted

Exhibit 21
Six-Month Analysis of Profit by Customer Group

	Six-Month Total	Shade Hills	Triad Builders	Other Builders	Replacement Business
Sales	1,051,200	453,600	422,880	93,120	81,600
Materials	476,160	204,240	192,240	40,800	38,880
Direct labor	315,840	131,760	122,712	25,728	35,640*
Gross Margin	259,200	117,600	107,928	26,592	7,080
Payroll costs	108,640				
Liability insurance	39,000				
Office expense	30,000				
Vehicle expenses	19,264				
Warehouse	17,496				
Other	27,520				
Pretax profit	17,280				

* Includes sales commission.

was an adequate return on his investment. He did not want to be involved with the daily operations of the business. Because of poor profit margin, he is considering selling his shares.

Piedmont Siding has two major customers, Shade Hills and Triad Builders. Both customers are large residential developers, and Piedmont Siding receives a large volume of their business in the Piedmont Triad. Piedmont Siding also works with small, independent contractors on new construction and competed for replacement vinyl installation contracts.

Piedmont Siding had three major cost categories: direct labor and direct materials, constituting 76 percent of costs; salaries and benefits, 14 percent of total costs; and all other general and administrative expenses. Because all materials are ordered on a job-by-job basis and all installation is done by subcontractors, direct materials and labor are easily traced to each job. With this information, Bill prepared the statement contained in Exhibit 21.

On Monday morning Thompson reviewed the figures in Exhibit 21 with Duane and Bill.

"See," Duane said, "we have over a 9 percent margin on replacement work. If we build volume, we can really improve the bottom line."

"What about these costs?" asked Thompson, as he pointed at the lines for payroll and general and administrative expenses. He continued, "Shouldn't we see if any of these costs can be attributed to any of the specific customer groups?"

Bill responded, "I don't know of any way to spread the costs other than to use a simple allocation base."

Fortunately, Thompson Jeffries served on the advisory council of a local university and asked Peter Johnson, one of the faculty members, for help on this project. Peter's suggestion was to have the company attempt to do an activity-based analysis of the items that appear on the income statement below gross margin. Since payroll represented the largest of the expense items, that was the starting point. The goal was to accurately determine how much time the employees spent performing various activities. However, management did not want to deal with the burdens of keeping detailed logs of activities. Instead, they simply estimated the amount of time spent on tasks that supported each broad group of customers. Exhibit 22 contains the results of the time analysis.

Exhibit 22
Results of Two-Stage Time Allocation

	President	Vice President	Scheduler-Purchaser	All Other Personnel
Shade Hills	30%	25%	33%	18%
Triad Builders	30%	25%	32%	19%
Small contractors	15%	25%	15%	33%
Replacement business	5%	10%	15%	20%
Other*	20%	15%	5%	10%
Annual salary & benefits	70,000	60,000	35,000	52,280

* Reviewing bids for proposals, directly overseeing one time large contracts, etc.

Required:

a. Using the information in Exhibits 21 and 22, recalculate the profit by customer group after assigning payroll costs.

b. In light of your results from requirement 21, evaluate Duane's plan to expand the replacement business.

c. Provide some suggestions as to what could be done with the general and other administrative costs to help complete this analysis.

d. How can an activity-based system help management develop a long-range business plan?

Case 3: Guys & Dolls.

Guys & Dolls Inc. specializes in producing miniature mechanical porcelain toy figurines. These figurines, used in retail displays and sold as collectors' items, use popular movie or cartoon characters such as Mickey Mouse, Goofy, and so on. Over the years there has been a steady increase in product variety. The company now makes many different products in various batch sizes. These products vary in number of details, special features such as movements or voice, parts needed, machines required to produce them, size of production runs, and quality inspections. In recent years Guys & Dolls has invested heavily in automated machinery and realized a steady decline in labor cost.

The company's manufacturing plant is organized into two production and two support departments. Production takes place in Machining and Assembly. Parts are ordered, stocked, and moved into production by the Material Department. The other support department, Maintenance, does the entire repair and upkeep of the machinery.

A conventional cost system is in use. Overhead costs are budgeted by the four departments and a sequential (step) method of allocation is used to allocate manufacturing overhead from support to production departments. The following allocation bases are used:

Property taxes:	square footage
Utilities:	kilowatt hours
Material Dept:	requisitions
Machine Dept:	machine hours

Overhead is charged to products using machine hours as a base in Machining and Direct Labor Hours as a base in Assembly. The company expects all products to earn a minimum of 10% profit margin (i.e., Profit ÷ Sales Revenue). The estimated marketing and G&A costs are approximately $2,000,000 per year for these two products. These costs are added to the manufacturing costs to arrive at product prices. Both products require the

141

same marketing and G&A effort. The expected cost is applied to manufacturing costs to arrive at product prices. The budgeted overhead costs and bases for 1997 are:

Budgeted Costs and Bases For 1997					
Costs	Materials	Maintenance	Machining	Assembly	Total
Property taxes					140,000
Utilities					250,000
Salaries	560,000	250,000	350,000	440,000	1,600,000
Supplies	80,000	150,000	220,000	60,000	510,000
Depreciation	120,000	360,000	840,000	180,000	1,500,000
Total	760,000	760,000	1,410,000	680,000	4,000,000
Bases					
Square footage	20,000	5,000	15,000	20,000	60,000
Kilowatt hours	5,000	15,000	50,000	30,000	100,000
Material requisitions		800	4,800	2,400	8,000
Machine hours		10,000	35,000	5,000	50,000
Direct labor hours			12,000	28,000	40,000

In recent years the company has been facing stiff competition from overseas manufacturers. Cost and manufacturing efficiency have become very important. Leslie Newcome, president of Guys & Dolls, has been studying the possibilities of using some modern manufacturing methods and activity-based cost systems (ABC). In particular, he was struck by two ideas: reorganizing manufacturing into "focused manufacturing cells" instead of functional departments, and using activity-based cost pools and drivers for cost allocation. Newcome discussed this plan with his VP of production and manager of cost analysis and asked them to study and recommend changes.

After an extended study, the two reported back to Newcome with a plan to reorganize production into two manufacturing cells and to create seven cost pools. According to the new plan, the two manufacturing cells would do their own maintenance and would have two operations—machining and assembly. The work cells would share space and utilities with other departments. These costs did not vary by products. A common staff would handle materials, production setups, and quality assurance. Accordingly, cost pools were created for quality control and production setups. The Materials Department, however, was split into two cost pools: procurement related and materials handling related. Two other cost pools created were Detail and Feature. The Detail cost pool represented costs associated with the number of details, such as colors and expressions in a product. The Feature pool included the cost of adding different voice and movements to a figurine. This was done because beyond the *basic* product, additional details and features added costs to a production run. Since there was little significant cost difference between details and features, these cost pools were identified as a lump sum based on details and features used in the past. The following cost pool data and associated drivers were identified:

142

Activity/Operation Pools	Cost	Drivers	
Work cell occupancy costs	$300,000	Square feet	60,000
Materials handling	400,000	No. of material moves	50,000
Materials procurement	360,000	No. of parts	2,000
Quality control	500,000	No. of inspections	5,000
Production setups	340,000	No. of setups	1,700
Detail related costs	900,000	No. of details	15
Feature related costs	1,200,000	No. of features	12
Total budgeted overhead costs	4,000,000		

In 1997, two of the items going into production were the Flintstone and the Lion King figurines based on recent popular movies. The Company expected to produce 20,000 of *each* of these figurines and sell them at a price of $125 and $90 per unit, respectively. The following production data was collected:

	Flintstone	Lion King
Production quantity	20,000	20,000
Direct materials + conversion operations cost	$200,000	$180,000
Selling and Administration costs	$1,000,000	$1,000,000
Machine hours	10,000	8,000
Direct labor hours	5,000	5,000
Square feet required	6,000	2,000
No. of materials moves	15,000	3,000
No. of parts	400	100
No. of quality control inspections	60	20
No. of product runs (setups)	25	5
No. of details	5	2
No. of features	6	2

Required:

a. Compare the production and total cost and profit margin per unit for the two products using departmental overhead allocations with those using the new activity-based cost pools.

b. Do both products meet the target return (10%) requirement of the company?

c. Which set of numbers are you using to answer the previous question? Why? Support your answer with arguments.

d. Assume that some of the products in the company are not currently meeting their profit targets. Suggest steps that you can take to ensure that they meet their profit targets in the future.

MODULE

Standard Costing as a Cost Management Tool

VERSION
2.0

AUTHORS

Shahid Ansari and Jan Bell
California State University Northridge

Thomas Klammer
University of North Texas

SERIES CONCEPT DEVELOPED BY:

Shahid Ansari • Jan Bell • Thomas Klammer • Carol Lawrence

Standard Costing as a Cost Management Tool

CANDLES LOSES ITS SPARKLE

Performance is on the agenda and tensions are high at the monthly meeting of Sparkling Candles' departmental managers.

Josie Johnson, the cost manager greets the participants and begins her presentation. "Good morning everybody! You all have copies of this month's variance report. We seem to have the same problems we've had in the previous months. Our production costs are too high and there are persistent unfavorable variances on the monthly standard cost report. We need to discuss how to improve performance, better control costs, and eliminate these variances."

Sam Potter, the production manager for specialty candles and a recent MBA pipes up, "Josie, can we take the gloves off and speak freely?"

"You bet Sam, that's why we're here!"

"Good! That standard cost system of yours is a big part of the problem. The variances the financial staff compute and report every month aren't very useful for those of us in operations. The information is late and it is not very informative. In addition, we spend considerable effort and time identifying and reporting who's responsible, and the result is our current work often suffers. I don't know who established those standards! Some of them don't even reflect the realities of our current operating environment. We also have no control over lots of the variances. Frankly, the monthly standard cost variance reports don't help us identify and correct problems. The standard costing system seems to be working against us."

"There's certainly some truth in your comments, Sam. However, making comparisons between actual and expected results is critical for controlling costs. Perhaps we need to update our standards. We also need to spend time digging deeper into the root causes of these variances. We are interested in controlling costs and not simply generating paperwork. It may be time for us to reevaluate our standard cost system and make sure we're generating and using the information properly! Here's what I'd like to do. Let's study and redesign the system. I'll make some of my staff available, if you're willing to be part of this effort."

"That's a good idea, Josie," replied Sam, "We could start by looking at the information for our large fancy-cut candles. There are always variances in materials and in the hand-carving labor cost for this product. There are also a lot of useless variances reported!"

■ STRATEGIC VALUE OF STANDARD COSTING

A standard cost is a predetermined per unit cost. It represents an organization's expectation of the resources that should be consumed in producing a unit of output under specified (usually optimal) operating conditions. A variance is the difference between the actual cost incurred and the standard cost.[1] Making comparisons between planned and actual costs is

---

[1] In accounting, the term *variance* means the deviation between a standard and an actual cost. It should not be confused with the use of the term *variance* in statistics

147

an essential part of the cost management process. Consider an auto repair shop that sets a wage standard of $15 per hour for its technicians. If an oil change should take 15 minutes of a technician's time, the standard cost of labor is $3.75 (15/60 minutes × $15 per hour). Assume that the shop actually paid $16 per hour and an oil change required 17 minutes; that means that the actual labor cost was $4.533 (17/60 minutes × $16 per hour). The unfavorable variance of $.78 has two sources; a higher wage rate and more time used during the oil change. When a variance is significant, we need to determine the underlying causes for that variance.

Standard cost systems (SCS) are strategically important. They help organizations provide customers with what they want (quality) at an affordable price (cost), and when they want it (time.) Standards incorporate expectations of quality, cost, and time (QCT). For example, an ice cream manufacturer has to control the amount of fat content and flavor to suit their customers' tastes. They also have to make sure that the cost is equal to or below what customers are willing to pay and what competitors charge for similar quantity and quality of ice cream. Finally, they must ensure that the ice cream has the necessary shelf life to sit on grocery shelves without losing flavor (time). Variances from standards may indicate that those QCT expectations have not been met allowing the ice cream manufacturer to take corrective measures. This kind of information is critical for any organization that operates in a highly competitive environment.

■ MODULE LEARNING OBJECTIVES

This module focuses primarily on the value and limitations of standard costing systems (SCS) for cost management. It illustrates the fundamental process of setting standards, measuring variances, and evaluating differences between actual and expected results. After studying this module, you should be able to:

- ■ Understand the difference between cost maintenance and cost reduction systems.
- ■ Identify when to use standard costing.
- ■ Apply the five steps in using standard costing to manage costs. These steps include:
  - ■ Developing standards
  - ■ Collecting actual cost data
  - ■ Computing variances
  - ■ Investigating variances
  - ■ Taking corrective action
- ■ Appreciate the behavioral and cultural attributes of a good standard costing system.

■ COST REDUCTION VERSUS COST MAINTENANCE SYSTEMS

Organizations use two types of cost management tools. The first category is designed to *reduce costs* and includes tools such as target costing and *kaizen* costing. The second category of tools, which includes traditional budgeting and standard costing, are designed to *maintain* or contain costs within a predetermined range.

In systems theory, a cost maintenance system is an *error-controlled feedback* system. This type of system works on the principle of using errors to take corrective actions. The process sets a predetermined standard or value for the variable being controlled. Actual performance is measured and compared against the predetermined standard. When the deviation between actual performance and the predetermined standard exceeds an acceptable range, corrective action is taken.

A thermostat is often used as an example of this type of system. The purpose of a thermostat is to maintain desired room temperature. It does this by measuring room temperature and comparing it against the desired temperature. If the room gets too hot or cold, the thermostat trips the heating or air conditioning unit to turn on or off. It is the information about errors (deviations from standard) that allows the thermostat to do its job and restore the system back to its desired state.

Exhibit 1 shows that a standard cost system works in much the same way as a thermostat. In a standard cost system, the variable of interest is cost and the standard represents the desired level for this variable. The system compares actual costs against this preset standard cost. The resulting deviations (variances) are used to take corrective action when they depart significantly from the standard cost.

Exhibit 1
SCS as a Cost Maintenance System

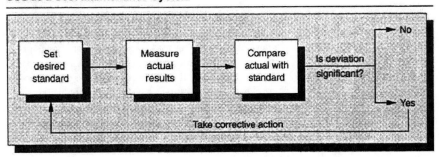

Unlike cost maintenance, cost reduction systems such as *kaizen,* continually seek to reduce cost. (*Kaizen* is the Japanese word for *continuous improvement.*) Exhibit 2 compares standard cost and *kaizen* costing systems.

Exhibit 2
***Kaizen* versus Standard Costing Systems**

Standard Costing System (SCS)	Kaizen Costing System
• Focus is on *maintaining* cost at predetermined level. • Assumes that existing process is *optimal.*	• Focus is on *reducing* cost. • Assumes that there is room to *improve* the existing process.
• Undertakes *discrete* periodic revisions of standards. • Goals are expressed in *financial* terms. • Breeds *complacency,* as meeting standards is good enough • *Reactive* effort designed to restore system back to equilibrium.	• Undertakes *continuous* improvement activity each day. • Goals are expressed in *operational* terms. • Mindset is one of continuous *change.* • *Proactive* effort to move the system forward.

149

If a SCS is a cost maintenance system, what products or services can benefit most by this system?

THINK ALONG

■ WHEN TO USE STANDARD COSTING

Standard costing is most useful in the later stages of a product's life cycle. In the early stages (development and testing) of a product's life cycle, both the product and the process used to produce it are subject to design changes. Without a final design in place, it is difficult to establish a desired cost standard. This also means that standard costing is most useful for products with long life cycles because such products have stable and repetitive processes that have been optimized over time. For example, Nabisco makes millions of Oreo cookies each year. Oreos are a well-established product with a long life cycle. The materials, labor, equipment, and process used to make Oreos does not change frequently. Engineers have established the optimum equipment layout, labor use, ingredient mix, cooking time, and packaging process. Having standards for each of these elements makes sense. Individuals buying the ingredients or making and packing the cookies can use variances from standards to identify and correct any problems in the cookie-making or material-purchasing processes.

If standard costing requires a stable process, it cannot be used for products that are still in development or that may be produced only once or a few times (e.g., a custom-built home). The production process used to provide the product or service would not be stable. Employees would still be learning about the process and searching for better ways to produce. Very little repetition would occur as the workers experimented with alternative production methods, and standards would not be meaningful. Likewise, when a product has a short life cycle, company engineers would not have time to establish optimal methods of production so standards would have little value.

A standard costing system is a system for maintaining costs in companies where products have long life cycles and the production process is stable and well understood.

KEY POINT

Standard costing is most effective for costs that can be managed through *immediate* corrective action. Typically, these are costs that vary with production volume, such as material and supplies, variable direct labor, and variable indirect costs. Sparkling Candles can monitor and compare the actual amount of wax and labor used in producing candles against preset standards. If variances exist, managers can investigate and respond quickly. Assume that excess wax and labor time is used in candle production. If the excesses are the result of improperly trained personnel, a short training session may improve the situation. If the variances are the result of too little supervision, the supervisor-to-worker ratio can be altered. If the excess use of wax and time results from poor quality wax, the purchasing agent can be instructed to increase wax specifications.

A standard costing system (SCS) is not an appropriate tool for managing fixed capacity costs, such as rent or depreciation, or for managing discretionary costs (costs that management can increase or decrease without affecting production quantity in the short run)

150

such as advertising. Capacity costs are incurred for longer periods. Once acquired, these costs cannot be changed with short-term variations in production. For example, there is no quick way to decrease factory rent when production declines. Sparkling Candles will have to renegotiate their lease in order to manage this cost. These types of costs are better managed with tools such as capacity costing, capital budgeting, and the theory of constraints.[2]

SCS and Product Costing.

A SCS also accumulates product cost and inventory valuation information that can be used for external financial reporting. Generally accepted accounting principles define product cost as the sum of actual direct materials, direct labor, and manufacturing overhead. Typically these are supposed to represent actual costs. However, production cycles rarely conform to reporting cycles in a business. This creates two problems.

First, at the end of any reporting period, firms typically have physical inventories of raw materials, work in process, and finished goods. They do not, however, know all of their costs. For example, the firm may not have been billed for its usage of electricity or may not have calculated all of its wages and salaries. Actual costs at this point may underestimate the real cost of inventory.

Second, in most businesses, costs fluctuate seasonally. For example, in cold climates the heating bill is higher during the winter months so the actual manufacturing overhead may be higher in the winter. Similarly, for businesses that use agricultural products such as fruits, there are seasonal crop variations and raw material prices may fluctuate. Even labor costs may be different if at certain times of the year labor has to be paid overtime wages.

THINK ALONG

> Why is it inappropriate to use actual costing when actual costs are either not available or there are seasonal fluctuations in costs?

When cost data is not available or when there are seasonal fluctuations in cost, the same identical product will have different costs in different periods. For example, the unit produced in winter may have a higher cost due to the higher heating cost or a lower cost because we did not have all our heating bills in time. This is highly misleading *because two products using the same inputs should not have different costs simply because they were produced at different times of the year.*

Standard costing helps to avoid these artificial fluctuations by setting annual cost standards based on the entire year. This allows a firm to match its cost cycle and data to the annual reporting cycle. Because predetermined amounts of materials, labor, and manufacturing overhead are established, product costs can be computed without the need for actual cost data. In addition, because the predetermined standards use an annual estimate, they smooth out seasonal fluctuations. Inventory accounts under a standard cost system include only the standard cost of materials, labor, and manufacturing overhead. As illustrated later in the module, variances (which represent inefficiencies) are isolated and kept separate

---

[2] See the *Capital Budgeting Process, Measuring and Managing Capacity Cost,* and *Theory of Constraints and Throughput Accounting* modules in this series.

151

from product cost. They are charged to the cost of goods sold as period costs and not shown on the balance sheet as an asset.

■ STANDARD COSTING STEPS

There are five major steps in standard costing. Careful application of these steps helps maximize the value of the SCS as a cost management tool and supports its supplemental objectives of inventory valuation and simplifying bookkeeping. The five steps are:

- ■ Step 1: Develop standards
- ■ Step 2: Accumulate actual information
- ■ Step 3: Compute variances
- ■ Step 4: Investigate variances
- ■ Step 5: Take corrective action

To illustrate the standard costing process steps, we focus on the material and labor used to make *fancy-cut candles,* one of the more popular products made by Sparkling Candles, the company in our opening story.

Step 1. Develop standards.

A standard cost represents the predetermined amount of resources necessary to produce a unit of output of a product or service. Therefore, standard costing begins with a good *understanding of the input-output relationships in a process.* To set standards, we must also decide how *difficult* they must be, what *data to use* as a basis for setting standards, and *who participates* in setting standards.

Understanding input-output relationships.
An analysis of the work activities in the candle-production process is the first step in setting standards. For example, consider the fancy-cut candle shown in Exhibit 3. It is one of the main products made by Sparkling Candles.

Exhibit 3
Sparkling Candles: A Sample Fancy Candle

Melting and mixing beeswax with scents and color is the first step in making candles. Special equipment inserts a wick into a reusable candle mold and then fills the mold with a liquid wax mixture. After the wax hardens, the unfinished candle is removed from the mold. A candle carver hand cuts fancy designs and shapes into the candle. After carving, candles are boxed and stored until they are shipped to customers. There are standard designs, but each candle varies slightly because of the hand-carving process and the skill of the carver. Exhibit 4 shows the flow diagram of the work process and major activities in that process.

Exhibit 4
Sparkling Candles Production Flow Diagram—Major Activities

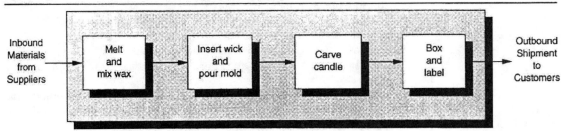

Knowledge of the production process can be translated into the quantity of material, labor, and other resources required for producing candles. When this information is combined with knowledge of market prices, accountants can set standard product costs for the materials, labor, and other short-term consumable resources.

Difficulty of standards.

Standards can be ideal or attainable. *Ideal standards* represent perfect operating conditions and therefore can be hard to achieve. For example, the ideal standard for a candle may be 9 kilograms of wax. The 9-kg standard quantity assumes no wax is ever spilled or wasted, the worker always measures perfectly, and the machines never get out of adjustment. Ideal standards have no *slack*—that is, no allowance for waste, breaks, or stress reduction.[3]

Recall from earlier that the standard time it should take to make an oil change was 15 minutes. Assuming this is an ideal standard, there is no margin for finding the right oil, dropping a tool, or talking to a customer. The use of ideal standards creates unfavorable variances, which can have a negative impact on employee morale. Even when attained, ideal standards can cause a high level of tension in the organization. It is for this reason that many researchers argue that some slack in standards is functional. For example, we may determine that allowing sixteen minutes for an oil change is more attainable.

---

[3] For a discussion of the effects of budgetary slack on performance see Hossein Nouri and Robert J. Parker, "The Effect of Organizational Commitment on the Relation Between Budgetary Participation and Budgetary Slack," *Behavioral Research In Accounting,* Vol 8, 1996.

An *attainable* or *practical standard* deliberately builds slack into the standard. It represents estimated cost under tight, but achievable conditions. Attainable standards can be reached with reasonable effort under existing operating conditions. The seventeen minutes it actually took to change oil in our earlier example would still be more than the attainable standard of sixteen minutes.

It may be useful for firms to use both ideal and attainable standards for cost management. The former focuses and challenges the organization to continually move the actual results closer to the ideal. The latter ensures that standards do not create unnecessary tension or lower employee morale.

Data used for setting standards.

Setting standards requires data. This data may come from engineering studies, external benchmarks, or past historical experience.

Engineering studies done by production engineers may help to determine the input-output relationships in a process. For example, engineering tests may show that exactly 9 kilograms of wax is required to make a candle when the process is totally controlled and 10 kilograms when work rules are relaxed. This data may be used to define ideal and attainable standards.

External benchmarking of firms in the same industry or firms in a different industry but with a similar process can also provide data for standards. For example, studies of labor processes in the candle-making industry may provide "best in class" information for the time it should take for dipping, inserting, pouring, and other steps in the manufacturing process. Such external comparisons have the added advantage of keeping a firm aware of what their competition is doing, and, they help the firm stay competitive.

Past historical data can be used for standard setting. For example, the 10-kilogram standard may represent the mean amount of wax used per candle during the past year. There are two dangers in using past data. We can institutionalize past inefficiency in the standards, and the past may not be a good guide to the future because of design changes in the product and/or the process.

Who participates in setting standards.

Standards may be *imposed* from the top or they may be set through a *participative* process of consultation with employees who are affected by the standard.

An *imposed standard,* which is set with little or no input from those responsible for meeting the standard, is used when it is desirable to ensure that all actions lead to a uniform strategic target. However, imposed standards do not create a sense of ownership on the part of employees. Motivating employees to achieve these standards, therefore, may be more difficult.

Participative standards use inputs from employees either affected by a standard or who have the best understanding of the process. Participation does *not* mean those responsible for meeting the standard get to set the standard. It does mean that employees have input in the standard-setting process.

KEY POINT

To set standards we must understand the input-output relationships in a process, decide how much slack to allow in standards, select the data to use as a basis for setting standards, and determine who should participate in setting standards.

The standard cost card.

A *standard cost card* summarizes the results of the standard setting process. It lists the expected quantity and expected price for each major cost component. Exhibit 5 is an example of the standard cost card for the production of a typical fancy candle for Sparkling Candles. It lists the direct material and direct labor costs for this product. Column 2 of Exhibit 5 shows the standard material price, and column 3 shows the standard quantity of materials and labor used in the fancy candle. Column 2 multiplied by column 3 provides the standard cost of each material and labor item required for the fancy candle.

Exhibit 5
Standard Cost Card per unit for White Rose Fancy Candle

Item	Standard Price	Standard Quantity	Standard Cost
Budgeted Production		50,000 candles	
Materials/Candle			
Wax	$.22 per kg	10 kg	$2.20
Other materials (wick, color, scent and box)	$.002 per cm	14 cm	0.028
Standard Material Cost			**$2.28**
Direct Labor/Candle			
Melting and Mixing	$12 per hour	1 minute	$0.20
Pouring	$12 per hour	0.75 minutes	.15
Carving	$15 per hour	20 minutes	5.00
Box and Label	$7.20 per hour	.5 minutes	.06
Standard Labor Cost			**$5.41**

Step 2. Accumulate actual information.

Standard cost systems compare actual and standard costs to make sure costs are under control. *This means that actual cost information must be collected and reported using the same categories as those used for setting standards.* For example, in Exhibit 5 we have separate standard costs for wax and other materials. What happens if in collecting actual data we lump the costs of the wick, color, scent, and box with the wax? In this case, we would have to manually separate the data or compare the cost of five items against the standard cost of wax only.

Managers use standards to manage costs by taking corrective actions when the process is out of control. For standard costing to be an effective cost management tool, the data on actual cost performance must be captured and reported in a *timely* fashion. The frequency of reporting depends upon how fast corrective action should and can be taken. If reporting is too late and the time for corrective action is over, standard cost and variance reports are not useful for cost management. You will recall that this lack of information was one of the complaints Sparkling Candles personnel raised about the existing system. Critical information that operating personnel need to actively manage operations is often captured and reported using other tools. This allows problems to be identified and solved before the standard cost variances are even reported. For example, observation, a

155

control chart, or an hourly quality report may show that more candles than normal are flawed. This information leads to immediate corrective action.

Exhibit 6 shows the actual current period cost data for the White Rose Fancy Candle produced by Sparkling Candles. Note that to keep our example simple, we are simply focusing on the most expensive material (wax) and the most expensive process (carving). Limiting our focus is not unrealistic since often the cost of recording and reporting data for minor materials such as wick and scents may exceed the benefit from tracking them.

KEY POINT

Actual information for computing and analyzing variances must be collected and reported in the *same categories* as the standards, and the information should be reported in a *timely* manner for corrective action to be taken quickly. When this is not possible, we must supplement standard costing with other real-time tools such as hourly display boards (see Exhibit 10) or control charts.

Exhibit 6
Actual Cost for White Rose Fancy Candle for November 2003

Item	Actual Price	Actual Quantity	Total Actual Cost
Number of Candles Produced		39,000	
Materials			
Wax Purchased	$.23 per kg	420,000 kgs.	$ 96,600
Wax Used	$.23 per kg	387,000 kgs.	$ 89,010
Direct Labor			
Carving	$15.20 per hour	12,000 hours	$182,400

Step 3. Compute variances.

A variance is a deviation from a predetermined standard cost. Since the cost of any item is the sum of the unit price multiplied by the total quantity purchased, mathematically a variance is the result of a deviation in the price paid, the quantity purchased, or both. In a typical organization, the responsibility for purchasing inputs and using those inputs is usually separate. For example, the procurement department negotiates and orders materials while the plant supervisors usually control usage of that material. In a responsibility accounting system, therefore, variances are used to assign responsibility to appropriate people who have control over that element of the cost and to draw their attention to the need for corrective action.

Based on this mathematical and organizational logic, most standard cost systems compute and report four major variances. In the list below the terms in parentheses are other names used for the same variance. The four major variances are called:

- Material-Price Variance (MPV)
- Material-Quantity (Usage) Variance (MQV)
- Labor-Price (Rate) Variance (LPV)
- Labor-Quantity (Usage) Variance (LQV)

The overall formula for computing any variance is the same. It is simply the deviation or delta (Δ) between standard and actual prices and quantities. To illustrate the computation of variances, we will use the following notation:

AP = Actual price per unit
SP = Standard price per unit
AQ = Actual quantity
SQ = Standard or Flexible Budget Quantity
Δ = (Actual – Standard)

The production budget for any period represents the unit standard cost multiplied by the budgeted production quantity. For example, if Sparkling Candles expects to produce 50,000 candles this next period, the wax part of its production budget will be $110,000 ($2.20 $\times$ 50,000).[4] If the actual production is more or less than 50,000 candles, we must first calculate the *flexible budget* for that level of production before computing variances. *A flexible budget is the amount of spending <u>allowed</u> based on the unit standard cost for the actual level of production.* We can illustrate this numerically as follows. Exhibit 6 shows that Sparkling's actual production during the current period was 39,000 candles. Therefore, they were *allowed* to spend $85,800 (39,000 $\times$ $2.20) on wax. Similarly, the *flexible budget* for carving labor is $195,000 (39,000 $\times$ $5.00).

KEY POINT

A *flexible budget* is the amount of inputs that should be consumed by a given level of production volume. It applies only to costs that vary with production levels such as direct material, direct labor, factory utilities, and supplies.

Material-price variance (MPV).
As Exhibit 6 shows, 420,000 kilograms of wax were purchased in November at a cost of $96,600 at a cost of $0.23 per kilogram. The material-price variance for November is computed as follows:

MPV = ΔP $\times$ AQ Purchased

(AP – SP) $\times$ AQ Purchased

($0.23 – $0.22) $\times$ 420,000 kilograms

$0.01 $\times$ 420,000

MPV = $4,200 Unfavorable

---

[4] The budgeted cost for wax comes from Exhibit 5.

KEY POINT

The traditional way for computing variances is to subtract the standard price or quantity from the actual price or quantity. This means that a positive amount is unfavorable and a negative amount is favorable. Do not let the sign (+/–) confuse you. When identifying variances, you should ignore the mathematical sign and simply consider the nature of the variance. If a firm paid or used more than expected, we have an unfavorable variance.

The material-price variance is unfavorable because the actual cost of wax in November was $0.01 more per kilogram than the expected or standard cost.

THINK ALONG

Why did we use the quantity **purchased** (420,000 kg) rather than the quantity **used** (387,000 kg) to compute the material-price variance?

The material-price variance uses the actual quantity purchased because the company has to pay for the entire quantity it bought. Just because some of the material is in inventory does not change the fact that the cost has already been incurred. Not waiting for the material to be used also allows for timely reporting and corrective action to remove the cause of this variance.

Material-quantity variance (MQV).

Exhibit 6 shows that the actual quantity of wax used to produce 39,000 fancy candles in November was 387,000 kilograms. To compute the quantity variance, however, we must first compute the flexible budget quantity of wax for the production of 39,000 candles. Since each candle requires 10 kg of wax, the flexible budget quantity for 39,000 candles is 390,000 kilograms of wax. This information allows us to compute the material-quantity variance for November as follows:

$$MQV = \Delta Q \times SP$$
$$(AQ - SQ) \times SP$$
$$(387{,}000 - 390{,}000) \times \$0.22 \text{ per kilogram}$$
$$MQV = \textbf{\$660 Favorable}$$

The material-quantity variance is favorable because the actual quantity of wax used in November to make 39,000 candles was 3,000 kilograms less than expected (387,000 – 390,000).

Total-material variance.

According to Exhibit 5, the budgeted material cost for November is $2.20. For making 39,000 candles, the standard material cost is $85,800. The actual cost for November (Exhibit 6) is $96,600. The total variance, therefore, is $10,800 unfavorable. If we add the two material variances, price and quantity, they total $3,540 Unfavorable ($4,200 U + 660 F).

Reconcile the difference of $7,260 between ($10,800 and $3,540) the total material variance and the material and quantity price variances.

The remaining difference of $7,260 U represents the inventory of 33,000 kg of wax (420,000 purchased – 387,000 used). The 33,000 kilograms multiplied by the standard price of $0.22 equals the $7,260. Since not all of the material is used, the $7,260 is still in inventory. It might be useful to report this amount as a *materials-inventory variance* to signal to management that inventory levels are high. While it does not measure the cost of keeping inventory, the signal may start a conversation about whether the high inventory levels are justified.

Labor-price variance (LPV).

Exhibit 6 shows that the actual wage rate paid to carvers is $15.20 per hour. The standard carver labor rate per hour is $15.00 per hour. The labor-price or wage-rate variance for November is:

$$LPV = \Delta P \times AQ$$
$$(AP - SP) \times AQ$$
$$(\$15.20 - \$15.00) \times 12{,}000 \text{ hours}$$
$$LPV = \mathbf{\$2{,}400\ U}$$

The price variance is unfavorable because the actual hourly wage rate in November was $.20 more per hour ($15.20 – $15.00) than the expected wage rate.

Labor-quantity variance.

In November, the actual carver labor hours used for producing 39,000 candles were 12,000 (see Exhibit 6). Based on the standard carving time of 20 minutes per candle or three candles an hour, the flexible budget for carving labor hours is 13,000 hours. The carver labor–quantity variance for November's production of 39,000 candles is computed as follows:

$$LQV = \Delta Q \times SP$$
$$(AQ - SQ) \times SP$$
$$(12{,}000 - 13{,}000) \times \$15 \text{ per hour}$$
$$LQV = \mathbf{\$15{,}000\ F}$$

The variance is favorable because the actual hours carvers worked in November to carve 39,000 candles are 1,000 less than expected (12,000 – 13,000).

Total-labor variance.

The actual carver labor cost for November is $12,600 less than standard labor cost ($182,400 – $195,000). The standard labor cost of $195,000 is calculated as follows:

Carver labor cost per candle ($15 × 1/3 hour)	$ 5.00
Actual candles carved	× 39,000
Flexible labor cost budget at actual production level	$195,000

If the favorable carver labor–quantity variance of $15,000 is combined with the $2,400 unfavorable carver labor–price variances, we have accounted for the total carver–labor variance of $12,600. Unlike the total material-cost variance, the sum of the price and quantity variance for labor is equal the period's total labor variance because labor is acquired and used in the same period—that is, firms cannot have labor inventory.

Variable overhead-cost variances.

Firms often establish standards for variable production support costs such as electricity, supplies, and indirect labor. The variance computation for these elements is identical to the computations we showed you in the prior section. For example, if the actual cost of utilities is higher than standard, it could be because the electricity rates have gone up or because electricity usage is higher than expected. Similarly, the support labor cost could be higher because the rates paid exceeded the standard rates or more hours were used.

Assume that Sparkling Candles has set a standard of 5 kilowatt-hours (kWh) of electricity per labor hour and that the standard electricity rate is $0.30 per kWh. Exhibit 7 shows the flexible budget for the 12,000 actual labor hours.

The actual electricity cost for November is $20,650. The standard labor hours allowed for the production of 39,000 candles is 13,000. Therefore, the flexible budget for electricity is $19,500 (13,000 × 5 × $.30). There is a total unfavorable variance of $1,150 for electricity. As shown below, we can split this total unfavorable variance into two components— spending ($2,650 U) and efficiency ($1,500 F).

Exhibit 7
Budget and Actual Electricity Cost for November

Standard Electricity Rate	$0.30/kWh
Standard usage	5 kWh per labor hour
Flexible budget for actual production	60,000 kWh (5 x 12,000)
Actual usage	59,000 kWh
Actual rate	$0.35 kWh

$$\text{Electricity Spending Variance} = \text{Actual Spending} - \text{Budgeted Spending}$$
$$= (\$.35 \times 59,000) - (\$.30 \times 60,000)$$
$$= (\$20,650 - \$18,000)$$
$$= \mathbf{\$2,650\ U}$$

Note that the flexible electricity budget for 13,000 labor hours is 65,000 kWh. This is the quantity of labor allowed for the production of 39,000 candles. Since we are assuming that electricity use varies with labor hours, any efficiency in labor hours will also result in electricity savings as well. In November there was an efficiency variance of 1,000 labor hours (see labor-quantity variance). The 1,000 labor hour savings should also result in savings of 5,000 kWh (65,000 – 60,000). This difference between usage of electricity at the 12,000 and 13,000 labor hour levels, leads to an Electricity-Efficiency Variance of:

$$\text{Electricity-Efficiency Variance} = \Delta Q \times SP$$
$$= (60,000 - 65,000) \times \$0.3$$
$$= \mathbf{\$1,500\ F}$$

160

Note that the Spending Variance of $2,650 U can be further subdivided into price and quantity components as follows:

Electricity-Price Variance	$= \Delta P \times SQ$
	$= (0.35 - 0.30) \times 59,000$
	$= \textbf{\$2,950 U}$
Electricity-Usage Variance	$= \Delta Q \times SP$
	$= (59,000 - 60,000) \times \$0.30$
	$= \textbf{\$300 F}$

KEY POINT

> We can compute price, quantity, and efficiency variances for all *variable* overhead production costs as long as these costs vary with production volume.

Fixed overhead-cost variances.

Fixed costs do not change with volume and are typically budgeted once a year. Assume that Sparkling Candles has budgeted fixed overhead costs of $100,000 for its expected production volume of 50,000 candles per month. Further, assume that the actual fixed overhead costs for November are $110,000.

THINK ALONG

> What variance can you compute for cost management purposes?

The only meaningful variance that we can compute for fixed costs is a *spending* variance. The spending variance is the difference between the budget fixed cost level and the actual fixed cost level. For Sparkling Candles it is:

Fixed Overhead-Spending Variance = $110,000 - 100,000 = **$10,000 U**

A quantity or efficiency variance is unlikely since we have assumed that these costs are fixed no matter what the level of production. Therefore, the fixed overhead cost is $100,000 even though the actual production is 39,000 candles.

For product costing purposes, however, *fixed overhead costs are applied to products as if they were variable*. In our example, each candle will receive a fixed overhead cost of $2 ($100,000 ÷ 50,000 normal volume). The difference between the $78,000 applied overhead and the budgeted fixed overhead of $100,000 is called a **volume variance**. Exhibit 8 shows the traditional treatment of fixed overhead costs.

Exhibit 8
Sparkling Candles—Traditional Fixed Overhead Variances

1. Actual Fixed Overhead	$110,000
Fixed Overhead Applied or Absorbed by Products ($2 × 39,000 candles)	78,000
2. Under-applied or under-absorbed Overhead (1 – 2) (Charged to cost of goods sold on the income statement)	32,000
3. Spending Variance (110,000 – 100,000)	$10,000
4. Volume Variance (Traditionally computed)	$22,000

The volume variance allows us to reconcile the difference between actual and budgeted volume. However, we do not recommend computing and reporting a volume variance because it can lead to dysfunctional behaviors such as building inventory. For example, if Sparkling Candles were to produce 50,000 candles, there would be no volume variance but there would be finished goods inventory—an extremely costly proposition. We believe that fixed overhead costs are better handled with a capacity-management model.[5]

Variance reports.

All of the variances computed in the prior section are typically summarized in a *variance report* to management and first-level supervisors. The report may provide comparisons at any level of detail. For example, a firm might compare actual or expected labor costs on an overall basis, for each facility, for each department, for each work classification, and for each product. The SCS should provide variance reports customized to the level of detail needed to maintain control of costs.

Top management typically receives summary financial information on major variances by product, process, or cost factors in a quarterly report. Plant, product, or division managers receive monthly variance reports that summarize significant financial variances in major categories such as labor or material use or price.

Operating managers and supervisors receive detailed analysis of price and quantity variances for each material, labor, or variable overhead item that has a standard. These reports typically cover a week's activity. Exhibit 9 provides a sample weekly variance report.

Exhibit 9
Sparkling Candles—Weekly Variance Report

Budgeted Production	50,000			
Actual Production	39,000			
Flexible Budget Qty.	39,000			

Variance Analysis	Flexible Budget	Actual Cost	Dollar Variance	Percent of Budget
Material (Wax)	$ 85,800	$ 96,600	$10,800 U	
Price variance			4,200 U	4.89%
Quantity variance			660 F	0.77%
Inventory			7,260 U	8.46%
Labor (Carvers)	$195,000	$182,400	$12,600 F	
Price/Rate variance			2,400 U	1.23%
Quantity variance			15,000 F	7.69%
Variable Overhead	$ 19,500	$ 20,650	$ 1,150 F	
Price/Rate variance			2,950 U	15.13%
Quantity variance			300 F	1.54%
Efficiency variance			1,500 F	7.69%
Fixed Overhead	$100,000	$110,000	$10,000 U	
Spending Variance			10,000 U	10%

[5] See *Measuring and Managing Capacity* module in this series.

162

While dollar variances are useful to gauge the financial impact of deviating from plans, they may be too late to take corrective actions. Critical variables, such as quantity produced, are often monitored and reported daily, by shift, hourly, or even continually. Activities that are monitored more frequently are measured in operational and not financial terms. Exhibit 10 is an example of continuous monitoring

Exhibit 10
Continuous Monitoring of Production Cell

It shows how a Japanese manufacturer uses a lighted board to measure units produced. The variance of "–2" shows that the workstation is 2 units behind what it should have produced by that time of the day. It serves as a call for help. Other cell members who are ahead of their quota see the display and can help that particular cell catch up.

Step 4. Investigate variances.

The primary purpose of investigating reported variances is to manage costs. This requires identifying the root causes of variances and assigning responsibility for variances so corrective action may be taken. However, it takes employee time and the incurrence of other costs to investigate variances. Recall that one of the issues at Sparkling Candles is why answers seem to be required for every item on the variance report. The benefits of investigating a variance, therefore, should be greater than the cost of performing the analysis. Only those variances deemed significant should be investigated.

THINK ALONG

> Of the variances computed in the prior section (see Exhibit 9), which ones should be investigated?

Deciding which variances to investigate.
Given that investigation is costly, most firms use a management-by-exception system that focuses on variances that are large in *size* or show a *trend.* In addition, it may be useful to randomly select a small percentage of variances to investigate in order to ensure that cost controls remain adequate. It is also important to investigate both favorable and unfavorable variances. A favorable variance for a particular item may be unfavorable to the firm overall. For example, using less material than required creates a favorable quantity variance, but might make the product unsafe and lead to legal problems.

163

Size

The absolute or relative size of a variance is an important factor in the investigation decision. Often absolute size or percentage difference criteria are set and all variances that exceed these criteria are investigated. Assume the size criteria for variance investigation at Sparkling Candles is $5,000 and/or 5 percent of the budgeted cost. A review of Exhibit 9 shows that the labor quantity and the fixed overhead spending variances are greater than $5,000 and will be investigated. In addition, labor rate and variable overhead-efficiency variances are greater than 5 percent of the budget and will be investigated as well.

Trend

If a variance shows a trend that is getting larger period by period or is always negative or positive, further investigation may be warranted. Even though the size of the variance remains below preset-size criteria, the trend may be a warning that a particular part of a process may be deteriorating and may fail if corrective action is not taken.

KEY POINT

> It is important to investigate both favorable and unfavorable variances if they are large, exceed a certain percent of budget, or seem to indicate a trend.

Identifying root causes of variances.

Once accountants identify that a variance needs investigation, operating personnel must apply a systematic process to find out what causes these variances. Many firms such as Hewlett Packard and Toyota use a tool called *root-cause analysis*. Root-cause analysis is a method of linking a variance to the underlying cause of the variance. This technique requires that investigators ask "why" until they find the underlying cause of the variance. Most firms find it takes four or five levels of analysis to identify root causes. At Toyota, root-cause analysis simply takes the form of asking *"five whys"*—that is, they recommend asking "why" at least five times to determine the root cause of a problem or a variance.[6]

Assume that Sparkling Candles has a persistent problem with an unfavorable labor-quantity variance. Exhibit 11 provides a possible root-cause analysis for why the company has this unfavorable variance. Note that at the first level the answer is that more labor hours than were in the budget were used. This is not only obvious; it is also not very helpful. The second question asks why we used more hours. The answer, there was lots of inexperienced labor in the pool, is a little more helpful. The next "why" asks why inexperienced labor was used? The answer is that experienced labor was unavailable. The fourth "why" tells us that the reason little experienced labor was unavailable was because competitors are hiring this labor away. The fifth and last "why" tells us that the reason experienced workers leave is that they do not have career growth opportunities.

Note that root-cause analysis shows that the labor-quantity variance, a problem normally associated with manufacturing, is actually the result of the human resource policies of the firm. It reveals the process *linkages* that show how decisions in one area can adversely affect other areas. By understanding the root cause, we can attack the real source of the problem rather than simply putting pressure on the production supervisor—the normal outcome without root-cause analysis.

---

[6] For a discussion of how to use root-cause analysis as a quality management tool, see the module *Measuring and Managing Quality Costs* in this series.

KEY POINT

Root-cause analysis, which requires asking "why" several times, allows managers to understand and address the source of variances rather than their symptoms.

Exhibit 11
Root-Cause Analysis Using the 5-Why? Method

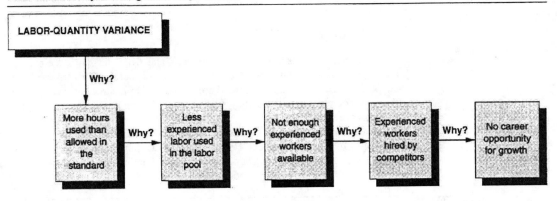

Step 5. Take corrective action.

The final step in the standard costing process is to use the information derived from the root-cause investigation to take corrective action. However, to select the appropriate corrective action, we must array the root causes by *source*—that is, where in the organization a root cause originates. A root cause can originate within a unit, from another unit, or from the external environment.

Assume that Sparkling Candles has done a complete root-cause analysis of all variances and that this analysis shows the following six root causes for the variances:

- Poor safety training for workers
- Improper storage of molds
- New hires poorly trained and inexperienced
- Incentives to accept the lowest bidder for materials
- Early retirement package to layoff workers
- Demand fluctuations making prediction difficult

Exhibit 12 places these causes in the three different cells depending on where these causes originate—within unit, inter-unit, or external environment. Within-unit causes are properly addressed by unit managers and first line supervisors. They have the primary responsibility for analyzing, investigating, and taking corrective action on such causes. If improper storage of molds is causing warping in candles, this is something that should be addressed by the molding department supervisor.

165

Exhibit 12
Classifying Root Causes by Source and Frequency

Source	Root Cause of Variances
Within Unit	1. Poor safety training for workers
	2. Improper storage of molds
Inter-unit	3. New hires poorly trained and inexperienced
	4. Incentives to accept the lowest bidder for materials
	5. Early retirement package to layoff workers
External environment	6. Demand fluctuations making prediction difficult

When variances result from actions that originate from other units, a cross-functional team is better suited to take care of this problem. This is because corrective action requires cooperation and coordination among these managers. If procurement is causing variances from poor purchasing policies, they need to be part of the production team to understand the consequences of their actions.

Finally, top management is best suited to handle causes that originate outside an organization—from its environment. For example, fluctuations in demand cause production schedules to go off. Stabilizing demand is not something the production managers can do even if the variances are in production costs.

KEY POINT

The source of a root cause determines whether the unit manager, a cross-functional team, or upper management can best handle it.

■ BEHAVIORAL AND CULTURAL ASPECTS OF SCS

A good SCS provides management and operating personnel with information they need to take corrective action in a timely manner. Without an SCS, it is difficult for an organization to provide a quality product at an affordable cost. The results of variance investigations, when arrayed properly, also help in understanding linkages between units and those that originate from the external environment.

However, in order to use SCS effectively, managers must understand the behavioral and cultural properties of these systems.

Behavioral Impact of SCS.

A SCS, if used properly, can help to motivate employees. This is because SCS can be used to affect aspiration levels and create a sense of empowerment. However, if used carelessly, standard costing can encourage negative or dysfunctional behaviors.

Affect aspiration levels.

Standards are targets. They can be challenging or they can be easy. Research shows that the level of goal difficulty has an impact on employee aspiration level and performance.

Higher aspiration levels lead to higher performance. However, aspiration levels are revised upward or downward based on past success or failure in achieving a goal. When a person sets a high aspiration and fails in reaching that goal, he or she tends to lower their aspiration in the next period. Conversely, if they succeed in meeting a goal easily, they tend to revise their expectations upward.

If standards are too difficult, they will result in variances. Employees may see variances as failure to achieve goals. This will lead to revising aspiration levels downward and, therefore, decrease the chance of meeting standards in the future. If the standards are too easy, employees may not be challenged to achieve them either. Setting standards at just the right level of difficulty is important to use standard costing effectively.

Sense of empowerment.

Standards that are imposed by top management or functional experts make individuals less likely to accept the legitimacy of the targets and fail to motivate employees to perform. When standard setting allows employees to participate, it can create a sense of empowerment. Research shows that participation can increase employee "buy in" and lead to less frustration, higher satisfaction, and better performance.[7] Recall that lack of meaningful participation in standard setting is part of the frustration expressed in the opening story. When individuals are involved in the process, they are more likely to take ownership of the standards, work to meet targets, and accept evaluations based on differences between standard and actual results.

On the downside, participation takes additional time and must be real, not "pseudo." Pseudo-participation can create a credibility gap and cause frustration if employees feel that management is simply going through the motions but is not interested in their input.

Encouraging dysfunctional employee behaviors.

SCS are often used to evaluate the performance of employees. When used carelessly, they often lead to dysfunctional behaviors in an organization. Here are a few examples of how this might happen.

Since SCS operates on a management-by-exception basis (that is, managers intervene only when things are going wrong), they accentuate focus on negative performance. Too much focus on negative variances and not enough reinforcement of positive accomplishments can cause frustration and lower employee satisfaction levels. Employees may start gaming to reduce variances rather than increase efforts to attain them.

Focus on assigning responsibility for variances may cause individuals to take short-term actions to avoid negative consequences. For example, a material-price variance may lead to substituting low-cost material that may be below quality. This will result in shifting variances from procurement to production that may have to deal with the consequences of low-cost material. You will recall that we recommended against computing fixed overhead-volume variance. This is because this variance can lead to unnecessary build up in inventory.

Pressure to meet quantity standards can lead to dysfunctional behaviors as well. Departments have been known to continue production to meet preset targets, even when the department receiving their output has broken equipment and has no need for the output. This leads to build up in work-in-process inventory.

---

[7] See for example, Brownell, P. "Participation in the Budgeting Process: When It Works and When It Doesn't," *Journal of Accounting Literature*, 1982. Chong, V. K. and C.W. Chong, "Effects of Budget Participation on Performance." *Behavioral Research in Accounting*, Vol 14, 2002.

Finally, pressure to meet standards can remove the incentive to share improvement ideas. Individuals will focus on meeting existing standards even if they are inefficient or easy rather than share process-improvement ideas that will change or increase standards.

Cultural Attributes.

A SCS can reflect and reinforce important cultural values. One important value is fairness. The process of setting standards and using variances to evaluate performance affects how operating personnel and managers view the system. A well-designed SCS is perceived as fair and can create a value system where quickly adjusting to variations from expectations becomes a way of life. If the standards are perceived as unfair, a negative culture grows and inhibits the organization's ability to meet its strategic objectives.

Developing and using standards is a signal that planning matters and that managing the actual results is important. Standards represent the type of rational calculated action that many industrial cultures value over impulse and instinct. The creation and use of standards provides organizations with a vehicle for demonstrating that it considers actions logically and rationally. The calculation and reporting of variances on a regular schedule celebrates rationality and the organization's commitment to rationality.

■ LESSONS LEARNED

- ■ Standard costing is a cost maintenance and not a cost reduction system. It also facilitates inventory valuation.
- ■ Standard costing is useful for cost management when products have long life cycles and are produced using stable and repetitive processes.
- ■ Standards may be imposed or participative, and the data used may be from engineering, benchmarking, or historical studies.
- ■ Actual cost information should be accumulated and reported on a timely basis in a format that permits comparison of actual and standard amounts.
- ■ Price and quantity variances should be computed and reported on a timely basis for all variable production costs.
- ■ Capacity management models are best suited to handle fixed costs.
- ■ Root-cause analysis should be used to determine the underlying causes for variances.
- ■ Corrective action should be matched to whether a variance originates within a unit, is an inter-unit variance, or is from the environment.
- ■ A SCS, if not used correctly, can lead to dysfunctional behaviors or fail to motivate employees.

APPENDIX A
MIX AND YIELD VARIANCES

Most products are a combination of different materials and several types of labor. For such products, particularly those that require precise recipes, the mix of materials and labor should not vary. Bottling plant managers are not allowed to tamper with the formula used to make Coca-Cola. Dairies mix precise amounts of chocolate and milk to produce chocolate-flavored milk. Some production environments, however, offer some flexibility. Different types of materials or classes of labor may be substituted in a product. For example, orange juice manufacturers can mix navel and valencia oranges in slightly different proportions. A fried chicken franchise may mix experienced, higher-paid cooks with low-paid helpers in their breading operation.

When materials or labor vary from their predetermined proportion, a mix variance results. A *mix variance* is the cost that results from the difference between an actual mix and a standard mix. Often mix changes can also impact the total output that is produced from a given amount of input. For example, substituting cooks for helpers may result in higher quantity of breaded chicken pieces because the cooks are faster and more experienced. A *yield variance* is the extra cost from the loss in quantity that results when there is a change in the mix material or labor.

To illustrate mix and yield variances, consider Reseda Electric Works—an electrical contractor who does new construction wiring. The typical crew consists of one experienced electrician and two apprentice electricians. An experienced electrician can wire 10 fixtures per hour while an apprentice can wire only 5 fixtures per hour. The standard and actual data is summarized in Exhibits 13 and 14.

Exhibit 13
Reseda Electric: Standard Cost Sheet for November

Labor	Standard Rate	Standard Crew Mix	Standard Hours	Standard Labor Cost	Standard Output in Fixtures
Apprentice Electricians	$15 per hour	2 (67%)	320	$ 4,800	1,600
Master Electricians	$40 per hour	1 (33%)	160	6,400	1,600
Total			480	$11,200	3,200

During November, Reseda Electric wired 3,600 fixtures at a total labor cost of $15,000. The detailed breakdown of the actual hours is shown in Exhibit 14.

Exhibit 14
Reseda Electric: Actual Results for November

Labor	Standard Rate	Actual Hours	Actual Output
Apprentice Electricians	$15/hour	240	1,440 fixtures
Master Electricians	$40/hour	240	2,160 fixtures
Total			

169

NOTE PAD

Compare Exhibits 13 and 14. What variances can you compute?

Comparing Exhibits 13 and 14, we can see that Reseda Electric has no labor-rate variance since the actual and standard rates are the same. (If these rates had been different, we would have computed the two labor rates or price variances using the formula introduced earlier in this module.) However, they have used a different crew mix and have produced more output than planned. The computation of the dollar amount of these variances follows.

NOTE PAD

Can you compute the two labor-quantity variances using the formula introduced earlier in the module?

■ LABOR-QUANTITY VARIANCE

To understand labor mix and yield variances, we will begin by computing the quantity variance for the two types of labor, apprentice and master. Exhibit 13 shows the standard wage rates and the budgeted hours (480) for a budgeted output of 3,200 fixtures. Since the actual output is 3,600 fixtures, the flexible budget or *earned hours* for this output is 540 hours [(3,600/3,200) × 480)]. Ignoring the mix, we can compute a quantity variance as simply the difference between actual hours and the flexible budget for the standard hours *earned* on the basis of the output of 3,600 fixtures. The labor-quantity variance for November is:

LQV (Apprentices) =   ΔQ × SP
                       (AQ − SQ) × SP
                       (240 − 360) × $15

LQV (Apprentices) =   **$1,800 F**

LQV (Master) =   ΔQ × SP
                       (AQ − SQ) × SP
                       (240 − 180) × $40

LQV (Master) =   **$2,400 U**

LQV (Combined) =   **$600 U**

■ MIX VARIANCE

Let us now consider the impact of a crew mix. For November, there is a mix variance because the actual labor mix used differed from the standard labor mix. The actual information shows that apprentice labor was 50 percent rather than the expected 67 percent and that the master electrician labor was 50 percent rather than 33 percent.

The mix variance measures the monetary effect of using a different mix. In our example, it is the higher-than-expected percentage of master electrician hours. The mix variance uses the actual hours, but assumes that they are distributed in the budgeted mix. *This is because we want to isolate the effect of a change in mix without adding the effect of a change in output as well.* The formula for computing the mix variance is as follows:

Mix Variance = AQ × (A% – M%) × SP

> where, AQ = Actual quantity of labor hours used
>
> A% = Actual mix percentage
>
> M% = Standard mix percentage
>
> SP = Standard price

The electrician crew–mix variance for November is computed as follows:

	ATQ (A% – M%) × SP	Mix Variance[8]
Apprentice	480 (.50 – .67) × $15	$1,200 F
Master	480 (.50 – .33) × $40	3,200 U
Total Crew Mix Variance		$2,000 U

The decrease in the percentage of apprentice labor used results in a favorable variance while the increase in the use of master labor results in a unfavorable mix variance. The net effect of the mix change is an unfavorable crew-mix variance of $2,000. Because the total mix must equal 100 percent, there is always at least one favorable and one unfavorable mix variance if there is any change in mix.

■ YIELD VARIANCE

The change in mix required more of the expensive master electricians. While this increased the total wages paid, master electricians work faster and the yield from the same 480 labor hours has gone up. Instead of the budgeted 3,200 fixtures we have 3,600 fixtures. In effect, the 480 hours at the new mix has yielded 540 labor hours worth of output. This impact can be captured in the yield variance, which shows us the productivity impact of the new mix. Again, to isolate the effect of a change in the yield, we will hold the mix constant and assume that the earned hours and the actual hours were both at the standard mix. The formula for computing the mix variance is as follows:

Crew Yield Variance = [(AQ × M%) – (SQ × M%)] × SP

> Where,
>
> AQ = Actual quantity used
>
> SQ = Flexible budget or earned quantity for output produced
>
> M% = Standard mix percentage
>
> SP = Standard price

The crew yield variance for November is computed as follows:

	[(AQ × M%) – (SQ × M%)] × SP	Yield Variance
Apprentice	[(480 × .67) – (540 × .67)] × $15	$ 603 F
Master	[(480 × .33) – (540 × .33)] × $40	792 F
Yield Variance		$1,395 F

---

[8] Note that your answers will be slightly off if you use the rounded values of .67 and .33 instead of 2/3 and 1/3.

Note that the mix and yield variances together give additional information about the causes of a quantity variance. When mix and yield variances are combined, they equal the quantity variance. In our example, the mix and yield equal the combined quantity variance of $645 Unfavorable.

Total mix variance	$2,040 U
Total yield variance	$1,395 F
Total quantity variance	$ 645 U

THINK ALONG

> Was it a wise decision to use more master electricians?

We can see that despite the increased productivity of the master electricians, the decision to substitute the higher paid labor has resulted in an overall unfavorable variance of $645. This was because unfavorable mix variance was larger than the favorable yield variance. Reseda is better off sticking to its standard crew mix and avoiding the type of tradeoff between using cheaper labor it did in November.

■ PROBLEMS AND CASES—INTRODUCTORY LEVEL

1. Self-test questions.
a. What is a standard? A variance?
b. What is a standard costing system?
c. Identify three ways standard costing can be used as a cost management tool.
d. Certain characteristics of a product or firm lend themselves to standard costing. Identify two such characteristics.
e. How does standard costing simplify inventory valuation?
f. What costs does a standard costing system help us manage?
g. List the five steps in the standard costing process.
h. Identify four of the primary uses of traditional standard costing.
i. Differentiate ideal standards from attainable standards.
j. Briefly explain the nature of engineered standards, benchmark standards, and historical analysis–based standards.
k. How do imposed and participative standards differ?
l. When would quantity standards change?
m. Why are standards often adjusted only quarterly or annually?
n. For a standard costing system to be useful for cost management, actual information must have certain characteristics. List two of these characteristics.
o. What is the general formula for computing a price variance?
p. What is the general formula for computing a quantity variance?
q. What is a mix variance? A yield variance?
r. Identify three reasons organizations need to analyze variances.
s. Identify two key factors that often influence when a variance is investigated.
t. Should two variances of equal size always be investigated?
u. What is root-cause analysis?
v. Identify three factors that make standard costing decisions relevant for managing costs.
w. Identify three behavioral attributes of standard costing.

Problem-solving suggestions:
■ When calculating a variance, always indicate whether it is favorable or unfavorable.
■ Show and label each computation required for getting an answer.

2. Hollywood Makeovers performs face-lifts. The labor time allowed (standard) for each face-lift is 2.3 hours. The standard wage rate for a staff surgeon is $265 per hour. During October, Hollywood Makeover surgeons performed 450 face-lifts. Surgery required 1,020 hours, and surgeon charges totaled $275,400.

Required:
a. How many hours should it take to complete 450 face-lifts?
b. What is the actual surgeon labor cost per hour?
c. Compute the total surgeon-time (quantity) variance for October.
d. Compute the total surgeon labor–price variance for October.
e. What is the total surgeon labor–variance for October?

3. The Climb-Up Company manufactures stepladders. Climb-Up personnel determined that each stepladder needs 35 feet of aluminum at an estimated cost of $4.05 a foot. During March, Climb-Up purchased 370,000 feet of aluminum at a cost of $1,580,000. During March the firm used 345,000 feet of aluminum and made 9,700 stepladders.

Required:

a. Compute the total raw material-price variance for the month of March.

b. Compute the total raw material-quantity variance for the month of March.

c. Compute the inventory variance for the month of March.

d. Explain why actual purchases are used to compute the price variance.

e. How would you suggest that a manufacturing company like Climb-Up develop their material-use standard?

f. A review of the variance records indicates that Climb-Up always has unfavorable aluminum-quantity variances. Discuss possible reasons why this variance may be consistently unfavorable.

4. Quick Shelter, an international relief agency, provides tents that serve as temporary shelters after natural disasters. A local group sews tent fabric into the proper size for these tents. The following information is available about one part of the tent-sewing operation.

Standard Cost	
Material—tent fabric	9.5 yards per tent at $5 per yard
Labor	2.5 hours per tent at $8.25 per hour

Actual Results—May	
Production	12,000 tents
Labor used	28,500 tents at a cost of $242,250
Material used	112,800 yards
Material purchased	122,500 yards for $637,000

Required:

a. Compute the following variances (total, not per unit) and indicate whether the variance is favorable or unfavorable.

1. Material-price variance

2. Material-quantity variance

3. Labor-price variance

4. Labor-quantity variance

b. Based on your variance computations, do you think the material- and labor-quantity standards are attainable standards or are set too high? Why?

c. Why would a charitable organization want to use standards and compute variances?

5. The quality-inspection group at Mega Manufacturing conducts a detailed inspection of 2 percent of each year's widget production. The standard inspection cost is $27 for each inspection and assumes an inspection will take 90 minutes. The inspection budget for the current year was $540,000 based on a planned production of 1,000,000 widgets.

Actual inspection cost during the year was $579,500. The quality supervisor was asked to explain the $39,500 difference between the actual and budget cost. In response, the quality supervisor stated the increase was caused by the increase in production volume and suggested that manufacturing be made responsible for this added cost because actual production was 1,050,000 widgets. Analysis shows the department completed 21,000 inspections in 30,500 hours. Inspectors actually earned $19 an hour during the year.

Required:

a. Provide a more complete analysis of the $39,500 quality inspection difference.

b. Discuss who is responsible for the variances identified.

c. Explain why the supervisor might not have wanted to take responsibility for the extra cost.

6. Your boss just spilled coffee on the monthly variance report and you have been summoned to reconstruct the missing information. You know that all of the material purchased during the period was used in production. (Hint: You can't solve in order. Use the basic standard costing formula and determine missing information.)

	Labor	Materials
Standard quantity per unit	A	D
Standard price per hour or pound	$12.00 per hour	E
Actual production	15,000 units	15,000 units
Actual quantity per unit	B	4 pounds
Actual price	$12.50 per hour	$6.25 per pound
Price variance	$15,000 U	F
Quantity variance	C	9,000 U
Total labor or material variance	$3,000 F	24,000 U

7. Smoky River Manufacturing uses a standard cost system. Standards for power usage are based on direct labor hours. The remaining overhead costs are fixed. The following information is available for January.

Standard power cost	$0.40 per kilowatt hour
Standard power usage	8 kilowatt hours per labor hour
Standard labor hours	4 hours per unit
Budgeted production	15,000 units
Budgeted fixed overhead	$180,000
Actual units produced	16,000 units
Actual labor hours used	63,000 hours
Actual power usage	515,500 kilowatt hours
Actual power cost	$0.42 per kilowatt hour
Actual "other" overhead	$188,000

175

Required:

a. Calculate the variable overhead spending variance for power and subdivide it into the price, and usage variances. Also calculate the efficiency variance for power at Smoky River.

b. How much fixed overhead is applied? How much is the over- or under-applied overhead. Compute the fixed overhead-spending variance and overhead-volume variance for Smoky River?

c. Explain why computing and reporting overhead-volume variances may lead to undesirable behavior.

8. Metallica Fabricators produces parts for the automobile industry such as wheel bearings, axles, and wheel rims. It is a high-quality supplier and in the past the firm has been able to gain business on its quality reputation. This reputation exists mainly because the firm has relied on introducing new technology faster than other metal shops supplying the auto industry. With growing competition in the auto industry, however, parts suppliers such as Metallica are now under pressure to reduce their costs. Metallica is considering the installation of a standard cost system to respond to this challenge.

Required:

Do you think that a standard cost system is the right way for Metallica to manage its costs? Why or why not? What might you recommend instead of standard costing?

9. "What do I think about the standard costing system? Not much! The standard cost reports I get require me to spend several hours every month explaining old differences to people who don't understand the pressures we face here in production. When there is a production problem, we deal with it, long before this silly system tells us we have a problem. Why should I have to explain it again a month later? When marketing underestimates sales estimates, we get hit with rush orders and have to scramble for raw materials and the labor required. If marketing overestimates, we have to scale back production so we don't have excess finished goods and we end up with people not working. Either way I get blamed for spending too much or having inefficient workers. Why is it my fault?"

Required:

a. Identify some problems that these comments indicate might exist with the firm's standard costing system.

b. Prepare a proposal to management that includes some suggestions for fixing the problems you identified in the first part of the exercise. Include in your proposal why implementing these suggestions will make the standard costing system more useful.

10. Mary Sanders recently returned to the workforce to take over management of a small chain of flower shops that are owned by her aging parents. Mary knows that cost control has not been particularly effective in the shops. She has been reading about different cost management tools that are available and has asked you for some help in evaluating how a standard costing system might help in cost control. You are meeting with Mary for a pizza late this afternoon to discuss standard costing.

Required:

a. Develop a list of questions related to the flower shops that Mary should answer before adopting standard costing. Your question list should cover each step of the standard costing process outlined in the text.

b. Identify what Mary would need to do in order to implement a standard costing system that would help with cost control in the flower shops.

c. Discuss when standard costing might not be helpful for cost management in the flower shops.

d. Optional: Research flower shops using the Internet and use the information to determine what type of standard cost information might be particularly critical for this type of organization.

11. Wichita Falls Company is a new client that has asked for your help in modifying their standard costing process. You have spent some time with the company and gathered the following information.

a. Deliveries to customers are regularly late because the logistics manager refuses to allow suppliers to use overnight shipping when critical parts shortages arise.

b. Quality problems increased during the past year as purchasing managers have been required to take responsibility for material-price variances.

c. Experienced workers have been requesting transfers or are leaving the firm. Exit interviews indicate that they are frustrated with the constant pressure to explain major usage variances when they are working as hard as they can.

d. A recent review of how managers are using the monthly variance reports showed that the reports were looked at to see which variances would have to be explained, but they were seldom used in the production process. Observation and interviews indicate there are a number of informal systems that managers are using to monitor critical production variables.

Required:

Write a brief memo to the company president indicating why some of these problems may be occurring. Include suggested solutions for the problems. Your memo should focus explicitly on the behavioral and cultural attributes of a good standard costing system.

12. Many researchers argue that negative variances lower employee aspiration levels and therefore lower performance. Assuming this is true, consider the following suggestion. Companies should compute real variances from standards but not necessarily report these variances to employees. The reported variances should consider the possible behavioral effects and, if necessary, not report negative performance or at least massage the information so it does not have a damaging effect on employee aspiration levels. This way managers would know the real performance but employees would operate on "motivational" variances rather than real variances.

Required:

Evaluate the pros and cons of this proposal from a behavioral, cultural, and ethical perspective.

13. A local hospital operates several neighborhood urgent-care clinics. A standard costing system based on patients as the measure of activity is used to help monitor the cost management efforts at each clinic. For legal and quality-care reasons an adequate staff of attending and on-call physicians must always be available to serve patients. To date, each clinic has maintained a constant number of attending physicians, regardless of patient activity. Nurse scheduling has been varied with anticipated changes in patient volume. The hospital set a standard of one nurse for every four patient visits to an urgent-care clinic. Nurse pay varies with shift and scheduling. While the average pay is $22 an hour, the actual pay rates vary between $15 and $35 per hour. Medical supply costs are budgeted at $15 per nursing hour. A professional manager administers each clinic and is responsible for controlling costs. During February the following information is available for a clinic that is located in a high-crime section of the city.

	Budget	Actual
Patient visits	5,200	5,600
Nursing hours	1,300	1,500
Nursing cost	$28,600	$36,900
Supplies	$19,500	$24,700
Doctor wages	$75,000	$80,000

Required:

a. Compute the price and quantity variances for nursing costs.

b. Calculate the price and quantity variances for supplies.

c. Provide a possible explanation for the variances calculated in parts a and b.

d. The clinic administrator has suggested that the existing standards are not reasonable for his clinic and has requested a review of how the standards are set for each clinic. Develop a set of suggestions for setting standards and evaluating variances for nursing and supplies at the clinics. Explain how your suggestions would make the standard cost and variance information more useful to the clinic administrator and the hospital management.

e. Doctors represent the largest labor cost at each clinic. It has been suggested that standards similar to those established for nurses be established. Discuss the potential ramifications of this extension of the current cost system.

14. For each of the situations listed below, assume that you are a consultant and have been called in to help management understand more about standard costing.

A. An airline is considering establishing standards for agents who answer calls made to the airline's phone reservation system.

B. A dental clinic is interested in evaluating a standard costing for the work of dental hygienists who clean teeth.

C. The Social Security Administration is exploring establishing standards for its retirement benefit–claims coordinators.

D. A bottled water company is considering standard costing for its store-delivery people who also set up displays.

Required:

For each of the situations above explain the following:

  a. Would standard costing be a good cost management tool? Why or why not?

  b. If yes, what information would be needed to develop a standard?

  c. How would you get the information?

  d. What would be the value of variance information for cost management?

  e. What are the potential negative behavioral consequences of using a standard cost system for this type of work?

15. In many industries, such as automobiles, aircraft, household appliances, and oil and gas exploration, a large part of the product cost consists of purchased parts and services. Material prices (and thus variances) are particularly important for such industries and can, if not carefully controlled, cause a major increase in product costs. A major automobile company rewards its purchasing agents on the amount of favorable price variances. Agents keep 10 percent of any favorable material-price variance as part of their incentive pay.

Required:

  a. Discuss the behavioral effects, positive and negative, that are likely to be generated by this incentive system?

  b. Do you think that material-price variance is the best way to manage the costs of purchased components and services?

  c. What cost management approach would you recommend?

■ PROBLEMS AND CASES—ADVANCED LEVEL

16. Loan Facilitator, Inc. does loan reviews for small financial institutions throughout the United States. It uses a standardized loan review and approval system to accept or deny loans.

    The firm has been quite profitable. However, Loan Facilitators is facing more competition from larger financial institutions, which have developed their own loan-analysis software and are making it available to other firms.

    Recently the loan reviewers have requested substantial wage increases and the owners wonder how to evaluate the employees' request. The owners have hired a consultant who has suggested the firm implement a standard cost system. The consultant believes that the calculation of variances will aid management in setting responsibility for labor's performance.

    The loan-processing managers believe that under normal conditions a loan can be reviewed and a recommendation for approval or disapproval made in 80 minutes at a cost of $15 per hour. The consultant has also assembled labor-cost information for the most recent month and would like your advice in calculating direct-labor variances.

    During the month, the actual loan processor wages paid were $192,500 for 12,600 hours of work. There were 9,000 loans reviewed during the month. (CMA adopted and modified)

Required:

  a. Compute for management's consideration the direct-labor variances.

  b. Are the variances computed consistent with your expectations based on the problem facts? Why or why not.

c. Provide management with a list of possible reasons that variances may occur in this type of activity.

d. Discuss how standards might be set in this type of organization.

e. What are the benefits of having standards for managing labor costs and evaluating potential wage increases?

17. Lock Nut has a standard costing system for all manufactured items as part of its cost control and management system. A standard cost for each item is set at the beginning of the fiscal year. Standards are not revised during the year. However, planned variances are included in Lock Nut's monthly operating budgets to reflect changes in costs related to modifications in the material and labor inputs or by changes in the manufacturing process.

The table below shows the labor standards for one of Lock Nut's products for the current fiscal year.

Assembler – 2nd class (6 hr @ $12)	$ 72
Assembler – 1st class (3 hr @ $16)	$ 48
Master Machinist (2 hr @ $20)	$ 40
Standard cost per 100 units	$160

The budget standard was based on a labor team that includes six people with assembler second-class skills, three people with assembler first-class skills, and two people with master machinist skills. This team represents the most efficient use of the company's skilled employees. The labor standard also assumed that the quality of materials would remain the same as that used in prior years.

For the first seven months of the fiscal year, actual manufacturing costs at Lock Nut have been close to the established standards. Recently, the company has won several large new orders. The firm does not have enough skilled workers available to support the production increases needed using the typical work team. Management has chosen to restructure the work teams used. Beginning in month eight, the production teams will consist of nine people with assembler second-class skills, one person with assembler first-class skills, and one person with master machinist skills. The reorganized teams will work more slowly than the normal teams. As a result only 80 good units will be produced in the same time period 100 units would normally be produced. The overall quality of the production units is expected to remain extremely high with the reorganized teams.

Its major material supplier has notified Lock Nut that due to shortages, lower-quality materials will be supplied beginning at the start of month eight. Normally, one unit of raw materials is required for each good unit produced, and no units are lost due to defective material. Lock Nut estimates that 10 percent of the units manufactured starting in month eight will be rejected in the final inspection process due to defective material. (CMA adapted and modified)

Required:

a. What is the amount of budgeted cost per good quality batch produced?

b. Determine the number of units of lower-quality material that Lock Nut must start into production in order to produce 62,000 good finished units.

c. How many hours of each class of labor must be used to manufacture 62,000 good finished units using the modified work teams?

d. Determine the amount that should be included in Lock Nut's operating budget for the planned labor variance caused by the reorganization of the labor teams and the lower-quality material.

e. Discuss how the modified standard cost information could be used for cost management. Include in your discussion the profit implications of the proposed change and any recommendations for change that management might consider.

f. Assuming the change is made, should new standards be adopted now rather than waiting until the new fiscal year? Why?

18. Rolling Wheels, a manufacturer of high-end leisure equipment, has been in business for fifteen years. Competitive cost pressures caused the firm's controller to implement a standard cost system. Reports are issued monthly to help managers track performance. All negative variances are further investigated.

The roller blade production manager complained that the standards are unrealistic, stifle motivation by concentrating only on negative variances, and that standards are quickly out of date. He noted that a recent switch to synthetic wheels for the roller blades resulted in higher materials costs but decreased labor hours used in assembly. The net result was no increase in the total cost of producing roller blades. The monthly reports continue to show a negative material-price variance and a positive labor-quantity variance, despite indications that the assembly workers are slowing down.

Required:

a. Should the company use a standard cost system to manage its costs. Explain your reasons.

b. Briefly discuss the possible behavioral impact of their standard costing system on employee morale.

19. (Appendix) Sweet Green Company makes and supplies products to lawn and garden centers. A new growth enhancer, *Quick Grow,* is being introduced. The following information is available on *Quick Grow.* Because of the nature of the chemicals being used, the firm buys only what it will use during a certain time period.

A. In making *Quick Grow,* two chemicals, *Go Green,* a liquid, and *Blue,* a solid, are heated and mixed while at 290 degrees. A 30 percent loss in volume occurs for *Go Green* and a 10 percent loss for *Blue.* The resulting liquid mixture is put into 10-liter containers that contain 9.8 liters of *Go Green* and 8.1 kilograms of *Blue.*

B. During the cooling process, 6 kilograms of *Primp* is added to each 10-liter batch of *Quick Grow.* The addition of the *Primp* does not affect the total liquid volume. The resulting solution is capped and placed in cold storage while the reaction process works.

C. *Quick Grow* is highly unstable until the reaction process is completed. Two of every 10-liter containers are rejected during final inspection. Rejected batches have no commercial value, but they can be safely discarded.

D. Workers are expected to process one batch of *Quick Grow* every six minutes that they actually work on the product. Employees work an eight-hour day, with one hour per day set aside for rest breaks and cleanup.

181

E. When the price of *Blue*, and *Primp* change, the firm sometimes uses an alternative formula for these two items when making a 10-liter container of *Quick Grow*. The following information is available to you about the quantity of each material used last month when 4,000 containers of *Quick Grow* was made.

■ *Blue* quantity used was 40,000 kilograms.

■ *Primp* quantity used was 16,000 kilograms.

■ The firm used exactly the amount of *Go Green* anticipated.

■ The standard prices for each of the raw materials are given below.

Go Green	$.75 per liter
Blue	$.48 per kilogram
Primp	$.90 per kilogram

Required:

a. Determine the standard quantity for each of the raw materials needed to produce an acceptable 10-liter container of *Quick Grow*.

b. Determine the standard labor time allowed to produce an acceptable 10-liter container of *Quick Grow*.

c. Determine the standard cost to produce an acceptable 10-liter container of *Quick Grow*.

d. Compute the mix and yield variance for this situation for *Blue* and *Primp*.

20. (Appendix) BTU Company produces, Miles More, a gasoline additive that increases engine efficiency, lowers emissions because of more complete gasoline combustion, and improves gas mileage. The production process must be carefully controlled to ensure that the proper mix of input chemicals is used and to minimize evaporation. If the controls are not effective there can be a loss of output, efficiency, and less emission reduction.

The standard material cost of producing a 1,000-liter batch of Miles More is $305. The standard materials mix and cost of each secret chemical used in a 1,000 liter batch is as follows:

Chemical	Standard Input Quantity (liters)	Standard Cost Per liter	Total Cost
X-4	400	$.300	$120.00
Y-7	200	.625	125.00
A-2	500	.100	50.00
C-9	100	.200	20.00
	1,200		$315.00

The schedule on the next page shows the quantities of chemicals purchased and used during the current production period. The company made 408 batches of Miles More during the current production period. The company determines its cost and chemical usage variations at the end of each production period.

182

Chemical	Quantity Purchased (liters)	Total Purchase Price	Quantity Used (liters)
X-4	150,000	$46,500	160,800
Y-7	78,000	52,650	75,960
A-2	240,000	21,600	224,400
C-9	45,000	9,000	42,840
	513,000	$129,750	504,000

(CMA Adapted)

Required:

a. Calculate purchase-price variances for each chemical.

b. Calculate the quantity variance for each chemical.

c. Compute the materials-mix and yield variances.

d. Discuss possible explanations for variances. Include a discussion of why the mix might have been altered.

e. Discuss potential consequences of the mix alteration.

21. ELFGIP is a West African company in the oil and gas exploration and production business. Its budget for diesel fuel consumption is $100,000 per month. Its actual costs have been running close to $125,000 per month. Management is naturally concerned about this huge deficit.

Diesel fuel is consumed by boats that make journeys to offshore platforms carrying essential spare and replacement parts for oil-pumping equipment and underwater pipelines. Most boats make several journeys per day. They are typically 50–60 percent full. The company has several boats and many are often on standby duty. The underwater pipelines fail frequently because of salt-water corrosion and sections have to be replaced to avoid any leakage of oil into the ocean.

Required:

a. Prepare a simple root-cause diagram of the diesel cost variance using root-cause analysis.

b. What recommendations would you make to management to get better control over diesel costs?

22. Deep South Company makes electronic components for hospital and nursing home equipment. A standard costing system at Deep South is in use and separate standards exist for every component. The firm uses a flexible budget system based on direct labor hours to estimate and control overhead costs. Standard costs for each product are set once a year. Overhead rates are based on expected average monthly direct labor hours because variable overhead is primarily driven by direct labor hours.

Part 428—an AC e-bus—is a major component in many types of equipment. A partial standard cost sheet for Part 428 is shown on the next page (several materials are excluded for simplicity). Expected monthly direct labor hours are 15,000 for this product.

Component	Standards	Standard Unit Cost
Copper	2 pounds @ $6	$12.00
Direct labor	3 hours @ $14	42.00
Variable overhead	3 hours @ $8	24.00
Fixed overhead	3 hours @ $6	18.00

During March 4,500 units of Part 428 were manufactured. This quantity was below expectations because of a labor dispute over wages and safety conditions in the plant. After a settlement, overtime was scheduled to reduce the gap between expected and actual production. The following actual information is available for March.

Item	Purchased	Cost	Used
Copper	11,000 pounds	$5.90	9,800 pounds

Item	Quantity	Cost
Direct Labor	9,000 hours	$14.00 per hour
Direct Labor	5,000 hours	$14.50 per hour
Variable Overhead	13,700 hours	$116,450
Fixed Overhead		$ 96,000

During March, Deep South had 1,000 hours of overtime labor related to Part 428. The overtime premium of $7.25 per hour was included in variable overhead per company policy. (CMA adapted)

Required:

a. Compute the material-price and quantity variance.

b. Compute the direct labor–price and quantity variance.

c. Compute the variable-overhead spending and efficiency variance. Subdivide the spending variance into price and usage.

d. Determine the amount of over- or under-absorbed fixed overhead and compute the fixed spending and volume variance.

e. Based on your computations provide a partial evaluation of the variances. Include in your discussion at least your answers to the following questions.

   a. Which variances should be investigated further using a root-cause analysis?

   b. Are there risks associated with reporting a volume variance?

   c. If performance is evaluated by variances and different managers are responsible for materials, direct labor, variable overhead, and fixed overhead, what types of behavior might occur in this situation.

   d. What recommendations would you make to management?

Team or Individual Assignments.

23. Develop a list of the information you would need to set standards for a specific part of the functional area where you (or a member of your team) works. For example, what information would you need to prepare standards for sales clerks in a department store?

24. Contact a local business and identify an area where the firm uses standard costing. With permission of the appropriate management personnel, interview people and observe the production process. Prepare an analysis of how the firm uses the five-step standard costing process summarized in the module. Develop for your instructor a list of any suggestions for change that you might make.

25. Standard costs are increasingly being used in the health-care industry. The government has developed diagnostic-related groups (DRGs) for determining how much to reimburse doctors and hospitals for Medicare patients. Insurance companies and HMOs negotiate payment schedules and approve medical procedures based partially on standard practices and costs. Use an Internet search engine to see what information you can obtain about how insurance companies use DRGs or other standards in the medical area. You may choose to contact a local insurance firm or medical practice for some initial information.

  a. Find an example of a DRG or insurance-approved reimbursement for a medical procedure. Research how the reimbursement amount is set.

  b. Most medical practitioners argue that the reimbursement rate for procedures is too low. Research what type of behavior this is likely to drive.

  c. Health-care costs are a major concern. Use your research to evaluate whether the use of DRGs or insurance-approved reimbursement schedules are reasonable cost management tools.

  d. What are the cultural implications of setting standards for "professional procedures" such as medical practices?

Mini-Case 1: Cold Foods, Inc.

Cold Foods, Inc. is a specialty frozen-food processor located in the upper Midwest. The firm has long had a loyal clientele who have been willing to pay premium prices for high-quality frozen food prepared from specialized recipes. In the last two years, the company has experienced rapid sales growth in its operating region and has had many inquiries about supplying its products nationally. Cold Foods has expanded its processing capabilities, which resulted in increased production and distribution costs. The company has also been encountering pricing pressure from competitors outside its normal marketing region.

Cold Foods wants to continue its expansion and Matt London, CEO, has engaged a consulting firm to assist Cold Foods in determining its course of action. The consulting firm recommended instituting a standard costing system that would be used with a flexible budgeting system to better accommodate the expected changes in demand that will result from serving an expanded market area. London met with his management team and explained the consulting firm's recommendations before assigning the task of establishing standard costs to the team. After discussing the situation with their respective staffs, the management team met to review the matter.

185

Ann Foley, the purchasing manager, explained that additional expansion in production would necessitate obtaining basic food supplies from new suppliers rather than relying on Cold Food's traditional sources. Raw-material costs and shipping costs would increase and the quality of food supplies received might be lower. To maintain or reduce current costs, the increase in material costs would need to be made up in the processing department.

Ben Nygoni, the processing manager, countered that the need to accelerate processing cycles to increase production, coupled with the possibility of receiving lower-grade supplies, would reduce initial quality and thus lead to greater product rejection rates. This would mean that per-unit labor use could not be maintained or reduced and forecasting future unit-labor quantities would become more difficult.

Manual Lopez, the production engineer, advised that if the equipment is not properly maintained and thoroughly cleaned at prescribed daily intervals, the quality and unique taste of the frozen-food products would be affected. Gerald Snow, vice-president of sales, stated that if quality could not be maintained, Cold Foods could not expect to increase sales to the levels projected.

When London was apprised of the problems encountered by his management team, he advised them that if agreement could not be reached on the appropriate standards, he would arrange to have them set by the consulting firm and everyone would have to live with the results. *(CMA adapted)*

Required:

a. Identify the major advantages and disadvantages of using a standard costing system in this type of situation.

b. Identify the individuals who should participate in setting standards, and describe the benefits of their participation in the standard setting process. What could be the consequences if Matt London has the standards set by the outside consulting firm?

c. Assume the individuals involved in this scenario know that standard costs are often used as performance measures. Discuss how this may explain their arguments.

d. Discuss some of the problems associated with setting standards. Use the facts provided in the case as the starting point for this discussion. Include a discussion of the types of standards that should be used in this situation.

e. What characteristics of a standard costing system make it an effective tool for cost management?

f. What are the limitations of standard costing in the type of decision environment faced by this firm?

g. Discuss how standard costing can be useful in working with potential suppliers?

Mini-Case 2: Snap Together Manufacturing

Penny Sandminder is a manufacturing supervisor at Snap Together Manufacturing Company, a firm that makes a variety of plastic components that interlock. Some of these components are standard catalog items, while others are special designs for other companies. Sandminder receives a monthly performance report displaying the budget, actual activity for the month, and the variance between budget and actual activity. Part of

Sandminder's evaluation is based on her department's performance against budget. Snap Together's purchasing manager, Charles Boblet receives the same type of monthly performance reports and is evaluated in part on the basis of these reports.

It's the 18th and the prior month's reports have just been distributed. Sandminder and Boblet met in the hallway outside their offices. A scowling Sandminder says, "I see we have another monthly performance report hand-delivered by that arrogant junior employee from the budget office. It seems I am in trouble once again with my performance."

Boblet: "I got the same treatment. All I ever hear is about what I haven't done right. Now, I'll have to spend the rest of the week reviewing this month-old report and preparing explanations."

Sandminder: "My biggest complaint is that our production activity varies widely from month to month, but the annual budget's written in stone. Last month we were shut down for five days by a supplier strike that delayed delivery of the raw plastic. Since we carry little inventory, I didn't have much choice. You know about that since you called all over to find an alternative source of supply. When we finally found a supplier, we had to pay more than normal because it was a rush delivery."

Boblet: "I expect problems from time to time—that's part of my job—but now we'll both have to take a careful look at the variance report to see how the budget office showed that rush order. Every month, I spend more time making sure I'm properly charged for each item than I do making plans for my department's daily work. It's really frustrating to see all those charges for things I can't control."

Sandminder: "There's a lot of problems with the information we get also. I don't get copies of your reports, yet your department and several of our other departments influence a lot of what I do. Why do the budget and accounting people assume that I should only be told about my operations when the CEO keeps giving us pep talks about how we all need to work together as a team?"

Boblet: "I get more reports than I need and I am only asked to comment when top management calls me on the carpet because of my department's shortcomings. When's the last time you heard comments when your department had a great month?"

Sandminder: "Maybe they expect only good news. One of my problems is that the reports are all in dollars and cents. These don't help me as I work with people, machines, and materials. I need information about this month to solve this month's problems—not another report of the dollars I spent last month or the month before. (CMA adapted and modified)

Required:

a. Use the conversation between Penny Sandminder and Charles Boblet to describe what motivations and behaviors these two employees are likely to have as a result of the Snap Together variance reporting system.

b. Both employees and companies should benefit from properly implemented reporting systems. Describe the benefits that can be realized from using a variance reporting system.

c. Explain what is wrong with the standard costing system described above?

d. Does the existing standard costing system help the firm manage costs?

e. Based on the situation presented above, recommend ways Snap Together Manufacturing can improve its variance reporting system and increase employee motivation. What type of cultural changes may be required?

Mini-Case 3: Automotive Support Company
(From Management Accounting Practice—Volume 1—IMA 20)

The following transcript was prepared from a recording of a recent meeting of executives of the Automobile Support Company

Location: Seventh Floor Conference Room
Time: 10:00 Monday Morning
Meeting: Special Executive Meeting

Present:

Bob Sharp—President
Charlie Smith—Assistant Controller
Henry Wills—Sales Manager

Gloria Finan—Controller
Bill Plankton—Plant Manager
Julie Sheehan—Purchasing Manager

Bob Sharp: Good morning. As you recall, Thursday's operations-review meeting was chaotic. Many of the variances from standard costs that showed up in the interim financial statements did not seem to be controllable, and some of you questioned the entire accounting system. I asked Gloria to look into our standard costing methods and report back to us today. Gloria, have you come up with anything?

Gloria Finan: I think so, Bob. As you know, for many years we have used a standard costing system in which standards are only adjusted annually. At yearend, we determine the actual cost to produce the products then in inventory. These costs become the standards for the next year. This has worked well for the interim financial reports that we must provide to shareholders and others. We are able to create these reports without the need of expensive, and disruptive, interim costing of inventories. But the system has been less than satisfactory for internal purposes such as controlling costs through variance calculation and analysis. I asked my new assistant, Charlie Smith, to work out a system that would satisfy both stockholders and management. Charlie recently received an MBA from State University and has strong opinions about proper feedback and control. I brought Charlie with me today so that he could give us his recommendations in person. Charlie.

Charlie Smith: Thanks, Gloria. I think I have a solution that will satisfy everybody. The basic complaint about the present system is that the standards are out of date every time costs change. My proposal is simple—let's use two sets of standards. One set will be changed only once a year, as is our current practice and will be used for our interim financial statements. This will satisfy that need. The other set will be changed continually to keep material, labor, and overhead costs (and standard quantities) current. This will result in variances that reflect true efficiencies and inefficiencies, and that should satisfy our internal needs. I've worked out current standards and could implement them this week if you wish.

Bill Plankton: This looks very interesting, Charlie, but I wonder if I might ask a couple of questions?

Charlie Smith: Of course

Gloria (Aside to Charlie.): Look out!

Bill Plankton: Under your proposed system, two sets of books for inventories are needed. There will be two sets of variances that may differ in amount considerably, and two sets of inventory values for Raw Materials, Work in Process, and Finished Goods. Would this not be both confusing internally and a concern externally to tax officials, regulatory agencies, and even stockholders if word leaked out in the press about our having dual sets of books? I say we go with one system, and since we all understand the old one I see nothing wrong with sticking with it, imperfect though it may be.

188

While I'm at it, I may as well get something else off my chest. Our internal reports always show production inefficiencies as variances that are blamed on the plant, while the sales department gets none of the blame and all of the glory. Can't we have a system that shows variances from budget for (1) sales prices, (2) sales volume, and (3) changes in sales mix? Aren't these more important to the company's long-term success than cost variances, regardless of whether you look at them from a current or an old standard?

Charlie Smith: Well . . .

Henry Wills: Now Bill, let's not get worked up over things we can't control. Don't blame sales when the market is soft. Let's concentrate on controlling costs.

Bill Plankton: How can we control costs when we keep getting rush orders that we have to fill? Our guys have to interrupt production runs and work overtime two to three times a week just to help your salesmen keep their customers happy. And guess who gets blamed for those cost overruns?

Julie Sheehan: Well, I like Charlie's idea of using current standards, but I think in the future we should take his plan one step further. Why not develop "prospective" standards. By this I mean, when we set our standards at the beginning of the year, we should anticipate the cost increases that will occur during the year and build these into the standards. In the purchasing department, this would reward timely purchasing decisions with favorable price variances. Right now, the only time we get favorable price variances is when we get quantity discounts for purchasing in bulk.

Henry Wills: That might help with price variances, but it would not help with efficiency variances. It would also mean we would still need two sets of standards—current standards for use in providing sales with current product costs, and the prospective standards for the cost system.

Charlie Smith: We could set price standards prospectively and efficiency standards currently. The latter would require we devise a procedure to keep our book inventory from going out of whack. I agree we would need two sets of standards.

Gloria Finan: Since you brought it up, Julie, I must tell you that a number of purchasing's bulk orders have cost us more in inventory carrying costs than we have saved in price discounts. So even the favorable variances you mention were erroneous indicators of good performance. I don't think Charlie's plan addresses that issue, and it probably should.

Bob Sharp: Sorry Charlie, but I think there are a number of additional ideas mentioned today that deserve attention: the use of two sets of standards, the use of prospective standards, changing standards as costs change, and repricing inventories so inventory variances are not created. Gloria, could you and Charlie report back to us on Friday after considering the issues brought up today? Thank you. This meeting stands adjourned.

Charlie (To Gloria as they head back to their offices.): I thought you were on my side, Gloria.

Required:

a. Critique the standard costing system at Automobile Support Company. As part of the critique explain how the current system meets and does not satisfy the objectives of standard costing.

b. How would you suggest that standards be set at Automobile Support Company?

c. Does it appear that there is currently adequate investigation of the causes of variances at Automobile Support Company? Explain.

d. Prepare a set of recommendations for changes in the system. What implementation issues will be raised by your recommendations? How do your suggestions increase the focus on cost management for the company?